SOUTHERN REGIONAL FRENCH
A LINGUISTIC ANALYSIS OF LANGUAGE AND DIALECT CONTACT

LEGENDA

LEGENDA is the Modern Humanities Research Association's book imprint for new research in the Humanities. Founded in 1995 by Malcolm Bowie and others within the University of Oxford, Legenda has always been a collaborative publishing enterprise, directly governed by scholars. The Modern Humanities Research Association (MHRA) joined this collaboration in 1998, became half-owner in 2004, in partnership with Maney Publishing and then Routledge, and has since 2016 been sole owner. Titles range from medieval texts to contemporary cinema and form a widely comparative view of the modern humanities, including works on Arabic, Catalan, English, French, German, Greek, Italian, Portuguese, Russian, Spanish, and Yiddish literature. Editorial boards and committees of more than 60 leading academic specialists work in collaboration with bodies such as the Society for French Studies, the British Comparative Literature Association and the Association of Hispanists of Great Britain & Ireland.

The MHRA encourages and promotes advanced study and research in the field of the modern humanities, especially modern European languages and literature, including English, and also cinema. It aims to break down the barriers between scholars working in different disciplines and to maintain the unity of humanistic scholarship. The Association fulfils this purpose through the publication of journals, bibliographies, monographs, critical editions, and the MHRA Style Guide, and by making grants in support of research. Membership is open to all who work in the Humanities, whether independent or in a University post, and the participation of younger colleagues entering the field is especially welcomed.

ALSO PUBLISHED BY THE ASSOCIATION

Critical Texts
Tudor and Stuart Translations • *New Translations* • *European Translations*
MHRA Library of Medieval Welsh Literature

MHRA Bibliographies
Publications of the Modern Humanities Research Association

The Annual Bibliography of English Language & Literature
Austrian Studies
Modern Language Review
Portuguese Studies
The Slavonic and East European Review
Working Papers in the Humanities
The Yearbook of English Studies

www.mhra.org.uk
www.legendabooks.com

RESEARCH MONOGRAPHS IN FRENCH STUDIES

The *Research Monographs in French Studies* (RMFS) form a separate series within the Legenda programme and are published in association with the Society for French Studies. Individual members of the Society are entitled to purchase all RMFS titles at a discount.

The series seeks to publish the best new work in all areas of the literature, thought, theory, culture, film and language of the French-speaking world. Its distinctiveness lies in the relative brevity of its publications (50,000–60,000 words). As innovation is a priority of the series, volumes should predominantly consist of new material, although, subject to appropriate modification, previously published research may form up to one third of the whole. Proposals may include critical editions as well as critical studies. They should be sent with one or two sample chapters for consideration to Professor Diana Knight, Department of French and Francophone Studies, University of Nottingham, University Park, Nottingham NG7 2RD.

❖

PUBLISHED IN THIS SERIES

www.legendabooks.com

Southern Regional French

A Linguistic Analysis of
Language and Dialect Contact

❖

Damien Mooney

LEGENDA

Research Monographs in French Studies 47
Modern Humanities Research Association
2016

Published by Legenda
An imprint of the Modern Humanities Research Association
Salisbury House, Station Road, Cambridge CB1 2LA

ISBN 978-1-909662-89-6 (HB)
ISBN 978-1-78188-339-6 (PB)

First published 2016

Copy-Editor: Dr Anna J. Davies

CONTENTS

❖

ACKNOWLEDGEMENTS

❖

My special appreciation goes to my DPhil supervisor at Oxford, Dr Ros Temple, for her valuable guidance during the research project on which this book is based. I would also like to thank my DPhil examiners, Dr Ian Watson and Dr David Hornsby, for their essential feedback on my research and for their helpful suggestions when I began to write the present monograph. I would also like to acknowledge Professor John Coleman, Dr Peggy Renwick, and Dr Caroline Piercy who provided me with valuable advice during the data collection, data coding and statistical analysis stages of my research.

I would like to extend my thanks to Professor Janice Carruthers, my former colleague at Queen's University Belfast and member of the Editorial Board for the Research Monographs in French Studies series, for reading the original manuscript of this monograph and for her helpful comments and insights, and to Dr Graham Nelson and Professor Diana Knight at Legenda for their guidance.

I am indebted to the members of the *Institut Béarnais et Gascon*, and in particular to Mr Bernard Coustalat and Mr Jean-Marie Puyau. Their help in establishing initial contact with native speakers of Béarnais made this research possible. I would also like to thank Mr Justin Laban and Mr Yves Ginesta for allowing me to interview students at the *Collège-Lycée Saint Joseph Nay*. It is to my informants from the *communes* of Gan, Nay and Nousty that I owe my deepest thanks. The conversations I had with them have provided me, not only with the empirical data on which this book is based, but with unparalleled access to their linguistic and cultural heritage.

The research on which this book is based was funded by a Foley-Bejar Scholarship at Balliol College, Oxford and, in particular, by Mr Martin Foley, in addition to a Henry Hutchinson Stewart Literary Scholarship provided by Trinity College Dublin. I would also like to express my gratitude to the Faculty of Linguistics, Philology and Phonetics at the University of Oxford for providing me with multiple travel bursaries and, in the final year of my doctoral studies, a generous writing-up grant.

This monograph, and the thesis on which it is based, would not have been possible without the encouragement and friendship of my DPhil contemporaries in Oxford, my colleagues during my time in Belfast, and my friends and family; I therefore wish to thank Amanda Clarke, Erin Edgington, Maria Flood, Valentina Gosetti, James Harrington, Erica Mooney, Patrick Merrigan, Aisling O'Loughlin, and Richard Spavin. Finally, this book is lovingly dedicated to my wonderful mother, Jennifer Johnston, for her never-ending love and support.

D.M., Bristol, June 2016

INTRODUCTION

❖

Certains, pour se battre au service de la juste cause de l'antinationalisme, pensent qu'il faut se précipiter vers la langue universelle, vers la transparence, vers l'effacement des différences. Je voudrais penser le contraire.

JACQUES DERRIDA, *La langue n'appartient pas*, 2001

Diatopic variation in contemporary varieties of French has received relatively little attention when compared with the large body of sociolinguistic literature on geographically-based variation and change in English and other languages. This book provides a systematic analysis of the genesis and evolution of a variety of language often referred to as *français régional* or regional French (RF), focusing in particular on the south of France; it analyses the emergence of southern RF in a situation of bilingualism as well as change taking place in the variety as a result of exposure to non-local varieties of French. Crucially, few adequate theoretical analyses of RF exist and, with the exception of a small number of recent studies undertaken in the north of France, we have often been left wondering about the precise origins and exact nature of these varieties, particularly in the *Midi*.

Regional varieties of French are often assumed to have resulted from contact between the national language and local varieties present in the regions before French was imposed: 'In the first half of the twentieth century, as French began to make significant inroads into areas of provincial France where it had not previously been spoken, new varieties emerged from contact between local and national norms' (Hornsby, 2006: 3). RF was first defined in this way by Dauzat: 'Le français s'est d'abord implanté dans les centres urbains et dans les classes riches: modifié sous l'influence du milieu, il constitue ce que j'appellerai le français régional' (1906: 203), but Hornsby (2006: 3) notes that a similar notion, defined as *français provincial* was advanced by Gilliéron some twenty years beforehand: 'Le français provincial est le français importé dans les contrées où le langage indigène est un patois, français qui se développe selon ses propres germes et moyens de développement, et s'altère sous l'influence des patois' (1886: 290). The use of the term *français provincial* to mean *français régional* was common in the late nineteenth and early twentieth centuries but from 1940 onwards, *français régional* predominates. Tuaillon defines RF simply: 'Par cette appellation commode, on a coutume de désigner l'ensemble des particularités géolinguistiques qui marquent les usages de la langue française, dans chacune des parties de la France et de la francophonie' (1988: 291). Despite this apparent interest in the definition of RF from as early as the nineteenth century, there exists to this day no full analytical account of how RF actually emerges from these contact situations. Indeed, Hornsby notes that the concept of *français régional* remains extremely ill-defined and poorly understood (2006: 3).

While there has been a strong dialectological tradition in France since the nineteenth century (see *Atlas Linguistique de la France* (ALF) and other linguistic atlases),[1] the linguistic documentation of regional variation has traditionally focused on the regional languages and dialects of France and not on regional varieties of the French language: 'Until the 1970s [...], dialectologists, some as eminent as Brun (1933) [*sic*], Dauzat (1935) [and] Séguy (1950) only occasionally afforded themselves the luxury of excursi into the realm of French regionalisms' (Pooley, 2000: 118). Arguably, this lack of RF in some of the earlier linguistic atlases was largely a function of the absence of proficient French speakers in rural areas until the period following the First World War. Indeed, in the ALF, French regionalisms were included if they were in use and no explicit line was drawn between what was or was not French (in terms of varieties). It is also possible, however, that the reluctance to single out RF as an object worthy of study in its own right was strongly linked to the long-standing ideologisation of French as a static, logical and pure variety of language: 'ramasser des gasconismes,[2] le projet pourra paraître bizzare. On observe, on recueille les bonnes choses; on néglige, on abandonne les mauvaises' (Desgrouais, 1801: 5). Jones notes that early comments on RF are both disparaging and prescriptive (2011: 507), essentially designating geographical variation as a failed attempt to speak the standard language:

> Il n'y a qu'un bon langage et [...] les manières vicieuses de s'exprimer sont incalculables. [...] Parce qu'il n'y a qu'un chemin qui mène à la vérité, et qu'il y en a mille qui conduisent à l'erreur. (Molard, 1810: 10)

Molard's description of RF as a collection of 'manières vicieuses' may, again, be linked to some genuine lack of proficiency in French amongst rural populations in the nineteenth century: in a sense, some early varieties of RF may have been so heavily influenced by local languages that they were not readily recognisable as French. These derogatory definitions of RF continue, however, throughout the nineteenth and twentieth centuries, even after the advent of French into rural areas of France:

> Le monde des patois et des dialectes est fondé sur la tolérance et sur la liberté d'être de son village; le monde du français est celui de la discipline linguistique sévère. Les régionalismes du français sont des manquements à cette discipline; ils marquent les points où l'unification linguistique n'a pas encore atteint à la perfection. (Tuaillon, 1988: 299)

Various definitions of RF have been proposed and almost all of them agree that RF preserves features from local varieties with which it is/was in contact. Perhaps the most famous example of this is Tuaillon's assertion that RF is 'ce qui reste du dialecte quand le dialecte a disparu' (1974: 576). The notion of linguistic 'residue' in French from moribund substrate languages and dialects leads to the conception of RF as what Hornsby (2006) calls a 'halfway house' variety:

> Ces langues expliquent les particularités des usages français dans les régions où elles sont parlées, elles ont des liens très étroits avec le français, mais quand on conserve dans son discours trop de traits de ces langues, on ne parle pas tout à fait en français. (Tuaillon, 1988: 294)

> Un niveau supplémentaire, intermédiaire entre la langue régionale qu'ils
> parlaient et le français commun qu'ils voulaient parler. (Müller, 1985: 58–59)

While it is clear that substrate influence has a role to play in the emergence of RF from contact, the exact mechanisms by which linguistic 'residue' from local languages may be preserved in RF have not yet been fully elaborated. The influence of local language varieties on RF is all too frequently adduced as a catch-all explanation for non-standard forms in the emergent variety of French. Indeed, it is commonly accepted that bilingualism results in the most readily identifiable varieties of RF: 'the most highly differentiated varieties [of RF] are found in the speech of regional-language dominant bilinguals' (Armstrong and Pooley, 2010: 156). While there appears to be some truth in this, the linguistic mechanisms which facilitate or inhibit linguistic transfer in situations of bilingualism have not yet been explored empirically with reference to RF.

Another reason why regional varieties of French have received little attention is that they have been largely considered to be transitional ephemera and of little theoretical interest (Hornsby, 2006: 4). There is a widespread perception, both historically and more recently, that regional variation in French is 'unstable' or 'unfocused' and that homogenisation processes will eventually lead to its attrition:

> C'est une langue de nature éphémère, inconsistante, individuelle, et dont l'indi-
> vidualité est de plus en plus marquée à mesure qu'on pénètre plus profondément
> dans les couches les moins cultivées de la société. (Gilliéron, 1886: 290)

> Des français régionaux spécifiques [se trouvent] dans un processus de franci-
> sation qui aboutira en définitive à la généralisation de la langue zéro. (Müller,
> 1985: 137)

This view of RF as ephemeral is, at least in part, born of the fact that it is almost always compared to more standardised forms of the language: 'des déviations qui apparaissent dans le français "provincial" et qu'on juge telles par référence à une norme très floue: "le bon usage"' (Lerond, 1973: 4). Regional varieties of French are invariably presented in direct opposition to Parisian French which must be considered as 'le modèle pour un français commun le plus unitaire possible' (Tuaillon, 1988: 291–92).

Social changes, particularly those related to the centralising forces of Paris, are taken to be the reason for this 'tendance à l'uniformisation de la prononciation[3] en France métropolitaine' (Borrell et Billières, 1989: 55). Hornsby notes that increasing urbanisation in France over the past century has gone hand in hand with geolinguistic homogenisation, particularly in the north of France, while Armstrong and Pooley view the 'hypercephalic' demography of France as promoting the adoption of Parisian speech forms. With reference to pronunciation specifically, they note that RF speakers who do not speak local languages are likely to avoid substrate features in their speech and that regional features which are maintained are likely to be less markedly associated with a traditional regional language (2010: 156–58). While sociolinguistic studies of French undertaken over the past two decades have provided concrete evidence to suggest that RF variation in northern France is being reduced in favour of more standard varieties of French (cf. Pooley,

1996; Hornsby, 2006; Hall, 2008), the RF of the south of France remains markedly understudied in this respect.

Based on the findings of Wanner (1993) and Kuiper (2005), it is commonly assumed that younger speakers in southern regions of France are systematically adopting a non-local accent, what Hornsby and Pooley refer to as 'le manque de méridionalité dans la prononciation des jeunes méridionaux' (2001: 510). Armstrong and Pooley (2010) adduce high levels of migration to the south of France as a motivational factor in the adoption by young *Méridionaux* of a northern accent. While the evidence available is suggestive of large-scale homogenisation throughout France, the nature of the RF of young southern speakers has not yet been systematically described and the mechanisms of linguistic change active in their variety of French have not yet been identified.

Many studies of RF have been concerned with the location of an exact linguistic boundary between RF and the substrate dialects which are assumed to have influenced its formation. Carton (1981), for example, advanced the idea that there is a linguistic continuum between *patois* (or regional dialect), on one hand, and standard French (SF), on the other: *français général — français régional — français local ou dialectal — patois local*. In this typology, 'français dialectal' is viewed as dialect speech which has been heavily influenced by French, a function of the pervasive contact between the varieties. Hornsby notes, however, that there is 'no clear qualitative or quantitative threshold' between what Carton terms *français dialectal* and *français régional* (2006: 7). Carton's typology, based on contact between French and a Picard substratum, is only theoretically applicable to contact situations in the *langue d'oïl* area of the north of France. This is because of the typological similarity between French and the other *langue d'oïl* dialects. In the south of France, on the other hand, contact between French and *langue d'oc* substrata is quite clearly an instance of language contact, with clear structural separation between the varieties (Lodge, 1993: 74). Boyer (1986) has, nonetheless, proposed a similar typology for language contact in the south of France: *français officiel — français colloquial importé — argot français — français d'Oc — francitan — occitan résiduel — occitan reconstitué*. Pooley also notes that 'distinctiveness' is an issue when comparing French with all Gallo-Romance varieties (2000: 118). I will argue, however, that the typological and structural separation between *langue d'oc* and *langue d'oïl* varieties provides less evidence for a linguistic continuum between French and local *langue d'oc* substrata and that the issue of 'distinctiveness' is dramatically reduced in the south of France.

Research Hypotheses

Traditional definitions of RF have led to the over-simplified assumption that, firstly, it consists primarily of residual substrate features and, secondly, that these features are ephemeral and will be lost in favour of more standard features as time advances. The studies presented in this book aim to test two general hypotheses, henceforth referred to as 'the residue hypothesis' and the 'the ephemeral hypothesis': RF constitutes dialect residue from moribund substrate varieties; RF is ephemeral and subject to large-scale homogenisation processes. The analysis will identify, through close and systematic linguistic examination, the mechanisms active in the creation of RF during language contact as well as those active during its subsequent development over time, as it comes into contact with other non-local dialects of French.

The RF of Béarn, in southwestern France, will be offered as a case study. The region of Béarn is primarily rural and the variety of French presented is characteristic of semi-rural areas around the regional capital, Pau. The issues addressed here, namely the 'residue' and 'ephemeral' hypotheses, have also been examined by Hornsby (2006) in a situation of bidialectalism in Avion, northern France. Two main contextual factors differ, however, between the studies: Hornsby's study examines RF formation in a situation of dialect contact between two *langue d'oïl* varieties whereas the study presented in this book examines RF genesis in a situation of language contact between two typologically dissimilar varieties, one *langue d'oïl* and one *langue d'oc*; Hornsby examines change in RF in a new industrial town while the present study focuses on RF in semi-rural areas at some distance from Paris.

My examination of RF formation in a situation of bilingualism, as opposed to bidialectalism, aims to shed additional light on the issue of substrate influence, as raised by Hornsby (2006). The analysis focuses on transfer into French from the local language of the region, often referred to as 'Béarnais', and tackles the issue of 'residue' from a phonetic and phonological perspective, by exploiting acoustic phonetic techniques in order to explain more clearly the nature of substrate interference and by interpreting the findings using an analytical framework applied hitherto in studies of second language acquisition, but never with reference to RF. The examination of substrate residue acknowledges, from the outset, the lack of sufficient data on the nature of the variety of French to which bilingual speakers were exposed: it is most likely that southerners first encountered French through contact with other southerners rather than with native speakers from Paris.

In the examination of change taking place in RF as a result of exposure to other non-local varieties of French, acoustic phonetic techniques are also employed: the analysis of fine-grained phonetic data permits the analysis to examine the exact levels of convergence, among younger generations, towards the northern French norm. Hornsby's study identified, in the RF of younger speakers, forms which appeared to be diffusing from Paris but notes that RF varieties at some distance from Paris may be better equipped to resist the loss of local features in favour of non-local forms (2006: 137). This analysis aims to challenge the received view that RF is made up of transitional ephemera, focusing on a geographical area some 800 km from Paris (compared to 200 km for Avion), and provides evidence from the south of France that young speakers are not simply adopting northern forms at the expense of local ones.

Structure of the Book

Through an examination of RF formation during language contact and of change over time in RF during dialect contact, this book offers a unique comparison of the differential outcomes of each contact situation in southern RF, with two sub-studies addressing the questions of genesis and evolution respectively.

Chapter 1 presents the varieties that are involved in language contact, French and

Béarnais, as well as the variety that has emerged from this language contact, RF. The chapter comprises an external history of the imposition of French in Béarn, a detailed overview of the remaining Béarnais speech community in the twentieth century, and a discussion of the linguistic and ideological definitions of Béarnais and RF as languages or dialects.

Chapter 2 provides a detailed phonological description of Béarnais, comparing it along the way to the phonology of standard French and the northern supralocal norm, with the aim of identifying features that have the potential to transfer during language contact or, conversely, to be adopted during dialect contact. Traditional accounts of RF phonology are then presented for the southwestern region and for the south of France more generally, drawing on a selection of available impressionistic data.

Chapter 3 focuses on methodology, presenting two studies which explicitly address the research hypotheses discussed above, and outlines the methodology employed in these empirical analyses of linguistic variation and change in RF: sample design, including fieldwork sites and informant selection procedures; data elicitation techniques used in both studies to build corpora for Béarnais and French; acoustic phonetic analysis; auditory analysis; and statistical modelling techniques. The language contact and dialect contact studies are both 'sociophonetic' in nature, involving an acoustic phonetic analysis with rigorous adherence both to analytic 'best practices' and to a Labovian sociolinguistic research methodology.

Chapter 4 presents the results of the language contact study and addresses the question of how the phonology of RF arises, focusing on phonological and phonetic transfer from Béarnais into French. The language contact study provides a systematic analysis of the Béarnais and French mid-vowel and nasal vowel systems focusing on data from elderly bilingual speakers. Evidence for phonetic and phonological transfer from Béarnais into French is advanced and the linguistic mechanisms, active during the formation of RF, which promote and inhibit substrate 'residue' are discussed in detail.

Chapter 5 discusses the mechanisms of change that are active when dialects of the same language come into contact, namely levelling and geographical diffusion. The analysis and results for the dialect contact study are presented, using the findings of the language contact study as a reference point: the French of the older bilingual speakers is compared to two younger generations of monolingual French speakers in order to examine language change in apparent time. The outcomes of contact between emergent RF and other contiguous and incoming varieties of French are assessed, focusing particularly on evidence for convergence towards the northern French norm in the speech of younger generations. Variation and change in both the mid- and nasal vowel systems is analysed separately and evidence for phonetic and phonological change identified in RF is interpreted using the theories of dialect levelling advanced by Kerswill (2003) in order to explain why some localised features of RF are lost while others have been retained.

Chapter 6 revisits the genesis and evolution of RF in light of the results presented, and provides a detailed comparison of the mechanisms of change active in Béarn and Avion, contrasting the situation in Béarn with Hornsby's (2006) application of the koinéization model to phonological data in a situation of dialect contact in northern France. This comparative discussion sheds light on the differential outcomes of language contact (in Béarn) and dialect contact (in Avion) during the formation of RF. It also permits an examination of subsequent supralocalisation in two areas with contrasting socio-demographic histories, at very different distances from the Parisian centre. Finally, Chapter 6 addresses the links between changing linguistic norms in Béarn and the postmodern focus on local identities, regionalism, and other related socio-political issues.

Notes to the Introduction

1. Gilliéron, J., and E. Edmont, E. 1902–10. *Atlas linguistique de la France* (Paris: Champion) and, for example, Gardette, P. 1950. *Atlas linguistique et ethnographique du Lyonnais* (Lyon: Institut de linguistique romane des facultés catholiques); Séguy, J., and J. Allières, 1954–1973. *Atlas linguistique et ethnographique de la Gascogne* (Paris: CNRS); Patrice, B. 1980. *Atlas linguistique et ethnographique normand* (Paris: CNRS), etc.

2. 'Gasconismes' was often used to denote solecisms in general, in addition to its more literal meaning: 'Tour, mot gascon employé en français' (*Le nouveau Petit Robert de la langue française*, 2009).

3. Some conceptions of RF consider it to comprise phonological, grammatical and lexical variation: 'les régionalismes du français affectent toutes les parties de la langue: la prononciation, la grammaire, les mots' (Tuaillon, 1988: 292). Many sociolinguistic descriptions of RF have tended, however, to focus on phonological and phonetic variation (see, for example, Martinet, 1945; Walter, 1982; Carton et al., 1983).

CHAPTER 1

❖

Research Context

La France et le Béarn, dit-on, sont deux royaumes distincts..., le Béarn est lié à la France à peu près comme l'Irlande à l'Angleterre.
Victor-Pierre Dubarat, *Document sur Betharam*, 1900

Language contact between French and Béarnais, the indigenous language of Béarn, is hypothesised to have resulted in a distinct contemporary variety of French in the region. This chapter will examine the sociohistorical situation within which this language contact has taken place. It begins by discussing externally the evolution of the contact varieties, Béarnais and French, from Vulgar Latin as well as the history of French within the region, focusing on the process of language shift which has led to the obsolescence of Béarnais under pressure from French. The sociolinguistic characteristics of modern Béarnais speakers in the region are then presented, ahead of a general discussion of the distinction between language and dialect death. Terminological ambiguity associated with many of the designations used to refer to language in this book are problematised and the social arena within which these ambiguities have come to exist are discussed.

1.1. Dialectal Fragmentation in Gallo-Romance

By the tenth century A.D., the varieties descended from the Vulgar Latin spoken in Gaul had become strongly diversified along regional lines. While this regional diversity is, to a certain extent, attributable to the settlement of large numbers of non-Latin speaking migrants in Roman Gaul during the fifth and sixth centuries, Lodge notes that varying rates of romanisation in the territory and contact between Latin and various indigenous substrate languages, such as Gaulish or Aquitainian languages, meant that even before the Germanic invasions, the Latin spoken in Gaul was not uniform (1993: 79). These external influences led to the development of three broad dialect areas and within those dialect areas, the development of sub-dialect areas (Hawkins, 1993: 58). The most significant division within Gallo-Romance is between the dialect area in the south, *langue d'oc*, and the dialect area in the north, *langue d'oïl*, with a third, eastern, dialect area, *francoprovençal*, often said to constitute a transition zone. These dialectal divisions have persisted into modern times and Lodge notes that 'a comparison of the geographical distribution of regional forms found in medieval texts with their distribution charted onto modern dialect atlases shows a remarkable degree of stability' (1993: 71). The main

FIG. 1.1. Gallo-Romance languages (© Damien Mooney)

FIG. 1.2. Gallo-Romance dialects and other regional languages (© Damien Mooney)

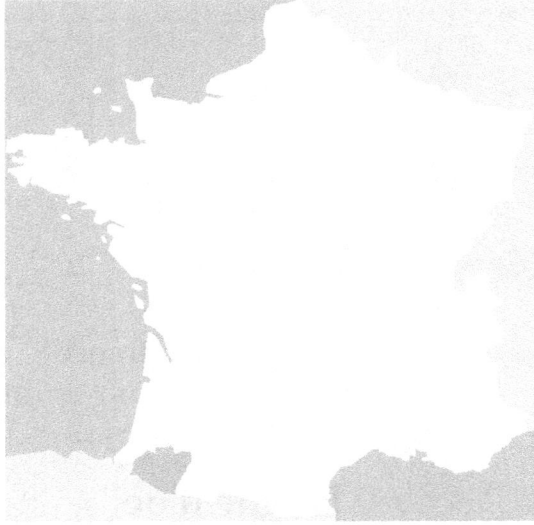

FIG. 1.3. The region of Béarn (© Wikimedia Commons user Thomas Gun)

dialect and sub-dialect areas for Gallo-Romance are illustrated in Figure 1.1. The transition zones between the *langue d'oc* and *langue d'oïl* areas are not clear-cut (Rickard, 1974: 25), but at the extreme ends of the *oc/oïl* continuum the dialects of the north may be considered as different from the dialects of the south as modern French is from modern Spanish (Hawkins, 1993: 58) and differences between them are evident at all levels of linguistic structure.

The modern *langue d'oc* dialect area covers thirty-one French *départements* and extends beyond France's national borders into Spain and Italy (Laroussi and Marcellesi, 1993: 90). The southern *langue d'oc* area is commonly divided into six main dialects that can be seen in Figure 1.2: Gascon in the southwest including the Béarnais and Aranese sub-dialects; Central Languedocian; Limousin and Auvergnat in the north of the *oc* region; Provençal in the southeast including the Nissart sub-dialect; Vivaro-Alpin or *provençal alpin* above the Provençal region. Bec (1963) sees these six *langue d'oc* dialects as forming three supra-groups: Southern Occitan (Languedocian and Provençal); Northern Occitan (Limousin, Auvergnat and Vivaro-Alpin); Gascon stands alone.

Within the *langue d'oc* area, Gascon is often singled out as a special case because it contains strongly marked regional features that are not found in any other dialects (Walter, 1988: 153). Indeed, Bec calls Gascon 'un lengatge estranh' [a strange/ foreign language] (1963: 48). Linguistic Gascony stretches from the Pyrenees to the Atlantic Ocean and from the Garonne river to the area around Toulouse (Bec, 1963: 48) with the exception of a small historically Basque-speaking area in the extreme southwest (see Figure 1.2). The explanation as to why Gascon contains such highly distinct linguistic features has been much debated. Lodge notes that numerous factors seem to be at play: the pre-Latin Aquitainian (rather than Gaulish) substratum; the post-Latin Basque superstratum resulting from the Basque invasion of the area between the Garonne and the Pyrenees from the sixth to the ninth centuries; and close communication networks with Romance-speaking populations south of the Pyrenees (1993: 68).

Béarn is the historically Romance-speaking part of the modern-day Pyrénées-Atlantiques *département* (see Figure 1.3). The *langue d'oc* variety historically spoken in Béarn is commonly referred to as Béarnais, and is a sub-dialect of Gascon. The number of Gascon speakers in southwestern France increases steadily from north (Bordeaux) to south (the Pyrenees) and because Béarn is the area of linguistic Gascony with the highest recorded number of Gascon speakers (cf. Moreux, 2004), Béarnais may be considered the principal surviving dialect of Gascon, and has thus become largely synonymous with it. Jean Lafitte describes the relationship between Béarnais and Gascon in romantic terms: 'le gascon, une langue à part entière, le béarnais, âme du gascon' (1996: 1).

1.2. External History of French in Béarn

From as early as the twelfth century A.D., all official documentation in Béarn was written in the local language, Béarnais, rather than in Latin (Keller, 1985: 65). Béarnais was thus firmly established as the prestige language at a time when official documentation written elsewhere, in the geographical space we know today as France, was largely written in Latin. Despite the predominance, elsewhere, of Latin in writing over all territorial vernaculars into the sixteenth century, the presence of French in Béarn can be attested as far back as 1387, when Gaston Fébus, Count of Foix and Viscount of Béarn, wrote his *Livre de Chasse*. However, Fébus notes in the epilogue that French is not his mother tongue and apologises for any errors in his writing: 'Et aussi ma langue n'est pas si bien duite de parler le franssois comme mon propre langayge' (cited in Tucoo-Chala, 1976: 171). He wrote many other works primarily in Béarnais and, at this time, French was almost unheard of in Béarn and was certainly far from posing any threat to, or competing in any way with, Béarnais.

In 1539, François I signed the *Ordonnances de Villers-Cotterêts* into law, one provision of which was to discontinue the use of Latin in official documentation within the geographical area governed by the French crown. The result was that over the 1540–1580 period, a very specific type of bilingualism[1] developed in many parts of the territory which followed a simple formula: 'le français est employé, quand on écrit, et l'idiome local, quand on parle' (Brun, 1923: 5). All official documentation, in the territory under French rule, was translated from Latin into French during this forty-year period. The implications of this for the largely illiterate masses were minimal and the majority continued to speak their local language variety. At the time of the *Ordonnances*, Béarn was a politically sovereign state, forming part of the *Royaume de Navarre*, and thus the legal stipulations of the *Ordonnances* did not impose any obligation. In the sixteenth century, official documentation in Béarn continued to be written in Béarnais. For example, the *Fors* (constitutional legislature) were printed in Béarnais in 1552 (Brun, 1923: 27). The queen regnant of Navarre, Jeanne d'Albret, mother of Henri IV of France, demanded that all judicial acts, patents and official documentation be written in Béarnais (Brun, 1923: 15) and, in 1568, that

Catholic mass be given to the population in Béarnais (Keller, 1985: 68). Despite this resistance to French at an official level in Béarn, a series of historical events took place resulting in situations favourable to its use in many domains. Jeanne d'Albret converted to Protestantism and introduced it to the region in the late sixteenth century. This introduction of the protestant faith involved high levels of in-migration to Béarn from Paris. The protestant preachers spoke French and, by virtue of their regional origins, their relative education, and the nomadic nature of their work, spreading their word throughout the region resulted in widespread contact between French and Béarnais. While it is almost certain that the nobility were using French during the protestant reform, there is evidence to suggest that the general population may have engaged with the protestant faith through Béarnais (Keller, 1985: 69).

Henri IV, *Roi de Navarre*, succeeded to the French throne in 1589. Following his succession, he granted continued sovereignty to Béarn and it thus remained an independent state, separate from France. Despite Béarn's independence, the reign of Henri IV (1589–1610) was characterised by a rise in the use of French in official acts and documentation. However, alternations in usage between French and Béarnais, in Béarn, were relatively infrequent with Béarnais remaining the dominant language. Béarnais remained the official language of the state and of address to the state or to those in authority and undoubtedly the language used in everyday communication by the masses. The *Fors* were again printed in Béarnais in 1602. By this stage, the rest of the south of France had renounced written usage of the local idiom in favour of French, a process almost certainly accelerated by the introduction of the printing press (Brun, 1923: 27).

The seventeenth century heralded a large number of political reforms that affected both national (Béarn, not France) and linguistic norms in Béarn. In 1610, with the succession to the French throne of Henri IV's son, Louis XIII, the status of Béarnais as official language of the sovereign state suffered as a result of the political unity with the French Kingdom. In 1620, Louis XIII incorporated Béarn into France by signing the *Édit d'Union* and ordered that all 'procédures de notre dite cour de Parlement soient expédiés en langage françois' (Brun, 1923: 32). While this legislation marks the shift from Béarnais to French at the court and for officialdom, Brun states that it is almost certain that at this time southern populations, beyond the court, were completely ignorant of French and unable to use it (1923: 6). By contrast, sufficient evidence exists to suggest that the nobility and the upper classes in Béarn were using French though their mother tongue was Béarnais (Brun, 1923: 19; Keller, 1985: 70). As a result of this, the people in Béarn who were speaking French were still highly dependent on Béarnais and spoke a French that was highly influenced by their mother tongue (Keller, 1985: 90).

From 1620 onwards, French was the official language of Béarn but there is evidence to suggest that, even for the officialdom, language shift was far from complete for a substantial period following the incorporation of Béarn into France. The *Fors* were re-printed in Béarnais throughout the seventeenth and eighteenth centuries (1625, 1673, 1715, 1723, 1781) (Keller, 1985: 70) whereas written documentation in the rest of Gascony, Provence and Languedoc had been in French since 1540. While writing in French gradually began to overtake Béarnais during the eighteenth century, the amount of documentation written in Béarnais was substantial, particularly in more rural areas such as the Pyrenean valleys (Brun, 1923: 52) and Béarnais remained the language of oral communication and some documentation until at least the eve of the Revolution. Brun states, in discussing the shift from Béarnais to French, 'et ce dénouement a été préparé et consommé non par l'intrusion de la monarchie française en Béarn, mais par celle des Béarnais dans les affaires de France' (1923: 17). The incorporation of Béarn into France did not, in and of itself, encourage the Béarnais people to speak French; in fact, it had little effect on the language of everyday communication. However, the increasing contact with Paris indirectly encouraged those who looked outside of the region to use French at the expense of Béarnais.

Upon the publication of the *Convocation des États Généraux* in 1789, many Béarnais nobles and bourgeois expressed nationalistic (Béarnais) sentiments, stating that the *Édit d'Union* (1620) was illegal as it had never been ratified by Béarn and had been imposed by force (Tucoo-Chala, 2009: 115). In fact, some notaries continued to write in Béarnais until 1815. However, from 1815 onwards, 'les Béarnais se contentèrent de suivre, toujours avec retard et avec modération, les implusions politiques venues de Paris' (Tucoo-Chala, 2009: 15). Post-Revolution, there is very little information available on the subsequent stages of language shift in Béarn. Keller discusses the increase of literacy in French as an indicator of the rate of decline of Béarnais over the course of the nineteenth century (1985: 71). Baron Dupin's (1826) *La carte de la France scolaire*, indicates that, in Pyrénées-Atlantiques, only one in fifteen boys of school-going age had received any formal education suggesting that at most 6% of the youngest generation *may* have spoken French. Victor Drury's (1864) similar survey found that between 70% and 80% of children attending school had some knowledge of French. This does not, however, account for those children who were not attending school.

The eventual shift from Béarnais to French was supported by the *Lois Jules Ferry* (1881–82) and the resultant introduction of national free and compulsory education between 1881 and 1886. The period immediately following the *Lois Jules Ferry* was not necessarily characterised by large levels of fluency and literacy in French among the general population. Weber takes the end of the First World War as the watershed in the fortunes of the traditional Romance dialects and regional languages of France (1979: 79), the shared experience of conscription having raised national consciousness and underlined the value of French as a *lingua franca* (Hornsby, 2006: 125). Moreux and Moreux (1989) note, however, that although the first signs of disaffection with Béarnais, in rural areas, appeared in the generation born during the First World War, the predominant daily use of French in Béarn began only with the generation born during the Second World War. The general shift from a rural to an urban-focused society in the twentieth century also supported the use of French in everyday communication. Even so, there are indications that the vitality of Béarnais continued for some time, particularly in rural areas. For example, Pottier's (1968) *Carte du bilinguisme en milieu rural* shows the majority of the rural areas of the Midi exhibiting a 'bilinguisme usuel' while only the Pyrenean borderlands and contiguous areas are credited with the label 'bilinguisme intense' (Kristol and Wüest, 1985: 2). The exact intensity of bilingualism in Béarn is open to interpretation. We can glean from this, however, that language contact in Béarn continued up until the mid-twentieth century, at least in rural areas. Indeed, in the mid-1980s, Kristol and Wüest, proclaimed that there were several rural sites in Béarn where intense bilingualism was still found and where we can study the language of the last generation of native speakers who arrived at school aged five, unable to speak French (1985: 4).

The contact period between Béarnais and French began on a large scale from 1826 to 1864 and continued, with Béarnais being transmitted as L1, up until some time between the two World Wars, a period of approximately eighty to one hundred years. Many of the last generation of Béarnais-French bilinguals are thus still alive today and in the cases of these speakers, of course, language contact has persisted up to the present day. The cessation of intergenerational transmission that occurred during the twentieth century, and concomitant completion of language shift to French, can thus be observed in apparent time, particularly in the urban and semi-urban areas of Béarn.

1.3. The Béarnais Speech Community

From the late nineteenth century onwards, and indeed over the course of the twentieth century, Béarnais found itself in an increasing state of language obsolescence. While there is some evidence to suggest that the last generation of native speakers were born in rural areas up until the eve of the Second World War (Moreux, 2004: 25), the state of the language in the latter half of the twentieth century displays the characteristics described by language obsolescence models: the language not being taught to children in the home; the number of speakers declining very rapidly, the entire population being bilingual, with French preferred in almost all situations; little or no literacy in the language (Bauman, 1980). In Dorian's terms, Béarnais is in a situation of 'gradual death' (1981: 107), but this definition specifies an age-governed proficiency continuum in the obsolescent variety: young speakers tend to be least proficient and older speakers most proficient with at least one generation of semi-speakers. Béarnais, however, has no marked age-governed proficiency continuum: native speakers are relatively easily locatable amongst Béarn-born inhabitants over the age of sixty-five in rural areas, but below this age, they are much more difficult to find and very few speakers are to be found under the age of forty.[2]

In the entire historically Gascon-speaking region, the number of speakers, at all levels of proficiency, varies from 3% of the population in Bordeaux to 30% in Béarn, approximately 500,000 speakers in total[3] (Moreux, 2004: 25). These numbers include fluent native speakers and semi-speakers. In some areas of Béarn, there are said to be many native speakers, an 'enormous pool of people with passive language competence' (Moreux, 2004: 29) and some parents who still transmit the language to their children. For the Béarn region, Moreux cites 16% of people aged over fourteen as saying that they spoke Béarnais well (fluent speakers) and 14% as saying that they spoke a little, giving a total of 30% for speakers of all levels of proficiency, or about 75,000 speakers. If we cautiously examine only the fluent speakers (approximately 40,000 speakers), we must note that over 50% of them are over the age of sixty and rural-dwellers and only 3.5% are between the ages of fourteen and twenty-four. All of the Béarnais speakers noted by Moreux were born in Béarn or in linguistic Gascony with INSEE (1994) showing that, in the late twentieth century, only a little over half of the people living in Béarn over the age of fourteen were actually born there. Finally, we may note that in Pau and its surrounding areas, where almost half of the population of Béarn now lives, Béarnais is almost totally absent (Moreux, 2004: 31). Any Béarnais speakers present in Pau are over the age of fifty and a minority even in this age group.

Béarnais is spoken only in closed tight-knit networks, usually made up of older people, who are very emotionally attached to their language, but few of whom make it an ideological issue or are preoccupied by its future (Moreux, 2004: 25). Béarnais is seen as a community-based and not a family-based language:

> Ce qui frappe, c'est que l'on utilise le béarnais avant tout dans les interactions sociales à l'intérieur de la communauté villageoise et que la famille n'est pas le lieu priviligié où on le parle le plus souvent. [...] Le béarnais est la langue de la communauté restreinte. (Müller et al., 1985: 103)

Kristol and Wüest (1985), referring to the domains of use of Béarnais, summarise the situation as follows: there are a limited number of domains where the language can be spoken, such as the market, for example, to the extent that using Béarnais in an unfamiliar context, such as an interview, can violate the speaker's sense of appropriate setting. Béarnais is thus highly restricted in its domains of use, which reduces its 'functional load'[4] and underlines its status as a dying language.

Nowadays, grandparents, especially grandfathers, may teach their grandchildren playful uses of Béarnais. However, these grandparents, who now seek to transmit *some* Béarnais, were the same parents who were careful not to speak any Béarnais to their children to avoid the shame of them starting school 'sans comprendre un mot de français' (Moreux, 2004: 37). Müller et al. (1985) observed that linguistic exogamy has been a major factor in driving language shift, in both rural and urban areas. In 1983, they observed that in Osse-en-Aspe, a small rural village in the Pyrenean *Vallée d'Aspe*, almost all of the non-Béarnais speakers had had at least one parent of non-Béarnais origin. By contrast, in families with both parents of Béarnais origin, intergenerational transmission was total for all informants surveyed. In the urban setting, notably in Oloron-Sainte-Marie, the largest town in western Béarn, and in Bédous, a large town nearby, non-transmission in families having two Béarnais-speaking parents was the cause of half the cases of monolingual French speakers, the other half being caused by linguistic exogamy (Müller et al., 1985). While we must exercise caution in interpreting these results owing to limited sample sizes and sampling techniques that targeted first language speakers, they indicate that there was a clear rural-urban divide in relation to intergenerational transmission as recently as the 1980s. In many of the rare cases where intergenerational transmission occurred at home, it was often imperfect and a highly marginal endeavour.

Since the 1980s, some public schools and private *Calandretas*, immersion-education schools, have been offering bilingual education at primary school level.

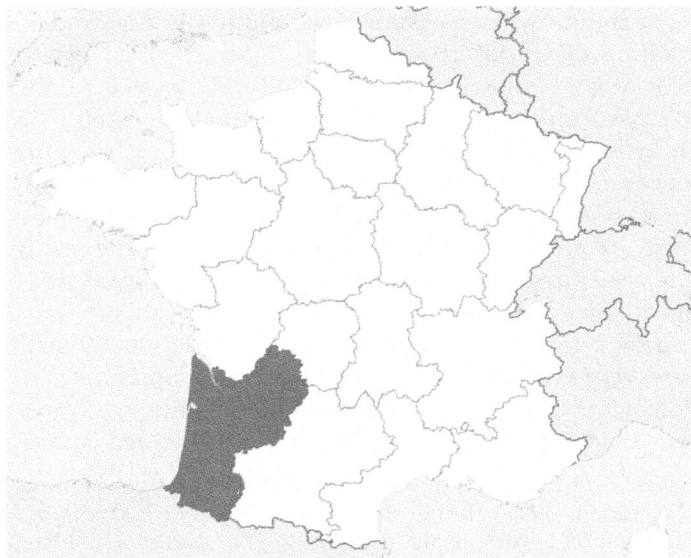

FIG. 1.4. The region of Aquitaine (© Wikimedia Commons user TUBS)

The language the children are taught at school, usually called Occitan, is said to be a 'bit different from the one they might hear at home' (Moreux, 2004: 33). The Pyrénées-Atlantiques *département* has been particularly progressive in terms of promoting primary competence amongst the young (Moreux and Puyau, 2002: 12). Of eleven *Calandretas* in Aquitaine (see Figure 1.4), eight were located in Pyrénées-Atlantiques[5] in 2002 (Coyos, 2004: 180). The *Calandretas* provide children, in theory, with the opportunity to strengthen ties with older generations in the region even if the language that they are taught at school is different from the one they may hear at home. Some cases have been reported, however, where for reasons of unintelligibility, communication between generations has been impeded (Moreux, 2004: 33; Moreux and Puyau, 2005: 4). The overall effect of these bilingual schools on the linguistic competence of the younger generations is almost negligible with only 1% of children attending these schools in Pyrénées-Atlantiques, roughly 2,000 children in total. This situation is further aggravated by the fact that most of the *Calandreta* pupils in urban areas rarely speak Occitan outside of the classroom and are less motivated to do so after they have left primary school (Moreux, 2004: 33).

1.4. 'Language' and 'Dialect' in Béarn

The question of what constitutes a language or a dialect has been widely discussed among linguists, largely because it seems impossible to distinguish between these terms on the basis of linguistic structure alone:

> Even if one rejects the flippant definition of a language as 'a dialect with an army and a navy', it is still undeniable that the distinction between language and dialect is primarily a sociological and psychological matter, rather than something that can be decided on purely linguistic grounds. (Matisoff, 1991:

193, cited in Jones, 2001: 40)

The notion of a language as being simply 'a dialect with an army and a navy' stresses the importance of political factors that lie behind perceived linguistic autonomy (Chambers and Trudgill, 1980: 12) and, indeed, 'language' cannot be considered a particularly linguistic notion at all:

> Linguistic features obviously come into it, but it is clear that we consider Norwegian, Swedish [and] Danish [...] to be single languages for reasons that are as much political, geographical, historical, sociological and cultural as linguistic. (Chambers and Trudgill, 1980: 5)

Defining Norwegian, Swedish and Danish, which have a high degree of mutual intelligibility between them, as 'languages' subverts the traditional definition of a language as a collection of mutually intelligible dialects. While this definition of a language is not always applicable, as illustrated above, it is useful to characterise dialects as subparts of a macro-variety, or language, in order to provide a criterion for distinguishing between one language variety and another (Chambers and Trudgill, 1980: 3).

From a linguistic perspective, the term 'dialect' refers to varieties which are grammatically (and perhaps lexically) as well as phonologically different from other varieties (Hawkins, 1993: 57) in that speakers of the same 'dialect' have a shared set of speech habits with reference to another group who have a different set of speech habits and thus, speak a different 'dialect'.[6] Chambers and Trudgill accept that standard varieties are as much dialects as any other form of the language (1980: 3) but they happen to have acquired the status of 'official dialect' in the countries in which they are spoken (Hawkins, 1993: 57). In being selected as the 'official dialect', these varieties may be said to have become languages, with such a transition highlighting the fact that the 'language' and 'dialect' definitions are intrinsically linked to socio-political phenomena. There is, of course, a distinction to be made between the linguist's problematic attempts to define 'language' and 'dialect' and the popular, often value-laden, use of the terms. In common usage, speakers often use 'language' to refer solely to the standardised varieties based on a common belief that language homogeneity, as represented by the standard, is beneficial to society. This belief is referred to by Milroy and Milroy (1985) as the 'ideology of the standard' and by Houdebine (1995) as the *imaginaire linguistique*. This subjective attitude towards the standard language is based on fictionalisations or rationalisations about the state of the standard language and its use. By contrast, 'dialect' may be employed in common usage to refer to: substandard or low status varieties associated with peasantry, the working class or other non-prestige groups of speakers; erroneous deviations from a standard language; varieties that have no written form, particularly those spoken in isolated parts of the world. These definitions of 'dialect' are generally negative and view dialects as mutations of the standard variety or as separate language varieties that are inferior to the idealised standard.

In France, the popular use of the term 'language' almost exclusively refers to standard French (SF). Houdebine (1995) sees the notion of SF as being born from a prescriptive and normative tradition, comprising an imaginary hierarchy based on a fictionalised representation of language. Such a SF language may be defined as the reference variety of French codified in grammars and dictionaries, and propagated through the education system as the national language of France. Hornsby refers to SF, by this definition, as the prestige norm or *français normatif* (2006: 78). Houdebine (1995) refutes the notion that *français normatif* exists in any real form because the French that is actually spoken in France is not a homogeneous entity but a rich collection of variant forms. This view, however, is not always shared by the general population who fail to recognise that the language they are actually speaking diverges from socially-constructed, idealised SF: 'the problem is that only in some cultures does the standard language and the prestige language amount to the same thing' (Milroy et al., 1994: 352).

The large majority of the French population speaks a variety of 'supralocal French' which Garmadi (1981) refers to as the *norme* and which stands in opposition to idealised SF, the *sur-norme*. Supralocal French is a levelled northern urban variety of French which is, in phonological terms, closely equivalent to what Carton et al. (1983) termed *français standardisé* (in opposition to *français standard*, in the normative sense). It is the variety of French used in urban settings in the area north of the

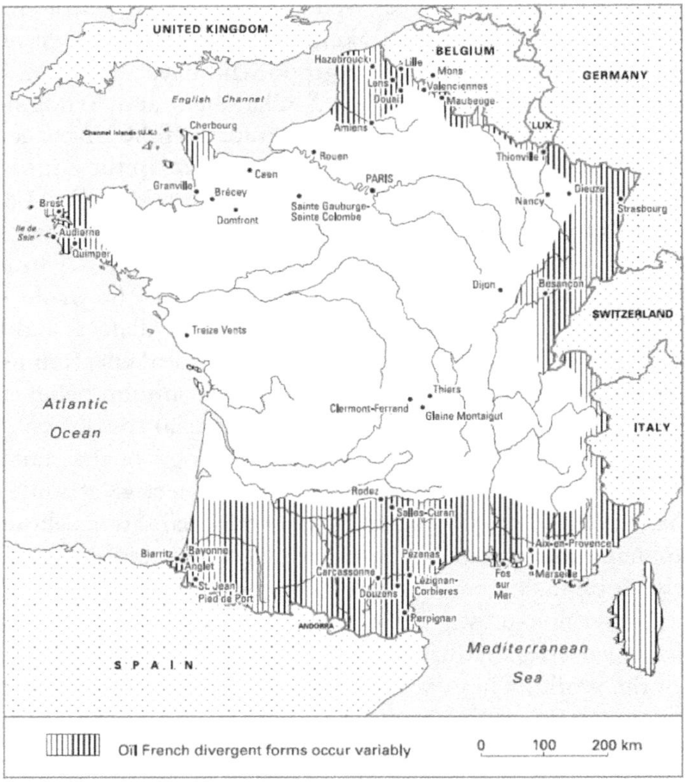

FIG. 1.5. The geographical spread of supralocal French in urban areas.
© Tim Pooley 2006. Source: 'On the geographical spread of Oïl French in France', *Journal of French Language Studies* (Cambridge University Press), p. 385.

Garonne and Massif Central, excluding the extreme peripheral areas to the east, the north and the Breton-speaking west (Armstrong, 2001: 2). Supralocal French constitutes a statistical norm, in that it is the everyday speech form of the majority of the population in the northern two thirds of France which differs from SF primarily in relation to its phonology (Pooley, 2007: 40). The regionally neutral supralocal variety of French has also spread southward into the northern *langue d'oc* regions, as illustrated in Figure 1.5, where the large white area represents a zone where regionally marked varieties are not used in towns.

The use of the term *dialecte* in the French context is notoriously difficult to pin down. *Dialecte* may be used by linguists to denote the Gallo-Romance varieties that emerged from the fragmentation of Vulgar Latin in Gaul (see Figure 1.1) (Hornsby, 2006: 21). In this case the language of which the Gallo-Romance varieties are *dialectes* would be Vulgar Latin. The term *dialecte* may also be used by linguists to refer explicitly to actual linguistic *dialectes de langue d'oïl* (e.g., *normand*, *gallo*, etc.) or *dialectes de langue d'oc* (e.g., *gascon*, *languedocien*, etc.). The popular use of the term *dialecte* may describe all of the Romance varieties of France that are not French; *langue d'oïl* varieties; *langue d'oc* varieties; *Ibero-Romance* (Catalan);[7] *Italo-Romance* (Corsican). In some cases, the term *dialecte* has also become extended to include all languages spoken in France that are not French, including the Romance varieties and the non-Romance varieties (see Figure 1.2).

From a purely linguistic perspective, we cannot say that the languages of France are dialects of French because, even for the *langue d'oïl* varieties to which it is closely related, they have not been derived from French and, for the majority of France's minority languages, they demonstrate varying degrees of typological dissimilarity and structural separation from French. For example, the following comparison illustrates the linguistic separation of French from Béarnais (Gascon) (Mooney, 2015a):

> Les jolies mains de la grand-mère, ridées par le temps, rendue rugueuses par les longs travaux, déformées par les souffrances! Je les vois tremblantes de vieillesse, tendues vers la douce chaleur du feu d'épis de maïs.
>
> Las beròjas mans de la mairana, froncidas per lo temps, bonhudas peus longs tribalhs, torçudas per las dolors! Que las vei, tremolantas de vielhèr, tenudas de cap l'aujor deus cabelhs de milhòc. (Pierre-Daniel Lafore, cited in Darrigrand 2012: 195–98)

In popular usage, the term *dialecte* is often interchangeable with *patois* where the latter may also be used to emphasise the localised characteristics of the *dialecte*. Linguists tend to shy away from the term *patois* because of its pejorative connotations: non-standard, backward, countrified, etc. When it is used, it may denote a highly localised variety of a particular *dialecte*, often spoken in an area no larger than a single village (Hornsby, 2006: 21). The term *patois* is also commonly used by speakers of local languages to refer familiarly to the variety they speak though it may be considered offensive when used by outsiders to the minority speech community. *Patois* is also used as the name for the Romance languages and the non-Romance languages, with both Breton and Béarnais speakers, for example, affirming that they speak *patois*.

Another use of the term *dialecte* refers to contemporary varieties of French. This usage of the term is almost exclusively reserved for specialists and is not widely used by lay-speakers. This type of *dialecte* may refer to any grammatical (and perhaps lexical) and/or phonological deviation from the accepted norm for SF or, equally, with reference to the supralocal norm (cf. Pooley, 2007). By this definition, *dialecte* corresponds broadly to 'dialect' in the Anglo-Saxon linguist's sense, though this usage has been slow to gain currency in France (Hornsby, 2006: 21). Armstrong and Blanchet state that this definition of *dialecte* refers to contemporary regional or social varieties of French, which have evolved since the fairly recent diffusion and adoption of the official language by the whole population (2006: 269). As such, regional varieties of French, or RF, are clearly dialects of French, from a linguistic perspective.

Finally, while the typological separation between Béarnais and French may allow us to define the former as a 'language' relative to French, we have seen that Béarnais is a sub-variety of Gascon which, in turn, forms part of the *langue d'oc* continuum (see Figure 1.2). From 1960 onwards, the *Institut d'Études Occitanes* in Béarn, which had existed elsewhere in the south of France since the eve of the Second World War, aimed to promote 'Occitan', the unifying name used to designate all varieties on the *langue d'oc* continuum, including Gascon and Béarnais, as a language. Subsequent corpus planning has led to the creation of standardised 'Occitan', which aims to unify all southern Gallo-Romance varieties by promoting the features that they have in common. If we accept the Occitanist agenda, then we must consider Gascon to be a dialect of Occitan, and Béarnais to be a sub-dialect of Gascon. Even if we reject standardised Occitan as a language, it seems plausible that, with reference to the *langue d'oc* continuum as a whole, Béarnais can be considered a dialect of southern Gallo-Romance owing to the common structural base that these varieties share from a historical perspective. However, various linguists have argued that elements of Gascon and Béarnais' linguistic structure (notably distinct sound changes and a complex verbal particle system) allow these varieties to be considered as distinct 'languages' with reference to the other *langue d'oc* varieties (Walter, 2008; Lafitte, 1996 ; Bec, 1963). Indeed, these arguments have spread beyond the level of linguistic analysis into the socio-political sphere in the region with the terms 'Béarnais' and 'Occitan' becoming the focus of a variety of ideological constructs which find themselves in conflict. Each term is linked to a set of militant discourses that, on one side, promote Béarnais as a language in its own right and, on the other, refute its autonomy and view Béarnais as a localised dialect of one particular language, Occitan (see Mooney, 2015a, and Moreux, 2004 for discussion).

1.5. Language and Dialect Death

The studies of contact presented in this book examine linguistic variation and change taking place in French, the dominant language variety in a situation of language contact. Any examination of linguistic transfer must, however, take account of the potential structural correlates of obsolescence in the variety that is being replaced, and from which linguistic features are hypothesised to have transferred into the dominant variety. A detailed and accurate description of changes which have taken place in the source language, Béarnais, is therefore essential in addition to an account of its historical representation. From a typological perspective, the level of structural similarity between the varieties in contact determines the nature and amount of linguistic transfer that may occur in a given situation. Linked to typological similarity are the separate but related processes of language and dialect death.

Language obsolescence may be defined as a process whereby a language is ousted from its territory by another language leading to a decline in speakers and 'during which gradual reduction in use, due to domain-restriction, may result in the emergence of historically inappropriate morphological and/or phonological forms together with extensive lexical borrowing' (Jones, 1998: 5). Language death may be seen as the end point of this obsolescence process which occurs at a superordinate level between distinct language varieties: structural separation and typological dissimilarity between the dominant and obsolescent language are largely maintained. It is important to note that language obsolescence is a combination of socio-political and linguistic changes and, indeed, the former gives rise to the latter. We have previously noted that, relative to French, Béarnais may be considered a language, owing to the typological dissimilarity and structural separation that exists between the varieties: the obsolescence of Béarnais from the late nineteenth century onwards can thus be considered a clear case of language death.

Dying languages generally undergo the same types of linguistic change as 'healthy' languages. The types of change that we observe in the structure of a dying language are not notably different from those well established in the study of language change in general, 'but the time span for change seems compressed and the amount of change seems relatively large' (Dorian, 1981: 154). Thus, in 'healthy' languages, a few changes will occur almost imperceptibly over a considerable period of time, but during language obsolescence, it is possible to witness many different types of change over a matter of generations (Dorian, 1981: 151). Structural changes that occur in obsolescent languages may or may not be directly attributable to the influence of an encroaching language. Many changes observed in formal language structure cannot necessarily be explained by external factors (Jones, 1998: 249): simplification leading to increases in regularity; the complete loss of structural elements, e.g. the loss of case distinctions in East Sutherland Gaelic (Dorian, 1981: 130); increases in transparency or the use of more analytic than synthetic structures; the generalisation of unmarked categories, e.g. loss of soft mutations in Welsh. Other changes may be a result of externally motivated transfer from the dominant language (Jones, 1998: 252–57): grammatical interference, e.g. syntactic calques; phonological interference; code-switching; lexical borrowing.

Dorian takes the view that the linguistic benchmark for the 'norm' in a dying language should not constitute the standard historical representations of the language but rather the internal conservative norm represented by the oldest local speakers (1981: 80). As the language shift advances, the historical norm serves as little more than a theoretical construct representing some 'pure' past version of the obsolescent language. Therefore, we must examine its contemporary structure in order to establish that the features we may expect to be involved in transfer are still present.

Dialect death, also known as 'dedialectalisation', is the process by which a specific localised variety of a language becomes obsolescent and dies out. It thus occurs on a subordinate level and does not involve a 'whole' language. For the purpose of this discussion, we may define a dialect linguistically, as a particular local variety of a larger superordinate language (Dorian, 1981: 8). Dialect death has been defined in a variety of different ways, three of which are discussed below, although these definitions are by no means exhaustive.

Dorian described East Sutherland Gaelic as a particular local dialect of the Scottish Gaelic language that is yielding to an equally particular local dialect of the English language, East Sutherland English (1981: 8). Scottish Gaelic will not become extinct with the loss of East Sutherland Gaelic and by this definition, only a particular local variety, and not a language will have died. Dorian herself points out that this definition of dialect death is problematic because the whole Scottish Gaelic language is threatened by (Scottish) English at a superordinate level. Therefore, the competition, at a national (Scottish) level, is between two typologically distinct languages, Gaelic and English; at a local level, the question is always which language, and not which dialect, to speak. Since, in the local context, the death of East Sutherland Gaelic will mean that a language, and not a dialect, will have died, this situation may more accurately be described as one of language death. By this definition, 'dialect death' is just one localised step in the language shift process: the gradual elimination of all dialects of Gaelic by English. The situation described by Dorian in Scotland parallels, in many ways, the situation in Béarn: the death of Béarnais at the hands of French, in the local context, is a case of language death, even if only one dialect of the larger *langue d'oc* continuum will have been eradicated. The other remaining dialects on this continuum are, of course, equally threatened by the dominant language.

A second type of dialect death sees a particular local variety of a language being replaced by a supralocal or national variety of the same language. In this case, dedialectalisation, at a subordinate level, leads to the replacement of local features with other non-local features of the same language. For example, Jones notes that since the introduction of Welsh-medium education in Wales, 'there is now occurring a phenomenon whereby local Welsh is being replaced by a Welsh that includes non-local features, most of them features of Standard Welsh but some also associated with other regional dialects' (1998: 260). It is also worth noting that, in the case of Welsh, as with Scottish Gaelic, these local varieties are also threatened by English at a superordinate level. We might expect similar processes to be active in Béarnais as a result of the Occitan standardisation movement and of Occitan-medium education, in which case the loss of localised features from Béarnais because of contact with the artificial standard would constitute a case of dialect obsolescence. Additionally, the loss of localised linguistic forms from regional varieties of the dominant language, French, may also be considered as 'dedialectalisation', as non-local or supralocal features are imported from Paris and/or other urban areas in the north of France.

A third definition of dialect death falls somewhere between those of Dorian and Jones. This type of dialect death, which comprises both language shift and dedialectalisation, has been discussed by Hornsby (2006) in relation to Picard and French which evolved, largely independently, from Latin and are historically bound to the regions of Ile-de-France[8] and Picardy respectively. They are both classified as *dialectes d'oïl* and they exhibit many structural similarities common to varieties of northern Gallo-Romance. Following the imposition of French as the national language, language contact led to high levels of linguistic convergence (phonological, morphosyntactic, lexical) towards French in Picard because of the typological similarity between the varieties (cf. Matras, 2010 : 68). This convergence is predominantly unidirectional ('advergence' or *Advergenz*; cf. Armstrong and Pooley, 2010: 10) and is said to be so great that 'it has fostered the perception that Picard is no more than a debased subvariety of French (Hornsby, 2006: 9). On this observation, Hornsby treats Picard obsolescence as a case of dialect death rather than language death even though Picard can not strictly be considered, from a historical perspective, to be a dialect of French. This 'dialect' has subsequently been ousted from its territory by French by the process of dedialectalisation, in the same way that regional varieties of Welsh are yielding to non-local Welsh forms. This definition of dialect death is, however, dependent on delineating some form of boundary at which one language may converge to the extent that it becomes another.

To summarise, contact between French and Béarnais must be considered to be a case of language contact because of the structural separation between the varieties as well as their independent historical developments from Latin. As such, the increasingly obsolescent nature of Béarnais may be considered a clear case of language death, as opposed to dialect death. When considered relative to standardised Occitan or to the *langue d'oc* continuum, the loss of Béarnais constitutes the loss of a single localised dialect and may thus be defined as dialect death, from a pan-regional perspective. Contact between regional and supralocal varieties of French is a case of dialect contact and the loss of contemporary regional varieties of French, as a result of encroachment from the supralocal norm, is a case of dialect death, or dedialectalisation, from a national perspective.

Notes to Chapter 1

1. The question of whether this type of bilingualism constitutes diglossia is beyond the scope of the present discussion. There is evidence to suggest, however, that even in the modern era, closely related varieties, such as French and Picard, represent separate grammars for bilingual speakers (Villeneuve and Auger, 2013).
2. See Jones (2001: 3) for a parallel situation in Jersey Norman French.
3. All speaker numbers are taken from Moreux (2004) who uses three reports entitled *Pratique(s), (présence) et représentations de l'occitan (ou langue occitane)* published between 1994 and 1997 after surveys were undertaken for the *Conseils Généraux* of the Pyrénées-Atlantiques *département* and for the Aquitaine *Conseil Régional*.
4. 'Functional load', is not used here in the same way as in functional phonology. It is used with the following meaning: 'a quantitative base to evaluate the notion of "power" of the languages in a society in order to distinguish between major and minor languages. The language that successfully functions in relatively more domains is considered to have a higher "functional load"' as specified in Pandharipande (2002: 1).

5. In the historically Basque-speaking region of Pyrénées-Atlantiques, Basque-French bilingual immersion schools, called *Ikastolas*, are the Basque equivalent of the *Calandretas*.

6. 'Accent' differs from 'dialect' in that it refers solely to pronunciation and therefore to a variety that is phonetically and/or phonologically different from other varieties. Chambers and Trudgill note, however, that 'accents' and 'dialects' frequently merge into one another without any discrete break (1980: 5).

7. The classification of Catalan as either Occitano-Romance (and thus Gallo-Romance) or as Ibero-Romance is a moot point amongst Romance Linguists (cf. Bec, 1963).

8. The emergence of French or 'francien' also involved high degrees contact and mixing with other northern Gallo-Romance varieties. It is thus not as straightforwardly localised as Picard (see Lodge, 1993).

CHAPTER 2

❖

Phonological Systems

*Sur les lèvres d'un homme du Midi et sur les lèvres d'un homme du Nord, les
mêmes mots n'ont pas les mêmes sons, la même harmonie, la même délicatesse,
ni en définitive le même caractère.*
Maxime Lanusse, *De l'influence du dialecte gascon*, 1891

This chapter provides a phonological description of Béarnais, comparing it to the
phonologies of both standard and supralocal French in order to identify the variants that have the most potential to transfer during language contact. The chapter also provides a description of changing RF phonologies in Gascony and the south of France more generally over the course of the twentieth century, drawing on a number of previous studies of RF. These phonological descriptions serve to contextualise the analyses of vocalic sub-systems that follow in Chapter 3 and to facilitate the reader's interpretation of the examples presented, particularly for Béarnais. Indeed, from a theoretical perspective, it is necessary to consider linguistic variation and change in individual variables with reference to the entire phonological system in which they occur:

> Les changements linguistiques ne prennent leur sens que si l'on considère tout
> l'ensemble du développement dont ils font partie [...] et il n'est jamais légitime
> d'essayer d'expliquer un détail en dehors de la considération du système général
> de la langue où il apparaît. (Meillet, 1906: 11)

Furthermore, it is hoped that these descriptions may function as a useful point of reference for students of French dialectology and for future analyses of Béarnais and of southern RF.

2.1. Béarnais Phonology

Graphic standardisation has been the main bone of contention between competing militant movements in the region of Béarn, with neither accepting the other's conventions. The Occitanist movement makes use of a standardised 'classical' orthography while more localised movements tend to use an orthographical system, codified in the *Dictionnaire du béarnais et du gascon moderne* (Palay, 1980), which reflects local pronunciations more closely. In the discussion that follows, these orthographies are used with the values attached to them by the regional and pan-regional movements, respectively: Palay (1980) for Béarnais; 'classical' orthography for Occitan.

Oral vowels

The Béarnais phonological inventory contains seven oral vowels that can appear in tonic[1] syllables (Bouzet, 1928; Bendel, 1934; Grosclaude, 1986; Moreux and Puyau, 2002, 2005; Molyneux, 2002). The oral vowel system is schematised in Figure 2.1, following the conventions of the International Phonetic Alphabet.

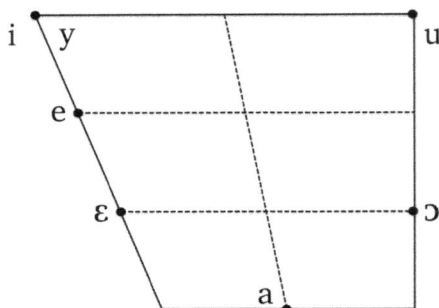

FIG. 2.1. The Béarnais oral vowel system (© Damien Mooney)

Béarnais has three close vowels, /i y u/, one close-mid vowel, /e/, two open-mid vowels, /ɛ ɔ/, and one open vowel, /a/. Vowels appearing to the left of a line, /i e ɛ a/, are unrounded vowels, and those to the right, /y u ɔ/, are rounded vowels. The standardised Occitan oral vowel system contains the same contrastive phonemes, as illustrated, with lexical examples, in Table 2.1.

Phoneme	Béarnais		Occitan
/i/	*pic* /pik/	('amer')	*picót* /pi'kɔt/
/y/	*pun* /pyn/	('point')	*punch* /pynʃ/
/e/	*péch* /peʃ/	('pêche')	*peis* /pes/
/ɛ/	*pè* /pɛ/	('pied')	*pè* /pɛ/
/a/	*pa* /pa/	('paire')	*par* /pa/
/ɔ/	*porc* /pɔrk/	('porc')	*pòrc* /pɔrk/
/u/	*poume* /'pumɔ/	('pomme')	*poma* /'pumɔ/

TABLE 2.1. Oral vowel phonemes of Béarnais and Occitan

The contemporary Béarnais and French oral vowel systems evolved, of course, from a common Latin root. A comparison of this evolution is provided here with the aim of examining the structural correspondences between the phonologies in contact for bilingual speakers in Béarn:

(i)   Latin Ī is retained as /i/ in Béarnais and French, e.g., VĪTAM > *bite* ['bitɔ] in Béarnais and *vie* [vi] in French.

(ii) Latin Ū became /y/ in Béarnais and French in stressed position, e.g., DURUM > *dur* [dyɾ] in Béarnais and *dur* [dyʁ] in French.

(iii) Latin Ē became /e/ and /ɛ/ in both languages, e.g., BELLUS > *bère* ['bɛɾɔ] in Béarnais and *belle* [bɛl] in French.

(iv)   Latin ā is preserved as /a/ in Béarnais but became /ɛ/ in French, e.g., MARE > *ma* [ma] in Béarnais and *mer* [mɛʁ] in French.

(v)   Latin −A (unstressed) became word-final post-tonic /-ɔ/ in Béarnais, e.g., HORA > *ore* [ˈɔɾɔ]. In modern SF, the reflex of word-final Latin −A, [ə] or the schwa, is now absent in word-final position, e.g., HORA > *heure* [œːʁ].

(vi)   Latin u (unstressed) became /ɔ/ in Béarnais but /u/ in French, e.g., BULLA > *bole* [ˈbɔlɔ] in Béarnais and *boule* [bul] in French.

(vii)   Latin ō became /u/ in Béarnais but /œ/ or /ø/ in French, e.g., FLOREM > *hlou* [ˈhlu] in Béarnais and *fleur* [flœːʁ] in French; NEPŌS > *nebout* [neˈbut] in Béarnais, but *neveu* [n(ə)ˈvø] in French.

(viii) Latin o (unstressed) also became /u/ in Béarnais, but /ɔ/ in French, e.g., PORTŌ > *pourtà* [purˈta] in Béarnais and *porter* [pɔʁte] in French.

These structural correspondences will be important in determining the parts of the phonological system of French where L1-to-L2 transfer has the potential to occur (see Sections 2.2 and 3.1).

Nasal units

The diachronic evolution of Latin VN (vowel + nasal consonant) sequences has also produced different results in Béarnais and French. The following points outline the historical development of their modern-day nasal unit systems, where 'nasal unit' is used here to mean 'any reflex of a historical VN sequence' (see Taylor, 1996):

(i)   Latin IN in closed or late-closed[2] syllables became /ĩ/ in Béarnais and /ɛ̃/ in French, e.g., FINUM > *fĩ* [fĩ] in Béarnais and *fin* [fɛ̃] in French. We may note that Old French did have a nasal /ĩ/ vowel (< Latin IN) which subsequently became modern /ɛ̃/ via a merger with Old French /ẽ/ and /ɛ̃/. When the Latin vowel remained in an open syllable, IN became /in/ in both Béarnais and French, e.g., FINAM > *fine* [ˈfinɔ] in Béarnais and *fine* [fin] in French.

(ii)   Latin EN in closed syllables became /en/ in Béarnais and /ã/ in French (via Old French /ã/; Rickard, 1974: 65), e.g., DENTUM > *dén* [den] in Béarnais and *dent* [dã] in French. In late-closed syllables, Latin EN became /ẽ/ in Béarnais and /ɛ̃/ in French, e.g., PLENUM > *plê* [plẽ] in Béarnais and *plein* [plɛ̃] in French. Finally, for open syllables, Latin EN became /en/ in Béarnais and /ɛn/ in French, e.g., PLENAM > *plene* [ˈplenɔ] in Béarnais and *pleine* [plɛn] in French.

(iii)   Latin AN in closed syllables became /an/ in Béarnais and /ã/ in French (via Old French /ã/), e.g., ANNUM > *an* [an] in Béarnais and *an* [ã] in French. In late-closed syllables, Latin AN became /ã/ in Béarnais and /ɛ̃/ in French, e.g., SANUM > *sâ* [sã] in Béarnais and *sain* [sɛ̃] in French. Latin AN in open syllables became /an/ in Béarnais and /ɛn/ in French, e.g., SANAM > *sane* [ˈsanɔ] in Béarnais and *saine* [sɛn] in French.

(iv)   Latin ON in closed syllables became /un/ in Béarnais and /ɔ̃/ in French (via Old French /ũ/; Rickard, 1974: 65), e.g., PONTEM > *poun* [pun] in Béarnais and *pont* [pɔ̃] in French. In late-closed syllables, Latin ON became /ũ/ in

Béarnais and /ɔ̃/ in French (via Old French /ũ/), e.g., BONUM > *boû* [bũ] in Béarnais and *bon* [bɔ̃] in French. Latin ON in open syllables became /un/ in Béarnais and /ɔn/ in French (via Old French /ũn/), e.g., BONAM > *boune* ['bunə] in Béarnais and *bonne* [bɔn] in French.

(v)   Latin UN in closed and late-closed syllables became /ỹ/ in Béarnais and /œ̃/ in French (via Old French /ỹ/), e.g., UNUS > *û* [ỹ] in Béarnais and *un* [œ̃] in French. There are, however, some instances of Latin UM in late-closed syllables becoming vowel + nasal consonant sequences in *langue d'oc*, e.g., PERFUMUM > *perhum* [per'hỹm] in Béarnais and *parfum* [paʁfœ̃] in French. In open syllables, Latin UN became /ỹ/ in Béarnais and /yn/ in French, e.g., UNA > *ûe* [ỹə] in Béarnais and *une* [yn] in French.

Therefore, Béarnais contains five phonemically nasal vowels /ĩ ỹ ẽ ã ũ/ and five vowel+nasal consonant (VN) sequences /iN yN eN aN uN/. The nasal consonant in nasal units /iN yN eN aN uN/ may surface as [n], [m], [ɲ], or [ŋ]. The vowel in each sequence is (variably) nasalised (Séguy and Allières, 1954–1973), e.g., *lìnye* ['lĩnje] ('linge'); *brun* ['brỹn] ('brun'); *toustém* [tus'tẽm] ('toujours'); *crampe* ['krãmpɔ] ('chambre'); *arrouncà* [arũŋ'ka] ('ronfler'). For this reason, the Béarnais VN nasal units are transcribed here and elsewhere with a nasal diacritic: /ĩN ỹN ẽN ãN ũN/. The phonemic status of the Béarnais VN nasal units is easily established as they exhibit meaningful contrasts with the oral vowels /i y e a u/: *pintà* /pĩn'ta/ ('pinter') ~ *pità* /pi'ta/ ('picorer'); *punte* /'pỹntɔ/ ('pointe') ~ *pute* /'pytɔ/ ('putain'); *crampe* / 'krãmpɔ/ ('chambre') ~ *crape* /'krapɔ/ ('chèvre'); *réndę* /'rẽnde/ ('rendre') ~ *rédę* / 'rede/ ('raide'); *soun* /sũn/ ('ils sont') ~ *sou* /su/ ('soleil').

Standardised Occitan does not have a nasal vowel system. The presence of such a system in Béarnais is the result of the historical deletion of Latin intervocalic −N- in (primarily) late-closed syllables. This development has not taken place in Occitan (or French) (Bendel, 1934: 74; Grosclaude, 1986: 58), e.g., LUNA > *lûe* [lỹɔ] in Béarnais, *luna* ['lynɔ] in Occitan and *lune* [lyn] in French; FENESTRA > *hièstre* ['hjestrɔ] in Béarnais, *finèstra* [fi'nɛstrɔ] in Occitan and, *fenêtre* [f(ə)nɛtʁ] in French. This is a prominent feature which distinguishes Béarnais and, other varieties of Gascon, from other *langue d'oc* dialects. The dropping of Latin N resulted in compensatory lengthening and nasalisation of the preceding vowel.

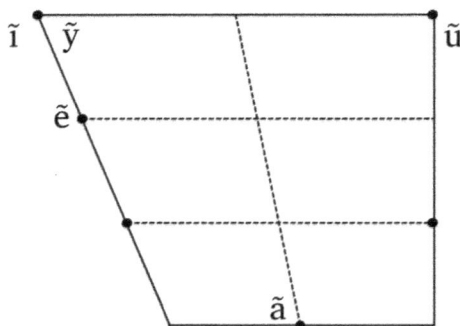

FIG. 2.2. The Béarnais nasal vowel system (© Damien Mooney)

The Béarnais five-term nasal vowel system /ĩ ỹ ẽ ã ũ/ is illustrated in Figure 2.2. The phonemic status of the nasal vowels is also easily established as they too are involved in meaningful contrasts with the oral vowels /i y e a u/: bî [bĩ] ('vin') ~ bi [bi] ('venir'); û [ỹ] ('un') ~ -u [y] ('le, lui'); hê [hẽ] ('foin') ~ hé [he] ('il fit'); pâ [pã] ('pain') ~ pa [pa] ('paire'); soû [sũ] ('son') ~ sou [su] ('soleil'). In some sub-varieties of Béarnais, these nasal vowels have become completely oral, thus neutralising these phonemic contrasts.

There are no minimal pairs in Béarnais that show the nasal vowels and vN nasal units to be in contrast with each other. Given this and the etymological relationship between the two systems, they may be considered as part of one Béarnais nasal unit system which has five phonemic elements /ĩN ỹN ẽN ãN ũN/ which alternate allophonically between [ĩN ỹN ẽN ãN ũN] (sequential nasal units) and [ĩ ỹ ẽ ã ũ] (non-sequential nasal units): [ĩN ỹN ẽN ãN ũN] occur in medial position, e.g., crampe ['krãmpɔ] ('chambre'), and in final closed syllables, e.g., téms ['tẽms]; in final open syllables, both [ĩN ỹN ẽN ãN ũN] and [ĩ ỹ ẽ ã ũ] can occur but the distribution is lexically specified, e.g., boû [bũ] ('bon') is never realised with a nasal consonant coda whereas poun [pũn] ('pont') always has a consonant. [ĩN ỹN ẽN ãN ũN] (sequential nasal units) and [ĩ ỹ ẽ ã ũ] (non-sequential nasal units) may therefore be seen to realise the same phonological unit, with the allophonic distribution governed by both contextual and lexical constraints. Since nasalisation of the vowel is variable in both sequential and non-sequential nasal units, nasal diacritics are always employed in the phonemic notation in order to indicate that the phonemic identity of the vowel in any given unit is nasal even if phonetically it may be realised as a denasalised, partially nasalised or fully nasalised vowel.

Glides

Standardised Occitan has three glide phonemes /j w ɥ/ while Béarnais, on the other hand, only has two glide phonemes /j w/[3] (Bouzet, 1928: 9). In Béarnais, /w/ is found in equivalent distributional patterns to /ɥ/ in Occitan, that is to say, /w/ and /ɥ/ have merged in Béarnais, in favour of /w/, e.g., HOC+DIE > oèy [wɛj] ('aujourd'hui') in Béarnais, but avuèi [a'βɥɛj] in Occitan. Accounts of diphthongs in Béarnais consider vowel + glide (or glide + vowel) sequences to be diphthongs (Bec, 1968: 48; Molyneux, 2002: 17; Moreux and Puyau, 2005: 9; see Mooney, 2014: 347 for discussion).

Consonants

The consonantal phonemes of Béarnais are presented in Table 2.2 (Bouzet, 1928; Bendel, 1934; Grosclaude; 1986; Moreux and Puyau, 2002, 2005; Molyneux, 2002).[4] Various divergences exist between the Béarnais and standardised Occitan consonantal inventories; a comparison of these systems reveals the following points of contrast:

Latin F became a fully aspirated glottal fricative, /h/, in Béarnais, e.g., FARINA > harîe /ha'rĩɔ/ ('farine'); CALEFACERE > cauhà /kaw'ha/ ('chauffer'), while it remains /f/ in Occitan, e.g., farina /fa'rinɔ/; calfar /kal'fa/.[5] When Latin F occurs in Béarnais, it is restricted to cult words or words borrowed from French, e.g., ['frɛzɔ] < French fraise [fʁɛz] is commonly used as an alternative to arrague [a'ragɔ] ('fraise') < FRAGA.

	Bilabial	Labio-dental	Alveolar	Post-alveolar	Palatal	Velar	Glottal
Plosive	p b		t d			k ɡ	
Affricate					t͡ç d͡ʝ		
Nasal	m		n		ɲ	(ŋ)	
Trill			r				
Tap			ɾ				
Fricative		(f v)	s z	ʃ (ʒ)			h
Lateral			l		ʎ		

TABLE 2.2. The Consonantal Phonemes of Béarnais

Additionally, the voiced labiodental fricative [v] is only present in Béarnais in loan words from French, e.g., *vélo* [veˈlɔ] < French *vélo* [velo]; *vaccî* [vakˈsĩ] < French *vaccin* [vaksɛ̃].

Latin –LL– became an apical tap or trill /ɾ r/ in Béarnais feminine nouns (Molyneux, 2002: 26), e.g., PULLA > *poure* /ˈpuɾɔ/ ('poule'); CAPPELLA > *capère* /kaˈpɛɾɔ/ ('chapelle'), while it becomes /l/ in Occitan (and French), e.g., *pola* /ˈpulɔ/; *capèla* /kaˈpɛlɔ/. In masculine nouns, root–final Latin –LL– became a palatalised affricate, /t͡ç/, in Béarnais when it occurred in coda position as a result of apocope (Grosclaude, 1986: 9), e.g., CASTELLUM > *castèth* /kasˈtɛt͡ç/ ('château') in Béarnais, and *castèl* /kasˈtɛl/ in Occitan; CAVALLUS > *cabath* /kaˈbat͡ç/ ('cheval') in Béarnais, and *caval* /kaˈbal/ in Occitan.

Béarnais has two palatalised affricate phonemes: voiceless /t͡ç/ (< Latin –LL) and voiced /d͡ʝ/, while Occitan has two post-alveolar affricate phonemes: /t͡ʃ/, and /d͡ʒ/. Latin –TC– sequences, that occurred as result of elision, such as VILLATICUM < VILLA, developed into /d͡ʝ/ in Béarnais, and /t͡ʃ/ in Occitan, e.g., *bilàdye* /biˈlad͡ʝe/ ('village') in Béarnais, and *vilatge* /biˈlat͡ʃe/ in Occitan. Occitan /d͡ʒ/ developed from Latin IU–, e.g., IUVENIS > JOVENIS > *jove* [ˈd͡ʒuβe] ('jeune'). The equivalent phoneme in Béarnais is /j/, realised as [j] or [ʒ] e.g., *yoén* [jwen] or [ʒwen]. The [ʒ] pronunciation is widespread in west-central Béarn and the Pyrenean valleys: /ʒ/ is a phoneme in these varieties but, when considering Béarnais as the sum of its sub-dialects, [ʒ] is a geographical variant of /j/.

2.2. Standard and Supralocal French Phonology

Standard and supralocal French differ primarily in relation to their phonological inventories, with many standard French phonemic contrasts involving vowels not maintained in the system of the statistical norm.

Oral vowels

The vowel system of conservative standard French is presented in Figure 2.3: the close vowels /i y u/; three pairs of mid-vowels /e/-/ɛ/, /ø/-/œ/ and /o/-/ɔ/; one pair of open vowels /a/-/ɑ/; the schwa /ə/.

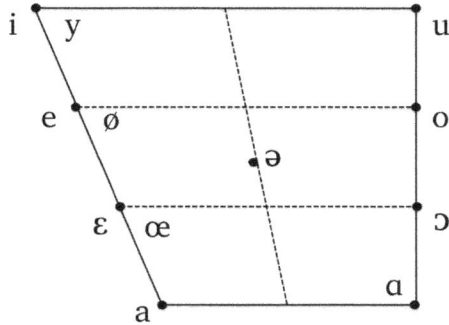

FIG. 2.3. The Standard French oral vowel system (© Damien Mooney)

The mid-vowels are involved in a number of phonemic oppositions as illustrated in the following examples: *vallée* /e/ ~ *valet* /ɛ/; *jeûne* /ø/ ~ *jeune* /œ/; *hôte* /o/ ~ *hotte* /ɔ/. In some contexts, there is evidence for a *loi de position* in SF whereby close-mid vowels [e ø o] occur in open syllables, e.g., *gai* [ge], *deux* [dø], and *dos* [do], while open-mid vowels [ɛ œ ɔ] occur in closed syllables, e.g., *sèche* [sɛʃ], *seul* [sœl], and *note* [nɔt] (Pooley, 2007: 47). The *loi de position* is by no means applied consistently in SF with each mid-vowel pair exhibiting numerous orthographical and phonetically motivated exceptions to this general pattern.

For the /e/-/ɛ/ mid-vowel pair, [ɛ] always occurs in closed syllables, e.g., *fête* [fɛt]; *serpent* [sɛʁpɑ̃]. In open syllables, the pronunciation can either be [e] or [ɛ] and this is lexically defined for the most part (see Price, 2005: 56–58): [ɛ] generally occurs with the following orthographies in open syllables: *-et, -ais, -ait, -aient, -aix*, e.g., *ballet* [balɛ]; *chantait* [ʃɑ̃tɛ]; [e] is used, for example, with the verbal endings of the future tense whereas [ɛ] is used for the verbal endings of the conditional, e.g., *j'irai* [ʒiʁe]; *j'irais* [ʒiʁɛ]. In non-final syllables the pattern observed follows the *loi de position*: [e] in open syllables and [ɛ] in closed syllables, e.g., *détruit* [detʁɥi] and *serpent* [sɛʁpɑ̃].

For the front rounded mid-vowels, /ø/-/œ/, the number of minimal pairs that exist is limited to only two: *veule* /vøl/ ~ *(ils) veulent* /vœl/; *jeûne* /ʒøn/ ~ *jeune* /ʒœn/. In final open syllables, the close-mid vowel is always used, e.g., *deux* [dø], *œufs* [ø]. In final closed syllables, on the other hand, the majority variant is the open-mid vowel, e.g., *seul* [sœl], *œuf* [œf]. In final position, this mid-vowel pair obeys the *loi de position*. The only exception to this is that in final closed syllables ending in /-z/, the vowel employed is lengthened close-mid [øː], e.g., *heureuse* [œʁøːz], *creuse* [kʁøːz]. In non-final syllables, the *loi de position* dictates which vowel will be used, e.g., *jeudi* [ʒødi], *meurtrir* [mœʁtʁiʁ].

For the back mid-vowels, /o/-/ɔ/, the pronunciation is always [o] in final open syllables, e.g., *beau* [bo], *chaud* [ʃo]. In final closed syllables, on the other hand, both /o/ and /ɔ/ can occur contrastively, e.g., *paume* /pom/ ~ *pomme* /pɔm/, *saute* /sot/ ~ *sotte* /sɔt/. There is a tendency for the *loi de position* to apply such that the open-mid variant [ɔ] occurs as the majority variant in final closed syllables, e.g., *école* [ekɔl], *note* [nɔt]. There are, however, numerous orthographical and phonetically motivated exceptions to this pattern. For example, the close-mid vowel [o] is used for graphic *au* in both open and closed syllables, e.g., *Pau* [po] and *paume* [pom], and in syllables closed by /-z/, e.g., *chose* [ʃoːz] and *rose* [ʁoːz]. The close-mid variant also occurs in closed syllables when a circumflex accent is present in the orthography, e.g., *hôte* [ot].

The open vowels, /a/-/ɑ/, are traditionally involved in a very small number of phonemic contrasts, e.g., *matin* /matɛ̃/ ~ *mâtin* /mɑtɛ̃/; *rat* /ʁa/ ~ *ras* /ʁɑ/. The back vowel is markedly less common than the front vowel in SF but when it does occur, it is usually in the following contexts: in monosyllabic words, e.g., *là* [lɑ]; in stressed position before /z/ where the vowel is lengthened, e.g., *phase* [fɑːz]; following [w] in monosyllabic words, e.g., *fois* [fwɑ].

The vocalic systems of SF and supralocal French differ substantially with regard to the mid-vowel contrasts, /e/~/ɛ/, /ø/~/œ/ and /o/~/ɔ/, and the open vowel contrast /a/~/ɑ/ in SF. The close vowels are generally considered to be 'stable' in supralocal French (Pooley, 2006: 360). In supralocal French, there is a tendency towards gradual diachronic neutralisation of these mid-vowel phonemic contrasts, though this applies variably to each of the contrasting pairs. In order to make clear the comparison between standard and supralocal French, the 'archiphonemic' symbols /E Œ O A/ are used for supralocal French, following, for example, Durand (2009: 6),[6] in order to indicate the neutralisation of phonemic contrasts present in SF (see Figure 2.4).

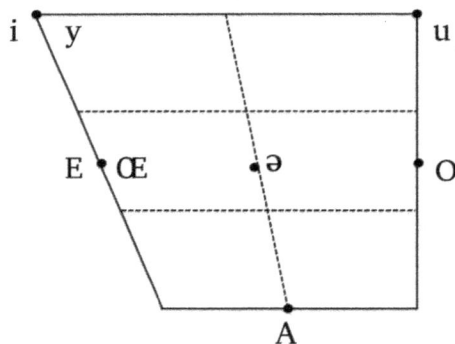

FIG. 2.4. The Supralocal French oral vowel system (© Damien Mooney)

The general supralocal pattern exhibits the following characteristics (Pooley, 2006: 360): /a/ and /ɑ/ are pronounced [a] in all positions, e.g., *pattes* [pat] and *pâtes* [pat]; /e/ and /ɛ/ are pronounced [e] in final open syllables, e.g., *(je) finirai* [finiʁe] and *(je) finirais* [finiʁe]; /ø/ and /œ/ are pronounced [œ] in closed syllables, e.g., *veule* [vœl] and *veulent* [vœl]. The /o/~/ɔ/ contrast, however, is said to be maintained in closed syllables, e.g., *hotte* [ɔt] ~ *hôte* [ot], and the majority realisation of the schwa /ə/ vowel is [ø] or [œ] with high rates of deletion in conversational speech.

Recent studies of these contrasts in supralocal French have revealed a significant amount of overlap in the distributions of the mid-vowels and low vowels. Hansen and Juillard (2011) consider these *voyelles à double timbre* and represent the Parisian French vocalic system as having three degrees of vowel height (as in Figure 2.4). Hansen and Juillard's study compared two corpora of spoken Parisian French: one collected between 1972 and 1974; one collected between 2001 and 2004. Their findings show a number of gradual phonetic mergers in Parisian French, with the

/a/-/ɑ/ merger being the most advanced, followed by /e/-/ɛ/, /ø/-/œ/ and finally, /o/-/ɔ/. These changes, however, are said to be far from completion (Hansen and Juillard, 2011: 351).

Nasal vowels

The conservative SF phonological inventory has, as we have seen, four nasal vowels /ɛ̃ œ̃ ɑ̃ ɔ̃/ (see Figure 2.5). These nasal vowels also alternate morphophonologically with a variety of VN sequences (from Latin open syllables). In the front of the vowel space, /ɛ̃/ and /œ̃/ are distinguished on the basis of lip-rounding, e.g., *brin* /bʁɛ̃/ ~ *brun* /bʁœ̃/. In the back of the vowel space, /ɑ̃/ and /ɔ̃/ are distinguished on the basis of vowel height and lip-rounding, e.g., *banc* /bɑ̃/ ~ *bon* /bɔ̃/.

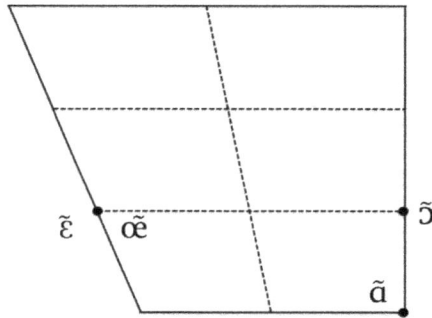

FIG. 2.5. The Standard French nasal vowel system (© Damien Mooney)

The supralocal French nasal vowel system is illustrated in Figure 2.6. In supralocal French, and particularly in Paris, the nasal vowel system has three phonemes /ɛ̃/, /ɑ̃/ and /ɔ̃/ owing to the merger of /ɛ̃/ and /œ̃/ (Pooley, 2006: 368). This means that the words *brin* and *brun* above are now pronounced [bʁɛ̃] by a majority of speakers in northern France. There have been some indications of possible mergers between /ɑ̃/ and /ɔ̃/ in supralocal French, though this change is said to be far further from completion than that of /ɛ̃/ and /œ̃/ (Hansen, 1998).

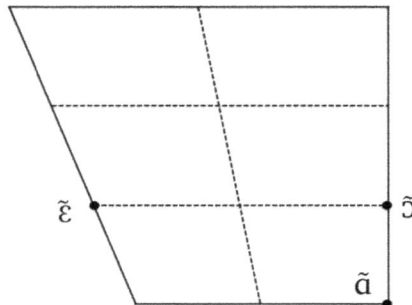

FIG. 2.6. The Supralocal French nasal vowel system (© Damien Mooney)

Additionally, in contemporary Parisian French, Hansen found that nasal vowels appear to be undergoing a counterclockwise chain shift in which the front unrounded vowel /ɛ̃/ approaches back unrounded vowel /ɑ̃/, the back unrounded vowel /ã/ approaches the back open-mid rounded vowel /ɔ̃/, and the back open-mid rounded vowel /ɔ̃/ becomes very rounded and close, e.g., *bain* → [ã], *banc* → [ɔ̃], *bon* → [õ] (2001: 210).

Glides

SF and supralocal French have three glide phonemes /j w ɥ/, e.g. *tiens* /tjɛ̃/, *fois* /fwa/, and *lui* /lɥi/. In French, vowel + glide (or glide + vowel) sequences are traditionally considered as a vowel followed by a glide rather than a diphthong; for these analyses, the glide is considered to be a separate phoneme rather than a component of the syllable nucleus.

Consonants

The consonantal phonemes of SF and supralocal French are presented in Table 2.3; these varieties do not differ with respect to their consonantal inventories. A comparison of the consonantal systems of Béarnais and French is provided below in order to identify the points at which the two languages diverge.

	Bilabial	Labio-dental	Dental	Post-alveolar	Palatal	Velar	Uvular
Plosive	p b		t d			k g	
Nasal	m		n		ɲ	ŋ	
Fricative		f v	s z	ʃ ʒ			ʁ
Lateral			l				

TABLE 2.3. The Consonantal Phonemes of Standard and Supralocal French

An inspection of the consonantal inventories reveals the following points of contrast (see Table 2.2 for Béarnais consonants):

(i)   SF does not have /h/. This is because French retains Latin F as /f/ while this evolved to /h/ in Béarnais, e.g., FUMARE > *humà* /hy'ma/ in Béarnais, and 'fumer' /fyme/ in French.

(ii) Both French and Béarnais have a /b/ phoneme but French /b/ derives from Latin B while Béarnais /b/ derives from both Latin B and Latin V, e.g., BELLA > *bère* ['bɛɾɔ] in Béarnais and *belle* [bɛl] in French; VIDERE > *béde* ['beðe] in Béarnais but *voir* [vwaʁ] in French. Thus, Latin B and V have merged to a single phoneme, /b/, in Béarnais and, as we have seen, Béanais only uses [v] in some loan words of French origin (Molyneux, 2002: 21; Bouzet, 1928: 10), e.g., *televisoû* [televizü] < French *télévision* [televizjɔ̃].

(iii) The velar nasal [ŋ] entered French during the twentieth century in a small number of borrowings from English (Jones, 2001: 30), such as *le parking* [lə paʁkiŋ] for *parc de stationnement*, and is now considered a phoneme of the language. The velar nasal occurs in Béarnais in borrowings from English via French, e.g., *lou parquing* [lu paʁ'kiŋ]. The phonemic status of /ŋ/ in Béarnais is debatable but [ŋ] regularly occurs as an allophone of /n/ before the velar plosives [k] and [g], e.g., *sanc* [saŋk] ('sang'); *engoère* [eŋ'gwɛɾɔ] ('encore').

(iv) SF /ʁ/ is a voiced uvular fricative [ʁ].[7] In Béarnais, the apical trill /r/ and apical tap /ɾ/ phonemes are involved in some phonemic contrasts, e.g., *pourét* [puˈret] ('poulet') ~ *pourrét* [puˈret] ('poireau'). The distribution of [r] and [ɾ] is somewhat constrained by their position within the syllable and with respect to word boundaries with a tendency for [r] to occur word-initially and as an onset after [n], and [ɾ] to occur in onset clusters and in the syllable coda, but this distribution is by no means categorical (Cardaillac Kelly, 1973: 32). Additionally, Béarnais rhotics are sometimes replaced by a uvular realisation [ʁ] which constitutes interference or transfer from French due to language contact.[8]

(v) The phonological inventory of Béarnais contains the voiced palatal lateral approximant /ʎ/ which is not present in French. This phoneme is generally represented in the orthography by *lh*, e.g., LECTUS > *lhéyt* [ʎejt] ('lait'). Historically, French had /ʎ/ in words like *paille, bouteille, grenouille* etc. but it was replaced by /j/ by the middle of the nineteenth century (Rickard, 1974: 126). The correspondence between Béarnais /ʎ/ and French /j/ can be seen in the following example using the feminine Latin –ULA suffix: VETULA > *biélhe* [ˈbjeʎɔ] in Béarnais, and *vielle* [vjɛj] in French.

(vi) SF has no affricates that have developed from Latin and when they do occur, as [t͡ʃ] and [d͡ʒ], they are borrowings (Jones, 2001: 30), e.g., *Tchèque* [t͡ʃɛk] < English *Czech* [t͡ʃɛk]; *gin* [d͡ʒin] < English *gin* [d͡ʒɪn]. The Béarnais /t͡ç/ affricate corresponds to /l/ in French (< Latin root-final –LL-) in words such as *cheval* [ʃəval] or *chapeau* [ʃapo] and *chateau* [ʃato] (formerly *chapel* [ʃapɛl] and *chastel* [ʃastɛl]) that owe their present form to back-formations from their plural forms during the Middle French period (Rickard, 1974: 68). Béarnais /d͡j/, on the other hand, corresponds to French /ʒ/, e.g., MATRIMONIUM > *maridàdyę* [maɾiˈðad͡je] in Béarnais, and *mariage* [maʁjaːʒ] in French.

2.3. Southern Regional French Phonology

The varieties of RF spoken in the southern third of France share noticeable similarities, mainly in pronunciation, although people from the different regions are said to be able to identify the differences between them (Armstrong and Blanchet, 2006: 264). We have seen that contact between French and the local languages and dialects of France is frequently assumed to have led to the emergence of contemporary regional varieties of French. In Béarn, RF appears to have emerged from contact between French and the local variety of *langue d'oc* spoken in the region, Béarnais.

The phonological inventories presented here for southern RF and for the RF of Béarn and Gascony are based on (largely qualitative) studies of these systems in the early and late twentieth century. Despite being outdated, Martinet's (1945) study provides some information on the nature of southern RF in the early twentieth century, albeit based on self-reported data from a small sample of relatively socially homogeneous male subjects. Martinet divides the south of France into two main areas: the Midi and the southwest sub-region (Gironde, Dordogne, Corrèze) (12 informants). The reason for this is sub-division is that there are often 'des caractéristiques plus septentrionales que méridionales' (1945: 29–30) in the data from the northerly part of the southwestern sub-region. More recent studies such as Walter (1982) and Carton et al. (1983) offer a greater number of regional subdivisions for southern varieties of French and all of Walter's informants were born into local families and spoke the autochthonous language appropriate to their area. Again, however, the sample sizes were limited. These data sets will, however, provide a reference point against which to examine modern-day variation in RF.

Oral vowels

Martinet (1945) reports the oral vowels of southern RF in final open and final closed syllables and these distributions are taken, by Pooley (2007: 43), to be indicative of the southern oral vowel systems in the first half of the twentieth century. Armstrong and Pooley refer to the patterns described by Martinet as forming part of the Dominant Southern Pattern (DSP): the phonological features common to the varieties of French used throughout the south of France (2010: 188).

In Martinet's data, the close vowels /i y u/ occur in all syllable types and this pattern parallels the vowel systems presented above for the standard and supralocal norms (see Figures 2.3 and 2.4). In the front of the vowel space, /e/ and /ɛ/ could occur in final open syllables, indicating the maintenance of standard contrasts. For the front rounded mid-vowels, on the other hand, the DSP follows the *loi de position* with [ø] in final open syllables and [œ] in closed and non-final syllables. This implies the neutralisation of contrasts present in the standard, e.g., *veule* /vøl/ and *veulent* /vœl/ both pronounced as [vœl]. The back mid-vowels also follow the *loi de position*, with close-mid [o] in open syllables and open-mid [ɔ] in closed syllables. Therefore, for /O/, allophonic variants conditioned by the *loi de position* are present in the DSP. Again, this implies the neutralisation of SF contrasts, e.g., *saute* /sot/ and *sotte* /sɔt/ both pronounced as [sɔt], and the regularisation of (standard) 'exceptions' in specified phonetic contexts, e.g., *chose* /ʃoz/ and *rose* /ʁoz/ pronounced as [ʃɔːz] and [ʁɔːz] respectively. The /a/~/ɑ/ contrast of SF is not used by Martinet's southern informants, with a centralised [a] used in all positions, e.g., SF *patte* /pat/ and *pâte* /pɑt/ both pronounced as [pät]. Based on this information, we can conclude that the DSP in the first half of the twentieth century (at least for Martinet's informants) contains the following oral vowel phonemes: /i y u e ɛ Œ O A/ and the schwa /ə/. As was the case for supralocal French (see Figure 2.4), the 'archiphonemic' symbols /Œ O A/ are used here to indicate a neutralisation of phonemic contrasts present in SF.

Later in the twentieth century, the general southern oral vowel system was described by Walter (1982) and Carton et al. (1983) for final open syllables and final closed syllables. The systems documented by these studies differ from those described by Martinet, indicating important changes in the DSP during the twentieth century. This data shows that the close vowels /i y u/ remain stable between 1945 and the 1980s. For the open vowels, /a/ and /ɑ/, the standard contrast is neutralised to [a], as was the case for Martinet's informants. Pooley notes, however, that the quality of this merged category varies geographically in final open position: intermediate

By the late twentieth century, the majority southern variants were uvular [ʁ] or pharyngeal [ʕ]. [r] was the majority variant used by older speakers in Gascony and Languedoc (Carton et al., 1983: 61) and this was also the case for Walter's informant from the Gers (1982: 183). Consonantal gemination (largely but not exclusively associated with [r]) is also cited by Martinet as a characteristic of southern RF, e.g., *serrer* /seʁe/ [serre]. In Walter and Carton et al.'s data, for the entire southern area, the gemination of /ʁ/ tended to co-occur with the realisation of the apical variant [r] and in word-initial position, e.g., *rat* /ʁa/ [rra], with singleton /ʁ/ in other contexts, e.g., *serrer* /seʁe/ [sere]. In Gascony, geminate apical [r] was realised both word-initially (Carton et al., 1983: 61), e.g., *royaux* /ʁwajo/ [rrwajo], and intervocalically (Walter, 1982: 183; Carton et al., 1983: 61), e.g., *les restes* /leʁɛst/ [lerrestə].

Word-final consonant devoicing was noted by Martinet as occurring with relatively low frequency (20% of southern informants) but comparisons between older and younger speakers suggested that devoiced variants were gaining ground, e.g., *rose* /ʁoz/ [rrɔːz̥]. Word-final consonant devoicing was only noted in Toulouse and the Gers by Walter (1982) and Carton et al., (1983).

Martinet notes the use of the palatal lateral [ʎ] as a regional variant of SF /j/, e.g., *travailler* /tʁavaje/ [travaʎe]. In the 1980s, this variant was only attested in the area near the Pyrenees (i.e. in southern Gascony). The /ɲ/~/nj/ contrast was maintained by the majority of Martinet's southern informants with the palatal [ɲ] variant reported particularly by southern, and especially southwestern informants, e.g., *l'agnelle* /laɲɛl/ ~ *la nielle* /lanjɛl/. In the 1980s data, [ɲ] also showed considerable vitality as a variant of /ɲ/ in all southern regions but particularly in the southwest.

Finally, Martinet notes that 10% of southern informants used the glottal fricative [h] in word-initial position, e.g., *haine* /ɛn/ [hɛn(ə)]. Armstrong and Pooley note that this is a minority feature that occurred only in the southwest, including Toulouse (2010: 190). In Walter (1982) and Carton et al.'s (1983) data, aspirated [h] had completely disappeared from the consonantal phonological inventory of southern RF apart from a very small area limited to the deep southwestern region of Gascony (i.e. Béarn) (Walter, 1982: 183).

The overview of the phonological inventories in contact in Béarn has highlighted the parallels and divergences, from an etymological and synchronic perspective, between Béarnais, Occitan, SF and supralocal French. The phonological description of southern RF, drawing primarily on the studies of Martinet (1945), Walter (1982) and Carton et al. (1983), identified divergences from standard and supralocal norms as well as, importantly, the degree of conformity of the southwestern RF vowel system to what Pooley (2007) refers to as the DSP. We have seen that variability in the mid- and nasal vowel systems traditionally distinguishes southern RF from the dominant supralocal norm (while regional consonantal variation was highly recessive) and so the language and dialect contact studies of Béarn RF will focus on these areas of RF phonology specifically, as they have been identified for some time as sites for linguistic variation and change.

Notes to Chapter 2

1. Béarnais is a stress-timed language (see Mooney, 2014: 347–48 for discussion).
2. Late-closed syllables are those which were open in Vulgar Latin but later closed owing to the loss of unstressed vowels in final syllables, e.g., SANUM > SAN > *sain* [sɛ̃].
3. In west-central Béarn and the Pyrenean valleys, and to a lesser extent, the central Pau region, /j/ is replaced by [ʒ] in all positions (word-initially, intervocalically and post-consonantally), e.g., EGO > *you* [ʒu] ('moi').
4. Table 2.2: brackets around IPA symbols indicate the ambiguous phonemic status of these sounds, from a historical perspective.
5. In some northeastern sub-dialects of Béarnais, /h/ also developed from Latin s when it occurs syllable finally before another consonant (Moreux and Puyau, 2002: 26), e.g., DIS+IEIUNO > disnà [disˈna] ('dîner') in Béarnais, pronounced [dihˈna]. This type of [s] debucalisation also occurred in French before the Old French period, but resultant [h] has since been lost, e.g., BESTIAM > bête [bɛt].
6. 'Les symboles E, Ø, O ne représentent pas des archiphonèmes au sens de Martinet mais des voyelles sous-spécifiées pour l'aperture [...] ou des classes de sons pour rester théoriquement plus neutre' (Durand, 2009: 6).
7. There is evidence to suggest that in modern-day supralocal speech, /ʁ/ is being realised increasingly as a voiced uvular approximant [ʁ] (Coveney, 2001: 57), particularly in final position (Fougeron and Smith, 1999: 80).
8. French had both [r] and [ɾ] until the eighteenth century but by the time of the Revolution, in Paris at least, they had largely been replaced by the uvular fricative [ʁ] (Rickard, 1974: 108).
9. The partially nasalised diacritic [˜] is not used in the IPA.
10. Walter and Carton et al. both note that pre-pausal [ŋ] is still common in Provence and Gascony, but receding in favour of [n] and [m] in Languedoc.

CHAPTER 3

❖

Theoretical and
Methodological Considerations

On était dépourvu d'instruments d'analyse phonétique sophistiqués [...] je
cherche à approfondir l'étude du système de la langue à partir du langage
concret [...] Les données les plus solides, les plus objectives, sont, je crois, les
données de la production spontanée.
WILLIAM LABOV, *Le changement linguistique*, 1983

The genesis and evolution of regional French in Béarn is examined in two sub-
studies: the language contact study and the dialect contact study. The former examines
linguistic transfer, from Béarnais into French, in a situation of bilingualism while
the latter investigates linguistic change and dialect levelling taking place in regional
French as a result of exposure to non-local varieties of French. For each study, the
theoretical frameworks used and linguistic variables examined are outlined, and
hypotheses are advanced regarding the potential outcomes of contact in each case.
The data collection and analysis techniques employed in each of these studies are
outlined in this chapter, and some of the methodological challenges involved in
investigating linguistic variation and change in this context are discussed.

3.1. The Language Contact Study

Bilinguals are seen to be the locus of change because competence in two languages is
a precondition for the adoption of material from one language into another (Hickey,
2010: 9). Transfer will normally arise when a bilingual identifies a phoneme of the
secondary system with one of the primary system and, in reproducing it, subjects
it to the phonetic rules of the primary language (Weinreich, 1968: 14). Flege's
(1988, 1990, 1991) Speech Learning Model (SLM) combines in a single explanatory
framework the linguistic mechanisms by which sounds or units of sound may
transfer from one language to another during bilingualism. During the acquisition
of an L2, the process of 'interlingual identification' causes words learnt in the
second language to be (initially) decomposed into categories based on familiar L1
sounds (Flege, 1995: 98). This (initial) association of L2 sounds with L1 categories is
the basis for the central tenet of the SLM: the categories making up the L1 and L2
subsystems of a bilingual exist in a 'common phonological space' and so have the
potential mutually to influence one another (Flege, 2007: 366).

Phonemes in the L1 and L2 that correspond structurally are termed 'cognate phonemes' and are said to be linked by 'equivalence classification'. Establishing equivalence classification is important in the SLM because production accuracy has been shown to depend crucially on whether new categories are created for L2 sounds not occurring in the L1 (Flege, 1997: 86). Category formation is directly linked to equivalence classification: if an L2 sound is equated with an L1 sound, new category formation will be inhibited; if an L2 sound is not equated with an L1 sound, a new phonetic category may be formed. Equivalence classification and category formation (which are mutually exclusive) determine the interaction of L1 and L2 phonetic subsystems to be governed by two different linguistic mechanisms: 'phonetic category assimilation' and 'phonetic category dissimilation', respectively.

The SLM proposes that the L1 and L2 phonetic subsystems will interact through the mechanism of phonetic category assimilation when new category formation has been blocked by equivalence classification. When a category is not formed for an L2 sound because it is 'too similar' to an L1 counterpart, the L1 and L2 sounds will assimilate, leading to a 'merged' L1-L2 category (Flege, 2005). For example, Flege et al. (1999) showed that Italian speakers of English assigned both Engish /i/ and /ɪ/ to a single /i/ phonetic category which existed in their L1. Within the merged category, the L2 sound will continue to resemble the L1 sound, and the L1 sound will begin to resemble the L2 sound (Flege, 2007: 368). The exact nature of these representations will reflect the levels of input acquired over a speaker's lifetime, with more recently encountered input being weighted more heavily than input encountered in the distant past (Sancier and Fowler, 1997). An important consequence of phonetic category assimilation is that both L1 and L2 sounds will eventually resemble each other in production and be realised phonetically as the same sound. Phonetic category dissimilation, on the other hand, occurs when a newly established L2 phonetic category is relatively close in phonetic space to a pre-existing L1 category (Flege, 2007: 375). This process of dispersion works to optimise the maintenance of phonetic contrast in the vowel space for separate phonetic categories, in much the same way that vowels in a single language disperse in the vowel space (Flege, 2007: 370).

The language contact study analyses phonological and phonetic transfer in the mid-vowels and nasal vowels of the variety of French spoken by a sample of bilingual Béarnais-French speakers, as these variables have been identified as sites of ongoing linguistic change in southern RF (see Chapter 2, Section 2.3) and are cognate or equivalent phonemes, or sequences of phonemes, in the bilinguals' mental representation of their languages; they are thus hypothesised by the SLM to be stored in a common phonological space.

Mid-vowels

The Béarnais and SF mid-vowel systems exhibit a one-to-one correspondence in the front of the vowel space, e.g., Béarnais /e/ with French /e/ and Béarnais /ɛ/ with French /ɛ/, while in the back of the vowel space, Béarnais /ɔ/ corresponds to both /o/ and /ɔ/ in French. The SLM predicts that the phonemes /e/ and /ɛ/ in Béarnais will be equated, via the process of equivalence classification, with

French /e/ and /ɛ/ in a common phonological space, facilitating their retention in emergent RF. This association would result in the French (L2) vowels being realised phonetically as instances of the Béarnais (L1) phonetic categories, [e] and [ɛ] (phonetic category assimilation). For the back mid-vowels, the SLM predicts that the existence of a single back mid-vowel phonemic category in Béarnais /ɔ/ will lead to the establishment of a single phonemic category in French for /o/ and /ɔ/ since equivalence classification would equate the two French sounds with the single sound in Béarnais. If such equivalence classification takes place, Béarnais /ɔ/ and French /o/ and /ɔ/ would be realised as phonetically identical, [ɔ]. An alternative hypothesis for the back mid-vowels is that L1 Béarnais speakers would perceive the phonetic difference between French /o/ and /ɔ/, leading them to establish a new L2 phonetic category for French /o/, and to realise French /ɔ/ as an instance of the Béarnais [ɔ].

Nasal vowels

While mapping the structural correspondences between the Béarnais and French mid-vowels was relatively straightforward, from both a diachronic and synchronic perspective, a comparison of the Béarnais nasal units and French nasal vowels revealed a complex array of structural equivalence classes which, for the most part, are not in one-to-one correspondence (see Chapter 2, Section 2.1).

The language contact study examines the five Béarnais nasal units /ĩN ỹN ẽN ãN ũN/, which may be realised as sequential [ĩN ỹN ẽN ãN ũN] or non-sequential [ĩ ỹ ẽ ã ũ] units. The analysis of French assumes as its staring point the four conservative nasal vowel phonemes, /ɛ̃ œ̃ ã ɔ̃/. From a historical perspective, the French nasal vowels /œ̃/ and /ɔ̃/ map directly onto the Béarnais nasal units /ỹN/ and /ũN/: there is a one-to-one correspondence between these phonological units in the surface phonologies. The SLM would predict these phonemic cognates to be equated and for L2 cognates to be realised as instances of L1 phonetic categories via phonetic category assimilation. The relationship between French /ɛ̃ ã/ and Béarnais /ĩN ẽN ãN/ is more complex. The evolution of French and Béarnais from Latin allowed us to identify the following systemic correspondences or potential equivalence classes: French /ɛ̃/ maps structurally onto Béarnais /ĩN/, /ẽN/ and /ãN/, e.g., French *vin* /vɛ̃/, *plein* /plɛ̃/, and *chien* /ʃɛ̃/, correspond to Béarnais *bî* /bĩN/, *plê* /plẽN/ and *câ* /kãN/; French /ã/ also maps structurally onto Béarnais /ẽN/ and /ãN/, e.g., French *cent* /sã/ and *sang* /sã/ correspond to Béarnais *cén* /sẽN/ and *sanc* /sãNk/.

Given the differences between the surface phonologies of Béarnais and French as well as the potential phonetic dissimilarity between the components of some structural equivalence classes, it is likely that processes other than equivalence classification (and phonetic category assimilation) may apply. When an L2 sound is sufficiently phonetically different from its structurally corresponding L1 sound, the SLM predicts that the L2 sound will be assigned to the nearest perceptually similar L1 phonetic category instead, thus blocking equivalence classification. As result of this, we might expect French /ɛ̃/ to be processed and produced as an instance of the Béarnais [ẽN] phonetic category given their perceptual similarity. Likewise, we might expect French /ã/ to be realised as a variant of the Béarnais [ãN] phonetic category. The L2 sounds would thus be dissociated from their underlying structural equivalents in the L1, in favour of one-to-one surface phonological correspondences. Alternatively, new category formation may cause the creation of a new L2 phonetic category for French sounds that are perceptually dissimilar from any L1 Béarnais sounds: it is possible the French /ɛ̃/ and /ɑ̃/ will form new phonetic categories in the bilingual vowel space, either because they are judged to be sufficiently phonetically different from any L1 nasal unit phonetic categories or because of the opacity of the complex structural relationship between the French and Béarnais systems for these units.

3.2. The Dialect Contact Study

The dialect contact study examines the evolution of RF over time by comparing the production of the mid- and nasal vowels of older bilingual speakers with that of two younger generations of speakers. The aim of this analysis is to track linguistic change in the variety after the 'dust of contact' has settled, to identify the mechanisms of change involved, and to address the question of whether it is accurate to characterise RF as ephemeral, that is to say that local features are lost in favour of northern supralocal forms (see Introduction). Linguistic changes identified in the dialect contact study are interpreted, in Chapter 5, using Kerswill's (2003) model of 'regional dialect levelling'.

When speakers of a local variety come into contact with speakers of other regional or non-local varieties, we often find that, over time, the differences between the varieties will be reduced. Kerswill calls this phenomenon 'regional dialect levelling' (RDL) or 'supralocalisation' which is claimed to be 'leading to the loss of localised features in urban and rural varieties of English in Britain, to be replaced with features found over a wider region' (2003: 223). The phenomenon of RDL arises from the interplay of at least two focusing[1] mechanisms: levelling 'proper' and geographical diffusion. Both of these processes are a result of 'speech accommodation', a social-psychological mechanism whereby speakers converge with, or diverge from, the variety spoken by their interlocutor in order to gain social favour or distinguish themselves socially (Trudgill 1986: 2). Trudgill argues that long-term linguistic changes occurring in dialect contact situations result from multiple such short-term, face-to-face interactions between individual speakers. The linguistic forms resulting from accommodation are not necessarily phonetically identical to the original form. Trudgill calls this accommodation 'imperfection', explaining that speakers in dyadic situations aim to reduce dissimilarity between their speech and that of their interlocutors while at the same time not imitating them slavishly (1986: 57). The occurrence of accommodation is dependent on the social network characteristics and the social mobility of the speakers involved with close-knit communities impeding change and loose social network ties favouring higher levels of interaction, more accommodation and thus, more linguistic change.

Levelling 'proper' is defined as a process promoting the 'reduction or attrition of marked variants' (Trudgill, 1986: 98), where marked refers to forms that are unusual or in the minority. In the regional context, this means that local varieties in contact with each other become more like one another and reduce the differences between them. Levelling 'proper' is facilitated by speech accommodation and often leads to the creation of a new variety, over a wider geographical space, that is characterised by the absence of highly local forms. At the structural level, the outcome of levelling is a 'reduction in exponents of phonological and morphological categories' between varieties in contact (Kerswill and Williams, 2005: 1024). Levelling 'proper' leads, over time, to the adoption of pan-regional forms: the use of new, regionally specific but geographically widespread features that retain majority regional features at the expense of local ones. Features that are common to a number of contiguous varieties are therefore more likely to survive the levelling process than those variants that have a specifically local affiliation. For example, Watt (2002) describes how the traditional Newcastle variant [ɪə] in words like *face* is being replaced by younger speakers with the monophthongal realisation [eː] which has wider geographical currency, in that it is a more widespread northern British English variant. This change, combined with others cases of monophthongisation, such as [oː] in words like *goat*, is symptomatic of pan-regionalisation: Newcastle English is becoming more like other northern varieties via levelling 'proper'.

Geographical diffusion is defined as the process by which linguistic features spread out from a populous and economically and culturally dominant centre (Kerswill 2003: 223), which is often, but does not have to be, the capital city. At an individual level, geographical diffusion is also motivated by speech accommodation as features spread via face-to-face interactions with other speakers, from elsewhere, who have already adopted the feature in question. The spread of diffusing linguistic features is wave-like, in that they radiate outwards from a central focus reaching geographically nearby locations before those at greater distances. This wave-like diffusion is often modified by the likelihood that nearby towns and cities will adopt the diffusing features before more rural areas in between (Kerswill, 2003: 223). This is termed 'urban hierarchical diffusion' which is explained by Trudgill's 'gravity model' (1986): linguistic innovations are said to be leaping or 'parachuting' according to a defined hierarchical pattern, beginning in the largest urban centre and spreading to rural areas via smaller and smaller 'satellite' towns (Trudgill, 1986: 39). Hierarchical diffusion therefore involves a demographic factor — the population size of the communities involved in the interaction — and a geographical factor — the distance between urban centres. For example, Kerswill (2003) presents evidence that TH-fronting, that is, the use of non-standard [f] for /θ/ and non-standard [v] for /ð/ in certain linguistic environments, is diffusing hierarchically from London. This change was adopted in geographically close urban centres first, for example, in Norwich before Newcastle, and in larger urban areas before rural areas in between, for example, in Derby (population, 236,000) before Wisbech (population, 19,000), although the latter is geographically closer to London.

Distinguishing between the processes of levelling and geographical diffusion in particular cases requires us to consider two types of information. Firstly, we must look for dialect-geographical evidence for the spread of a feature to see whether the apparently 'new' feature is diffusing gradually across geographical space or whether it is establishing itself simultaneously throughout a given area, in which case it would appear that levelling is present (Kerswill, 2003: 224). Kerswill also notes that the levelling mechanism is unlikely to apply over a large and demographically complex area such as Great Britain. Thus, if change is spread over expansive geographical space, we must suppose — other things being equal — that geographical diffusion is the more likely mechanism (2003: 236). The adoption into the RF of Béarn of DSP features would, for example, indicate that levelling 'proper' is taking place in the variety; the loss of marked local features in favour of unmarked features with broader, but still relatively local currency. The presence of supralocal French features, on the other hand, would indicate that geographical diffusion is the more likely mechanism of change.

Mid-vowels

In SF, the distribution of /e/ and /ɛ/ is dependent on syllable type: /ɛ/ always occurs in final closed syllables; the *loi de position* is observed in non-final syllables with [ɛ] in closed syllables and [e] in open syllables; /e/ and /ɛ/ are contrastive in final open syllables. In supralocal French, /ɛ/ occurs in final closed syllables; intermediate realisations are common in non-final syllables; in final open syllables, the contrast of SF is neutralised in favour of a close vowel, [e]. In the DSP, as observed in the 1980s, the front mid-vowels follow the *loi de position* in all contexts, [e] in open syllables and [ɛ] in closed syllables, thus neutralising the standard phonemic contrast in final open syllables. In the RF of Gascony, both Walter (1982) and Carton et al. (1983) suggest that [ɛ] was used in all syllable types in the speech of older informants: the standard contrast in final open syllables was thus neutralised to /ɛ/; the *loi de position* was not present. Moreux's (1985a, 1985b) findings in Béarn contradict this, suggesting that, while older informants maintained an /e/~/ɛ/ contrast in final open position, there was a strong tendency for speakers in the middle and younger generations to follow the *loi de position* and thus to neutralise the contrast. We must note that the oldest generation of speakers in the dialect contact study would have been aged between 38 and 59 when the data for the studies by Walter (1982), Carton et al. (1983), and Moreux (1985a, 1985b, 2006) were collected and are thus younger than the oldest speakers in those studies. They would, for example, have been included in the middle or 'intermediate' generation by Moreux.

The neutralisation of phonemic contrast in final open syllables for the front mid-vowels, characterised by the *loi de position*, in the RF of Gascony or Béarn would constitute evidence of levelling 'proper': the RF of Béarn would be adopting the majority southern variants for the front mid-vowels. A gradual reduction in the phonetic distinction between /e/ and /ɛ/ in non-final syllables would indicate, on the other hand, the mechanism of geographical diffusion whereby features of the supralocal norm are adopted into RF. Diffusion of the conservative standard, on the other hand, would see the adoption into RF of a contrastive distribution for the front mid-vowels in final open syllables and the use of the *loi de position* in non-final syllables.

In SF and supralocal French, the distribution of the back mid-vowels is condi-tioned by syllable type: /o/ always occurs in final open syllables; /o/ and /ɔ/

are contrastive in some final closed syllables; the *loi de position* applies in non-final syllables. There is evidence to suggest, however, that in supralocal French, intermediate variants are used in non-final syllables (cf. Hansen and Juillard, 2011). In the DSP, the back vowels follow the *loi de position* in all contexts, thus neutralising the standard and supralocal contrast in all final closed syllables. For Gascony, many speakers were shown to have the *loi de position* (following the DSP) while others used [ɔ] in all contexts (see Chapter 2, Section 2.3). The actual phonetic realisation of this vowel is said to be somewhere between [o] and [ɔ] (Carton et al., 1983; Moreux, 2006). While Moreux (1985a; 1985b) acknowledges the use of a single open back mid-vowel by some RF speakers in Béarn, he indicates, as for the front mid-vowels, that there is a tendency for most older speakers and younger generations of speakers to use the DSP pattern. The adoption of the *loi de position* for the back vowels may indicate the focusing mechanism of levelling 'proper' whereby the DSP feature is integrated into the RF of Béarn. Diffusion of SF, on the other hand, would be characterised by the use in RF of a close-mid vowel in final open syllables, the *loi de position* in non-final syllables and the maintenance of contrast in final closed syllables. The use of intermediate variants in non-final position would suggest the adoption of the supralocal system in RF via geographical diffusion.

Nasal vowels

From a phonological perspective, we have seen that the SF nasal vowel system contains four vowels /ɛ̃ œ̃ ɑ̃ ɔ̃/ while supralocal French has three vowels /ɛ̃ ɑ̃ ɔ̃/ as a result of the merger of /ɛ̃/ and /œ̃/. The DSP also has a four-term nasal vowel system and there is no evidence to suggest that the southwestern phonological pattern diverged from the DSP.

The standard and supralocal nasal vowels are realised phonetically as fully nasalised vowels: open-mid front unrounded [ɛ̃], open back unrounded [ɑ̃], open-mid back rounded [ɔ̃], and, for SF, open-mid front rounded [œ̃]. The southern vowels are generally held to have three variable phonetic parameters: vowel quality is traditionally modified such that /ɛ̃/ is higher [ẽ], /ɑ̃/ is central [ä] and /ɔ̃/ is more open [ɒ̃]; nasalisation is variable; nasal consonant codas frequently accompany nasal vowels, e.g., [ẽN], [œ̃N], [äN] and [ɒ̃N].

Evidence for supralocalisation in the nasal vowel system of the RF of Béarn may take two forms: either the retention of a four term nasal-vowel system in line with the DSP, via levelling 'proper', or a three-term supralocal system, adopted via geographical diffusion. Changes in vowel quality, the lowering of /ɛ̃/ from [ẽ] to [ɛ̃] and the backing of /ɑ̃/ from [ä] to [ɑ̃], may also indicate supralocalisation via diffusion. A reduction in the use of nasal consonant codas would also indicate diffusion of the supralocal norm whereas their retention would signal the (continued) use of the majority southern variant, or the DSP.

3.3. Data Collection

Fieldwork Sites

Pau is the second largest urban centre in the region of Aquitaine (see Figure 1.4), after Bordeaux, with a population of 84,763 in 2009 (INSEE, 2012) but its greater urban area has a population of approximately 198,000 inhabitants. The demographic evolution of Pau was rapid in the latter half of the twentieth century: it had a population of only 48,320 in 1954 (INSEE, 2012). This rapid growth is due to large-scale in-migration following the discovery of a supply of natural gas at nearby Lacq in the 1950s, the largest of its kind in Europe, which allowed France to be completely self-sufficient in natural gas for some thirty years afterwards. The gas discovery not only attracted manual labourers to the area but also led to the establishment of the *Total* scientific research institute, the largest research centre for the exploration and production of natural gas in Europe, which attracted many geo-scientists and skilled workers to Pau. Pau is served by an international airport and the *TGV Atlantique* high-speed rail network with links to Bordeaux in two hours. The national *TGV* network links Pau to Paris in five hours and intercity trains and motorways link it to other large urban centres such as Toulouse and the Bayonne-Anglet-Biarritz conurbation.

Three *communes* to the south and southwest of Pau, Pyrénées-Atlantiques, were chosen as fieldwork sites: Gan, Nousty, and Nay (see Figure 3.1). These semi-urban fieldwork sites were included in the study to allow for an analysis of both language

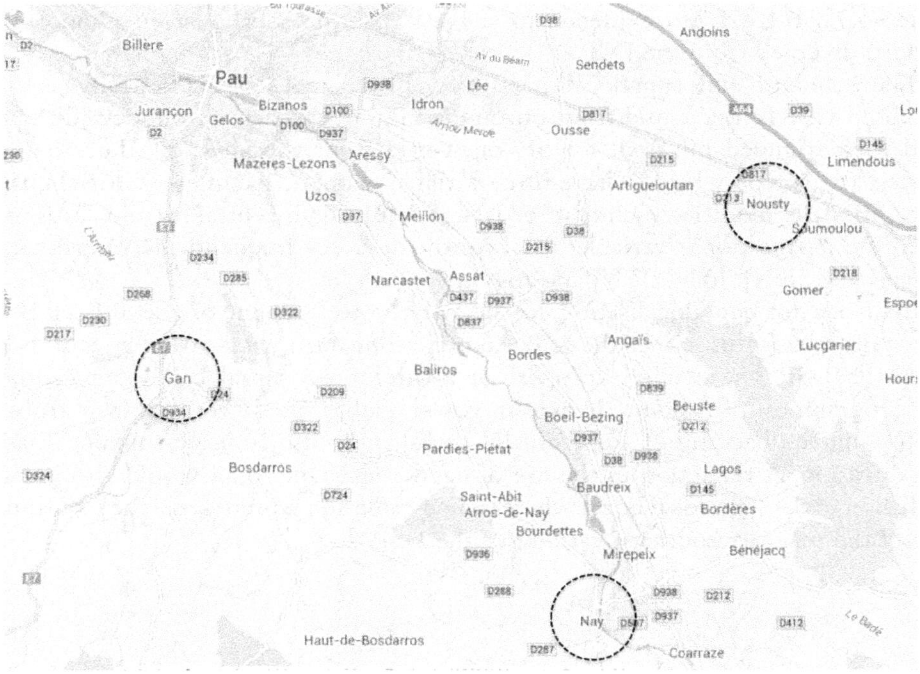

Fig. 3.1. Fieldwork sites (© Google Maps)

contact and dialect contact: each location needed to be sufficiently rural in order to facilitate the selection of an older generation of bilingual Béarnais-French informants (who are almost entirely absent from Pau).

Informant Selection

For the language contact study, informants were selected based on specified criteria: residents of semi-urban areas in the Pau region; native speakers of Béarnais; resident in Béarn for their entire life; parents and/or grandparents spoke Béarnais to them. The dialect contact study encompasses a much larger population: residents of semi-urban areas in the Pau region; have lived all their life in Béarn; parents also grew up in Béarn.

The definition of a 'native speaker' is problematic in many respects. Davies argues that the common-sense definition of what constitutes a native speaker is largely inadequate and that support needs to be drawn from the central linguistic disciplines (2003: 24): theoretical linguistics; psycholinguistics; sociolinguistics; bilingualism; language death theory; second language acquisition. In the language contact study, 'native speaker' is used to indicate that the 'first language' (L1) acquired by the informants was Béarnais and that French was acquired subsequently, as L2. This aligns with the definition of an L1 speaker often used in studies which have exploited the SLM, referring specifically to the first language acquired rather than to the speaker's dominant language.

The residency criterion, requiring participants to have lived in Béarn for their entire life, was included to control for exposure to non-local varieties of French that are not present in the region and for increased exposure to the supralocal norm due to, for example, extended periods of time spent in an area where the supralocal norm is dominant or where the effects of supralocalisation are more advanced. Accommodation to dialects of French not present in Béarn, or increased accommodation to the supralocal norm could potentially inflate the apparent effects of supralocalisation in the region and, additionally, such exposure may limit the comparability of all speakers within the selected sample; it would not be possible to account for the differential sociolinguistic histories of all participants because living outside of the region could involve residency in any number of places.

Finally, participants in the language contact study were required to have had parents who spoke Béarnais to them and participants in the dialect contact study all had local-born parents. This criterion for inclusion aimed to model reliably the transmission of regional phonological features from parent to child. Children are capable of replicating perfectly the language of previous generations (including sociolinguistic constraints) during the transmission process; any divergence from local norms can therefore be taken to indicate internally or externally motivated linguistic change (cf. Labov, 2007). It was necessary to model, as closely as possible, the natural chain of transmission in order to increase the applicability of the apparent-time construct used in the dialect contact study, which assumes differences in the language of successive generations to indicate change in real time. This inclusion criterion ensured, for example, that speakers in the oldest age group were *as like* the youngest generation's grandparents as possible.

The sample structure for the language contact study, stratified by biological sex, included five male and five female Béarnais-French bilinguals. The large majority of research undertaken using the SLM has focused predominantly on second language learners in the traditional sense, speakers who have learnt a language that is not normally spoken in their nation, and who are, in essence, speaking their L2 with a 'foreign accent'. Bilingual Béarnais-French speakers find themselves in a very different situation from this: the L1 and L2 varieties have been involved in long-term language contact; all speakers acquired their L2 at an early age; the levels of L1 and L2 input have varied over the course of the speakers' lifetimes; the L1 language has become restricted to a small number of highly specific domains of use; the L2 language is dominant, both socially and in terms of language use. Nevertheless, the principles governing transfer in the Béarnais-French situation are the same as those described by Flege and others in situations of foreign language learning. Examining the SLM in a situation of territorial language contact may also provide a new perspective on L1-to-L2 transfer through investigating its predictions in a different sociolinguistic context.

The SLM would classify Béarnais-French bilingual speakers as 'early learners' of their L2 as they began to acquire French when they entered primary education at the age of five or six. On this basis, the SLM would predict maximal ability to create new categories for L2 sounds as well as maximal ability to distinguish phonetic differences between L2 categories that are not meaningful in their L1, Béarnais. One methodological challenge involved in this study of language contact is that there is insufficient data available on the nature of the original French input to the bilingual's phonetic categories. It is very likely that it was not generally SF, since the primary input would have come from primary school teachers, normally from the region or from adjacent regions, as well as the highly accented speech of parents: 'Southerners' first contacts with French are more likely to have been through written documents and other Southerners than native speakers from Paris' (Morin, 2009: 411). Indeed, the nature of the French input (as well as the amount of French input) has evolved steadily over the course of the bilinguals' acquisition.

Each of the ten speakers from the language contact study was also included in the sample for the dialect contact study. Thus, as well as considering speaker sex as an independent variable, the dialect contact study also introduces the variable of age. Three broad-category generations have been used to classify speakers: older (65+ years); middle (30–50 years); young (16–18 years). These age groups were chosen to reflect different life-stages as recommended by Milroy and Gordon (2003): retirement, the working-world, and secondary school, respectively. The sample structure for the dialect contact study, with five speakers per cell, is presented in Table 3.1 and full participant details can be consulted in Appendix 1.

Age	Male	Female
Older (65+)	5	5
Middle (30–50)	5	5
Young (16–18)	5	5

TABLE 3.1. Sample structure for the dialect contact study

The recommended number of speakers to include per cell has been widely discussed in the sociolinguistics literature; a decision must always be made about the number of speakers to examine for every social factor included in the analysis. Tagliamonte (2006: 31) suggests, for example, two speakers per cell as a bare minimum but most other commentators agree that a figure in excess of five is desirable (Hoffmann, 2014). Indeed, Milroy and Gordon (2003: 28) argue, on the basis of statistical evidence from Guy (1980), that there is no need to include more than five or six speakers per cell in the analysis because the reliability of the results does not increase dramatically above this number; generalisations can thus be made about the presence at the community level of the linguistic phenomenon studied. There are also practical limitations on the number of speakers it is possible to include in a given study. Wolfram (2011: 299) notes that the nature of the linguistic variables examined may affect the number of speakers included and Llamas (2007: 14) argues that the level of detail involved in the analysis also has a role to play, as is the case for the language and dialect contact studies:

> If we are interested in the depth of the analysis (for example undertaking acoustic analyses of variants of phonological variables in numerous different linguistic environments) then we may lose something in terms of breath, as the number of speakers and the number of variables that can be analysed may be restricted owing to time constraints. (Llamas, 2007: 14)

Milroy and Gordon note that in minority language situations, 'random selection from a sample frame such as an electoral register will be both inadequate and inefficient' (2003: 27) because random sampling methods will often only locate monolingual speakers of the dominant language. Informants for the language and dialect contact studies were sourced using a 'quota sampling' technique. Quota sampling, or 'judgment sampling' involves 'a process of selection based on familiarity with the community in question, targeting sectors best representing the overall community' (Taylor, 1996: 29) whereby 'the researcher identifies in advance the types of speakers to be studied and then seeks out a quota of speakers who fit the specified categories' (Milroy and Gordon, 2003: 30). In order to fill the cells for the quota/judgment sample, I adopted a 'friend-of-a-friend' technique, also known as a 'snowball technique' or 'network sampling'. The technique involves entering the community and contacting potential informants via an intermediary and/or utilises the social networks of participants in the study to recruit potential new participants (Milroy and Gordon, 2003: 32). The motivation behind this technique is simple:

> If a stranger is identified as a friend of a friend, he may easily be drawn into the network's mesh of exchange and obligation relationships. His chances of observing and participating in prolonged interaction will be considerably increased. (Milroy, 1980:53)

Potential informants were proposed by contacts in the *Institut Béarnais et Gascon*, Pau, and were selected based on the specified inclusion criteria. The older bilingual group and the middle group were selected from all three of the fieldwork sites. The young group were all students at the *Collège-Lycée Saint Joseph* in Nay but originated from a variety of different places in the region. Nay is the only fieldwork site with secondary education facilities and it provides educational facilities for many of the surrounding *communes* in the central Béarn region.

The Corpus

Different data elicitation techniques were used for the language and dialect contact studies: in both studies, informants had a sociolinguistic interview in French and, for the language contact study, this was supplemented with a wordlist translation task from French into Béarnais.

A sociolinguistic interview was conducted with each speaker in the sample to elicit casual speech. The objective of a sociolinguistic interview is to observe the participant's relaxed, 'natural' or vernacular language use by encouraging them to engage in 'narratives of personal experience' (Tagliamonte, 2006: 38) by focusing the interview on a series of conversational 'modules' or 'resources' (Labov, 1973). These narratives of personal experience, or stories about the participants' own lives, are hypothesised to elicit speech reflecting their most normal usage, or at least the most normal usage possible while engaging in a recorded conversation with a relative stranger. The organisation of the sociolinguistic interview around conversational modules allows for a semi-structured method of data elicitation: the conversation appears relaxed and 'natural' between both the participant and the interviewer but may be directed and guided by the interviewer in order to focus the conversation and to keep it flowing. The choice of topics used with each participant varied depending on their age but modules that tended to elicit more casual speech included childhood, schooling, working, hobbies and family. In each module, questions progressed from being general (e.g. on childhood) to more specific or related topics (e.g. schooling), facilitating the organisation of modules into 'conversational networks' (Milroy and Gordon, 2003: 59; Labov, 1984: 35). In each of the thirty sociolinguistic interviews in the corpus, care was taken to allow the informant to talk as much as possible. Milroy and Gordon note that interviews should obtain between one to two hours of speech from each speaker but that it is difficult to be categorical about the appropriate length of an interview (2003: 58). Useful phonological data may be obtained in as little at twenty to thirty minutes but speakers are more likely to approximate their everyday usage over a longer period of time. All interviews ranged in length from forty-five minutes to one hour.

In the quest for casual speech, one must take account of the effect that the interviewer's presence in the conversation will have on the variety of speech produced by the participant, in terms of the dynamic process of speech accommodation. The fact that the interviewer may not be part of the speaker's normal environment can alter how the interviewee speaks, leading to Labov's observer's paradox: 'we want to observe how people speak when they are not being observed' (Milroy and Gordon, 2003: 49). I interviewed all informants in the corpus in order to control for the effect of changing the interviewer. I was a 26-year-old white Irish male who had lived in France for extended periods of time: Nice (2005–2006) and Paris (2008–2009). My hope was that, as a native English speaker, my variety of French would not trigger accommodation on the part of the informants (cf. Hoare, 2003,

Paltridge and Giles, 1984) and that any variation in my own accent would not be sociolinguistically salient for the informants. Llamas et al. found that the variety of a non-native speaker interviewer did not hold in-group or out-group associations that were meaningful to native-speaker participants (2009: 391). In this way, linguistic behaviour produced by participants in interviews with non-native speakers might arguably be seen as representing something closer to the default production patterns of the interviewee. It must be noted, however, that if my variety of French were classified relative to native-speaker norms, it would be SF or Parisian French given that I acquired French through an Anglo-Saxon educational system which focused exclusively on SF and I have spent an extended period of time in Paris. Beyond the issue of nativity, many different demographic characteristics of the interviewer may interact with those of the interviewee and influence the extent to which the participant approximates their vernacular usage. The general view is that the more similar two speakers are, the less likely the observer's paradox is to complicate the interview with the ideal situation being to have the interviewer from the same social group as the interviewee (Di Paolo and Yaeger-Dror, 2011: 10). However, Yaeger (1973) found that the more similar in age two speakers are, the more likely it is that demographic out-group status will influence the interaction. Thus, it is much less likely that my presence affected the speech of the older speakers than it is that my interactions with the younger informants, using a standard form of French, caused some accommodation on their part. Nonetheless, all interviewees in both studies were faced with the same non-native interviewer and even if the younger speakers were to accommodate towards my variety of French, that accommodation would be relative to any shifts, or stability, in the speech of the older and middle groups, presented with the same interactional stimulus.

All interviews with the older and middle informants were carried out in their homes and the interviews with the younger informants were carried out at the *Collège-Lycée Saint Joseph*. In order to mitigate the effect of being in a school environment, I systematically used the informal address pronoun *tu* with the younger informants and explained to them that I was not a teacher and that the interview was not a test.

At the end of the sociolinguistic interview each of the ten informants in the language contact study was asked to translate a wordlist from French into Béarnais in order to elicit phonological data on the Béarnais mid-vowel and nasal unit variables in specific contexts. The translation task collected baseline data on the phonetic and phonological variables in Béarnais that may potentially have transferred into each speaker's variety of French. This Béarnais data is thus compared, in the language contact study, to the French casual speech data for the ten bilingual informants. The use of the wordlist translation task to elicit baseline data for Béarnais phonological variables is open to criticism because informants are more likely to engage in transfer when translating from one language to another than when producing casual speech. However, the use of a translation task to gather phonological data on Béarnais is justifiable for the following reasons: the focus of the language contact study is on transfer from Béarnais into French, the opposite direction to transfer potentially induced by the act of translating; the systematic nature of the study means that it is essential that the same variables be examined in the speech of all informants; since all informants were translating, they were confronted with the same potential stimulus for transfer.

Comparing Béarnais wordlist data with French casual speech data may be criticised for two related reasons: firstly, the systems being compared and their acoustic characteristics could, of course, vary along a style continuum; secondly this comparison appears to conflate 'style' and 'language' in that all Béarnais data are 'formal' and all French data are 'casual'. There is evidence to suggest that, during language shift, obsolescent languages experience a reduction in their style repertoire (Dorian, 1981). In a typical scenario, where one language is being ousted by an incoming dominant language, the formal registers of the obsolescent language are lost as it becomes progressively restricted to intimate or informal domains. In this case, rather than using formal or informal stylistic variants, speakers of obsolescent languages frequently switch codes, switching to the dominant language to signal a change in register: the dominant and obsolescent languages are used as markers of style in discourse. Therefore, the effect of 'style' on the elicitation of the Béarnais data may be minimal, though this is speculative.

The translation task was always performed last in order to minimise observer's paradox considerations during the sociolinguistic interview. Informants were presented with individual French words, each written on a record card, and asked to provide a translation in Béarnais. The words were presented in a pseudo-randomised order which was the same for all speakers. The advantage of using a translation task to collect Béarnais data was that informants seemed to view themselves in a position of authority, providing information to the interviewer, rather than as objects of scrutiny.

In acoustic experiments carried out in laboratory conditions, it is common practice to have informants read a wordlist three times, in three random orders 'to counteract presentation order effects such as list intonation which affects word length and may influence individual segments' (Di Paolo and Yaeger-Dror, 2011: 15). This was not possible in the translation task as the informants were not reading a wordlist, but providing translations, and to ask them to repeat the words would have been unnatural and counter-productive, forcing them to pay more attention to their articulations, thus eliciting less vernacular-like tokens. Between the translation of each word, there was often meta-commentary on the lexical item produced and there was always a short delay as the next record card was shown to them by the interviewer. Because of the record cards, the informants were not aware of the length of the list, thus minimising potential listing effects, nor were they reading aloud. No fillers were inserted into the randomised list as eleven different target variables were originally contained in it and it was already quite substantial in length. Additionally, Di Paolo and Yaeger-Dror note that if a wordlist contains a number of different variables, 'the tokens of one variable may serve as fillers for the others, in the sense that they distract the participant from focusing on any one variable of interest' (2011: 14–15).

The words chosen for the wordlist translation task were, on the whole, those lexical items that contain structurally equivalent/corresponding phonemic categories in both the stimulus (French) and the target translation (Béarnais) for the mid-vowels and nasal units. For each French word stimulus, there was a corresponding Béarnais 'target' word. For example, if an informant was presented with the French word *chambre* /ʃɑ̃bʁ/, it was expected that they would provide the translation *crampe* /ˈkrampɔ/. The target words were drawn from the *Atlas Linguistique et Ethnographique de la Gascogne* (ALEG) (Séguy and Allières, 1954–1973). One hundred and twenty-five words, containing the variables under investigation, were analysed at two data points: Lasseube (692NE) and Gélos (685SE). The ALEG does not include data points at Pau, Gan, Nousty or Nay, so these data points were chosen because they are in the same, south-central Pau region. It was hoped that the data collected at these data points would be indicative of the 'target' translation words to be expected during the translation task given that these were the lexical items used at the time when the speakers in the language contact study were acquiring Béarnais.

3.4. Data Analysis

Segmentation of the casual speech files began at the same time-point for all thirty speakers: ten minutes from the beginning of the interview recording until sufficient token counts were extracted for all phonological contexts analysed. Fifteen tokens of each vowel variable were extracted for each speaker in each of three syllabic contexts: /Cv#/, /vCV(C)#/, and /CvC#/. For the nasal vowels, 45 tokens of each vowel were identified for each speaker in the study. For the mid-vowels, 45 tokens were segmented overall for each mid-vowel pair, /e/~/ɛ/ and /o/~/ɔ/, because of phonological constraints on the positions in which the individual vowels can occur, e.g. /ɔ/ does not occur in final closed syllables.

For the Béarnais wordlist, the target variable was segmented and included in the analysis when the translated Béarnais word provided approximated the 'target' translation expected for a given French stimulus. Lexical items that did not conform to the target word, and thus did not contain the target variable were excluded from the analysis. For example, for the stimulus *le sac*, the Béarnais target word expected was *lou sacòt*, containing the /ɔ/ variable. Speaker B, however, provided the Béarnais word *lou caba* which was excluded from the analysis.

Acoustic Analysis

Participants were interviewed individually and the corpus was recorded using a Marantz PMD661 Solid State Sound Recorder. The sampling rate used for the recordings of this corpus was 44.1 kHz (uncompressed linear PCM recording), using a 16-bit PCM sample size. Foulkes et al. note that an auditory analysis is relatively course-grained, imposing a pre-defined set of broad phonetic categories on the data which 'may miss fine-grained detail that is not easily perceivable, but which may nevertheless be identifiable instrumentally' (2011: 60). It is for this reason that the present study applies primarily instrumental techniques. The acoustic analysis employed here involves the continuous measurement of characteristic vocalic features (formant frequencies) in Praat version 5.2.21 (Boersma, 2001; Boersma and Weenink, 2012).

Segment duration was measured instrumentally for all vocalic variables with the primary aim of identifying the midpoint of each vowel. In the context of preceding and following plosives, taps or trills, vowel duration was measured by labelling the onset and offset of regular repeating glottal vibration in a Praat text grid; aspiration following plosive release in the preceding environment and consonantal closure in the following environment were systematically excluded from vowel duration measurements (see Figure 3.2).

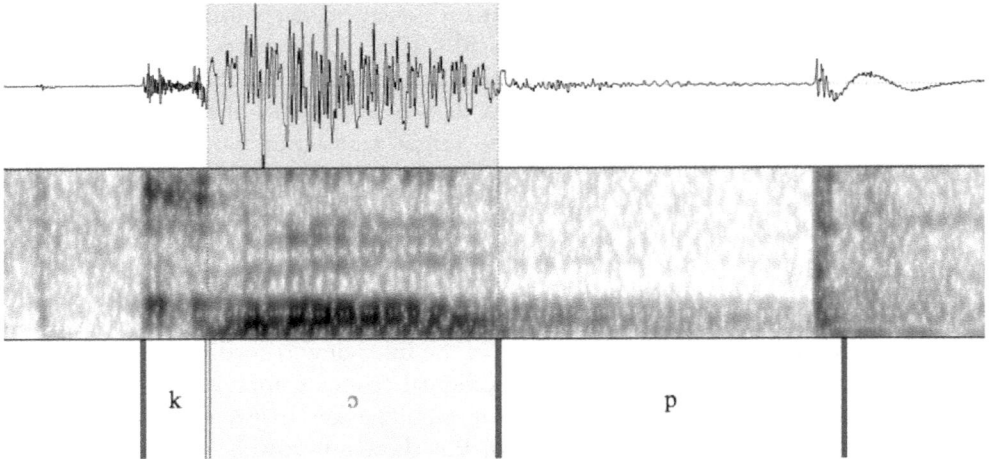

FIG. 3.2. Speaker H: spectrogram of word *cop* with labels for vowel onset and offset (© Damien Mooney)

For vowels preceded or followed by fricatives, fricative noise was never included in the vowel duration. Vowel onset and offset were determined at the points where aperiodic turbulence ended or began (or changed dramatically in intensity) and where higher formant structure became visible or invisible in the spectrogram window (see Figure 3.3).

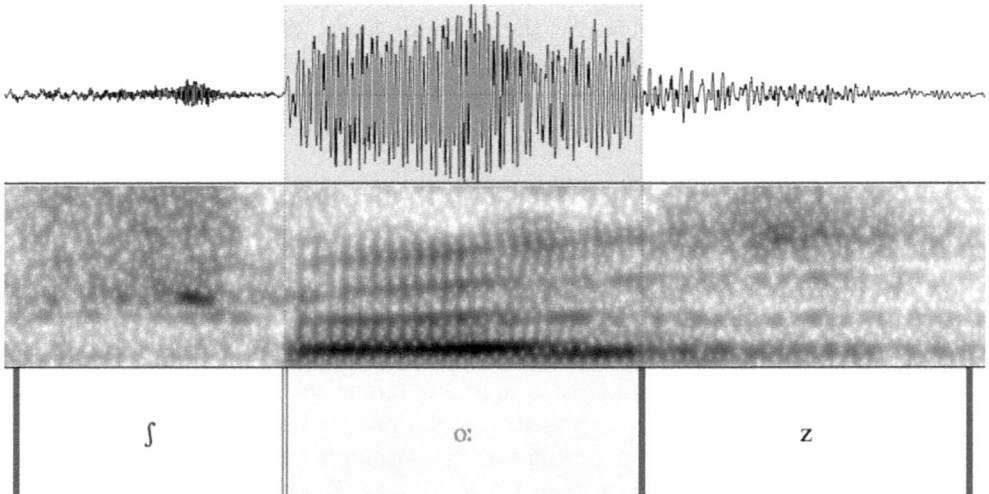

FIG. 3.3. Speaker U: spectrogram of word *chose* with labels for vowel onset and offset (© Damien Mooney)

For the nasal unit variables, in [ṽN] sequences, the boundaries between the vowels and following nasal consonant elements were determined at the point where sharp spectral changes occurred at the beginning of the period of oral closure. In this case, it was most useful to appeal to evidence in the spectrogram, notably a sudden drop in amplitude above fo, in order to establish the measurement point for the vowel offset (see Figure 3.4).

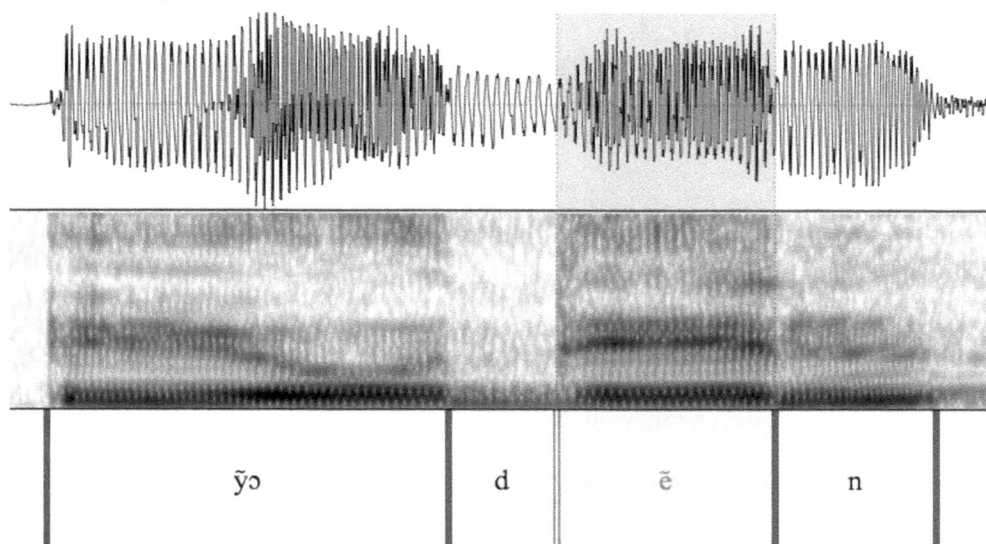

FIG. 3.4. Speaker D: spectrogram of words *ûe dén* with labels
for vowel onset and offset (© Damien Mooney)

In both studies and for both languages, the acoustic analysis of the mid-vowels and of vowels in nasal units investigated vowel quality on the basis of F1, F2 and, where necessary, F3 (for rounded segments). The traditional articulatory correlates of the formant frequencies are: F1 with tongue height; F2 with tongue frontness/ backness; F2 and F3 with lip-rounding. Various studies have, however, shown these values to be only approximate measures of articulatory configurations because other factors, such as the distance of the point of maximum constriction from the glottis, can also have an effect on all formant frequencies (e.g., Fant, 1960): these factors are not fully accounted for in the correlations outlined above. In sum, modelling the acoustic vowel space by plotting F1 against F2 may not be a wholly accurate indication of articulatory configuration during vowel production. Taking account of these complicating factors, and in line with the widespread interpretation of these correlations in sociophonetic studies of language variation and change, the studies of language and dialect contact nonetheless use the first three formant frequencies to model vowel quality.

The first, second and third formants were measured for each vowel token included in the analysis. These formants were estimated in Praat using the LPC (Linear Predictive Coding) algorithm, with a maximum of 4,000 Hz for male speakers and 4,500 Hz for female speakers. This instrumental adjustment based on

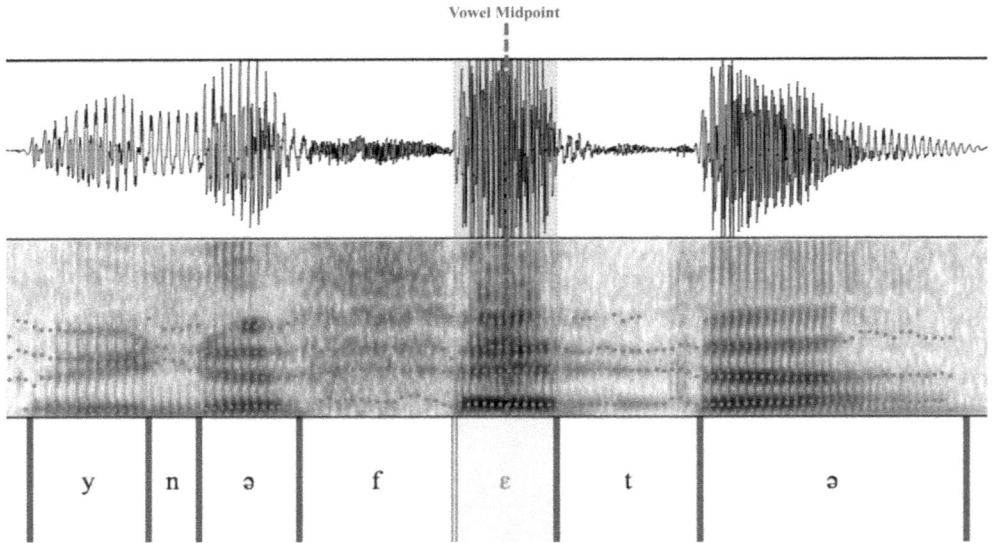

Fig. 3.5. Speaker R: spectrogram of words *une fête* with labels for vowel onset, vowel offset, vowel midpoint, and showing LPC formant tracker (F1–F4) (© Damien Mooney)

biological sex was included as formant trackers may accurately track three formants below 4,500 Hz for female speakers, but may be less accurate for male speakers who might have four formants in the 4,500 Hz range (Clopper, 2011: 195; Llamas et al., 2009: 392). A Praat script was used to automatically extract the value of F1, F2 and F3 at the vowel midpoint (see Figure 3.5).

Nasal and nasalised vowels are notoriously difficult to submit to acoustic analysis. This is primarily because of the effects of nasalisation on the vowel's spectral representation and because of the non-linear relationship between formant values and lingual configuration. The effect of articulatory gestures associated with nasalisation (such as, for example, velar aperture) on formant frequencies means that measures such as F1 and F2 (for vowels in nasal units) may no longer be wholly accurate correlates of tongue height and tongue frontness/backness. There is a perceptual confusion between formant changes due to adjustments of the velum, pharynx, and lips and formant changes due to lingual configuration. This may result in acoustic characteristics of vowel quality that result from nasal coupling, pharyngeal aperture, and labial configuration being misperceived as a result of articulatory changes in tongue position (Carignan et al., 2013). Additionally, F3 is severely affected by nasalisation whereby, owing to the presence of nasal anti-formants, F3 can be divided into two peaks of lesser intensity and/or shift towards higher frequencies, making instrumental measurement unreliable (De Mareüil et al., 2007). In light of these observations, we must take care when interpreting F1, F2 and F3 values for the vowels in nasal units as the acoustic properties of a given nasalised vowel may not be fully attributable to the articulatory configuration of the tongue's height, its frontness, or lip-rounding, respectively.

Auditory Analysis

The presence of a nasal consonant was examined for all Béarnais vowels in nasal units and French nasal vowels. As discussed in Chapter 2, the presence of a nasal consonant coda in Béarnais nasal units is lexically defined and, as such, the auditory analysis merely confirmed the presence of a nasal consonant where it was expected to occur. For French, on the other hand, we saw that the presence of a nasal consonant coda is variable. In both cases, however, the auditory analysis of consonant absence/presence provided a basis on which to split the Béarnais and French data sets according to the phonetic structure of the nasal unit: sequential [ṽN] or non-sequential [ṽ]. The separate examination of vowels in these different phonetic environments was necessary in order to take account of the potential coarticulatory effect of nasal consonant presence on vowel quality. Taylor (1996) has also shown nasal consonant presence to be negatively related to nasalisation: the presence or absence of a nasal consonant coda may further affect vowel quality owing to the effect of related nasopharyngeal coupling on formant frequency values. The auditory examination noted the presence or absence of a nasal consonant as well as the place of articulation of the nasal consonant when it was present in both Béarnais and French: dental [n]; bilabial [m]; palatal [ɲ]; velar [ŋ].

Statistical Analysis

Different speakers exhibit variation in the formant values they produce for a given phonological vowel because of physiological differences in their vocal tracts. These differences are most notable when comparing speakers of different biological sexes because of the greater size of the male vocal tract and the lower fundamental frequency (f0) of the source sound. In order to account for this sexual dimorphism, for the fact that no two speakers' vocal tracts share the same dimensions, and to reliably compare vowel tokens across speakers and sexes, all data were normalised using the Lobanov (1971) method before undertaking a statistical analysis of the data. Normalisation aims to eliminate variation caused by anatomical differences while preserving variation that is sociolinguistically significant. The Lobanov method involves calculating z-scores for individual data points which has the effect of transforming the original distribution to one in which the mean becomes zero and the standard deviation becomes 1. Oral vowels and vowels in nasal units were normalised separately as the analysis assumes them to pertain to different subsystems. During the normalisation procedure, univariate outliers were detected and removed from the data set. Outliers were identified as tokens with a z-score for F_1, F_2, or F_3 that was less than -2.5 or greater than +2.5. This means that tokens for which the z-score for any formant was greater than two and half standard deviations of the mean ($z > 2.5\sigma$) were excluded. The data were then re-normalised, using the raw F_1, F_2, and F_3 values for the remaining data points. The Lobanov normalisation method assumes that the limits of each speaker's vowels space, as represented by the extreme F_1, F_2 and F_3 values, are equivalent: the metric therefore maps each speaker's vowel space onto that of the other speakers in the data set. This assumption may be problematic for two reasons: the reference vowels used to represent the limits of the vowel space are taken from natural speech, not realisations of cardinal vowels; the acoustic difference between male and female speakers' reference vowels may not be a function of anatomical difference. In the latter case, these male-female differences, which may or may not be sociolinguistically meaningful, will be removed by the normalisation metric.

All target variables in the language and dialect contact studies were coded for a series of independent linguistic and extralinguistic factors that were hypo-thesised to constrain the variation under investigation: linguistic independent variables (preceding and following phonological environment, syllable type, lexical frequency); extralinguistic independent variables (speaker, age group, sex). For each dependent variable in the analysis, the preceding and following phonological environments were noted and coded in the token file. We may note that the 'phonological environment' and 'syllable type' factor groups were found to be collinear, or correlated with each other. Collinear dependent variables should never be considered together in statistical analyses because the results will not be reliable (Tagliamonte and Baayen, 2012: 163). Therefore, the regression analyses presented in Chapters 4 and 5 include only 'syllable type' as a factor group because the methodology used coding schemas that filled cells with tokens occurring in a defined set of syllable types. The number of tokens per cell (or factor) is thus much more evenly distributed for 'syllable type' than for the phonological context factor groups. This even distribution of tokens across the cells provides more reliable and robust statistical analyses overall.

Lexical frequency measurements were taken from the *Lexique* corpus (New et al., 2001; New et al., 2007), which is based on subtitles in French from 9474 films and TV programmes and contains approximately 50 million words. In the present study, the French word was searched in the *Lexique* database and the frequency was recorded in the token file as a continuous variable. *Lexique* distinguishes between morphologically inflected words such as *penser-pensons-pensez* and *grand-grande*. It also distinguishes between homonyms where morphological inflection is only indicated in the orthography such as *grand-grands*. During coding, words that differ phonetically were counted as different words (e.g., *bon* and *bonne*) and were listed separately even though they are forms of the same word from a morphological perspective. Inflected verbs were also included as separate entries (e.g., *chanter* and *chantons*) by the same logic. Homonymic verbal forms in the same tense but different persons (e.g., *rentre* and *rentrent*) were, however, counted separately in the initial coding phase as were verbs in different tenses and belonging to different parts of the verbal system (e.g., *arriver*, *arrivez*, and *arrivé*), following Hansen (2001: 244). Past participle forms with differential gender (marked in the orthography alone) were counted together (e.g, *parti* and *partie*). It has been shown that the processing of singular nouns is also influenced by the frequency of its plural (New et al., 2004) and for this reason, plural forms were included in the frequency estimate for singular nouns, with a composite lexical frequency score. The lexical frequency score for each word was log-transformed and the resulting values, representing a logarithmic function of lexical frequency per million words, were used in the statistical analyses.

For both the Béarnais and French mid-vowels and nasal units, the normalised formant frequency data were modelled statistically. Linear regression analyses for the continuous dependent variables (F1 and F2) were carried out in the R environment (version 2.15.3) using the Rbrul (version 2.06) text-based interface (Johnson, 2008). Rbrul is a variable rule programme which evaluates the effects of multiple language-internal and/or social factors on either a binary linguistic 'choice' or, as is the cases for most variables in this study, on a continuous dependent variable. For the French nasal vowels, the presence or absence of a nasal consonant appendage in the nasal unit was also modelled statistically using a logistic regression analysis for binary categorical variables. The specific technique employed for all statistical models was mixed-effects regression. Mixed-effects models make a distinction between two types of factor that can affect a response (dependent) variable. Firstly, fixed effects are factors that are replicable in another study, for example, speaker sex (male/female), stress (tonic/atonic), etc. Random effects, on the other hand, are factors drawn from a larger population which are not completely replicable (Johnson, 2009: 365), such as individual speakers and different lexical items. Coding for individual speakers allows the speaker variable to be included as a 'random effect' in mixed-effects statistical models which 'takes into account that some individuals might favour a linguistic outcome while others might disfavour it, over and above (or 'under and below') what their gender, age, social class, etc. would predict' (Johnson, 2009: 365). The mixed model will only return a significant result for a given factor, such as speaker sex, if the effect is strong enough to rise above the inter-speaker variation in the model. Likewise, including lexical item as a random effect takes into account the variation introduced into the model by individual words and only returns a significant result for internal independent variables when their effect is large enough to outweigh inter-lexical-item variation. If individual speakers and individual words are not included in the regression model as random effects, the results of the analysis will only be relevant for the individuals and words sampled and p-values may be too small and misleading to generalise to the larger population (Tagliamonte and Baayen, 2012: 143).

Note to Chapter 3

1. 'Focusing' denotes linguistic change in the direction of a relatively uniform, homogeneous, and socially unifying language norm (cf. Le Page, 1980).

CHAPTER 4

❖

Language Contact:
Evidence for Linguistic Transfer

Quand quelqu'un leur ouvre les yeux, et leur fait remarquer les fautes qu'ils font,
ils les reconnaissent avec surprise : ils sont étonnés d'avoir parlé ridiculement
toute leur vie. Ils sont les premiers à reconnaître la source du mal, *le patois*.
JEAN DESGROUAIS, *Les gasconismes corrigés*, 1801

This chapter presents the results of the language contact study: a systematic analysis
of the Béarnais and French mid-vowel and nasal unit systems focusing on data from
the oldest (65+) generation of speakers (five male, five female). The mid-vowel
system of Béarnais, the speakers' L1, is examined before that of French, the speakers'
L2; the nasal unit systems of each language are also presented separately. The
analysis of French parallels, as far as possible, that of Béarnais in order to facilitate
cross-linguistic comparison. Following the synchronic analyses of the mid-vowels
and nasal units in each language, evidence for phonetic and phonological transfer
from Béarnais into French is examined in the speech of the older bilingual speakers
and the applicability of Flege's SLM to the interference observed is discussed. The
final section of this chapter discusses the evidence for substrate residue, or influence
from Béarnais, in the RF of Béarn.

4.1. Transfer in the Mid-vowels

The statistical analyses of F1 and F2 for the Béarnais and French mid-vowels include
'speaker' and 'word' as random effects. All models also include 'phoneme', 'syllable
type', 'lexical frequency', and 'speaker sex' as fixed effects (see Table 4.1), and
distinguish the following significance levels: $p < 0.05$ and $p < 0.01$, for which chance
of observing the variation observed is less that 5% and 1%, respectively; $p < 0.001$
is highly significant; for $p < 0.0001$, the probability of observing the result is considered to be approximately zero (≈0), or 100%.

Béarnais Mid-vowels

Token counts for each of the three Béarnais mid-vowels, /e/, /ɛ/ and /ɔ/ are
presented in Table 4.2 for male and female Béarnais speakers. The lower number of
tokens for /ɛ/ is a consequence of its lower type frequency in Béarnais. The analyses
presented here focus on normalised F1/F2 acoustic data; the non-normalised data

Fixed effect	Factors
Phoneme	/e/ or /o/*
	/ɛ/ or /ɔ/
Syllable Type	/Cv#/
	/CvC#/
	/vCV(C)#/
Lexical Frequency	Continuous (log-transformed)
Speaker sex	Male
	Female

TABLE 4.1. Independent variables included in the statistical analyses of the Béarnais and French mid-vowels; * /o/ is included for French only.

(means and standard deviations) for the mid-vowels may be consulted in Appendix 2 (Tables A2.1–A2.2 for the front mid-vowels; Tables A2.3–A2.4 for the back mid-vowels).

Sex	/e/	/ɛ/	/ɔ/
Male	90	36	68
Female	90	37	76

TABLE 4.2. Token counts for Béarnais mid-vowels

Mean normalised F1 and F2 values and their respective standard deviations for these tokens are presented in Figure 4.1; there is minimal overlap between the normalised F1 values for /e/ and /ɛ/, indicating that vowel height is used by the Béarnais speakers to distinguish these vowels.

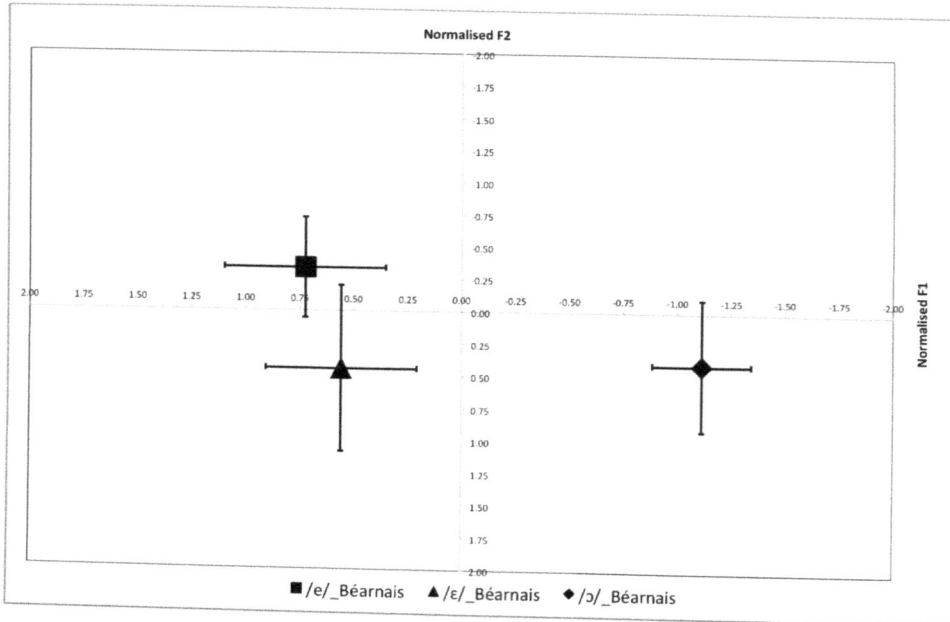

FIG. 4.1. Mean normalised F1 and F2 values for Béarnais mid-vowels (all speakers)

The regression model for the front mid-vowels, with F_1 as the dependent variable, is presented in Table 4.3. Phoneme is returned as a very highly significant independent variable ($p \approx 0$); the positive regression coefficient for /ɛ/ shows that higher F_1 values are favoured than for /e/, indicating that /ɛ/ is consistently articulated as more open than /e/. Lexical frequency is also returned as a significant independent variable ($p < 0.05$); the negative regression coefficient indicates that higher F_1 values, or more open vowels, are more common for lower frequency lexical items. In the regression model for F_2, no independent variables were returned as significant, indicating that while /e/ and /ɛ/ are distinguished in terms of vowel height (F_1), their locations on the front-back dimension (F_2) are not significantly different.

Dependent variable = F_1				
N = 253		Deviance: 326		
Grand mean = -0.11		Degrees of freedom: 10		
Factor Group	Factor	Coeff.	N	*p*-value
Phoneme	/e/	-0.342	180	0.000000159
	/ɛ/	+0.342	73	
Lexical Frequency	Continuous (log-transformed)	-0.14	253	0.0237
Non-significant factor groups were Speaker sex (p=0.247) and Syllable type (p=0.285).				

TABLE 4.3. All speakers: Mixed-effects regression for F_1 in the Béarnais front mid-vowels

For the statistical analyses of the back mid-vowel, the independent variables are the same as for the front mid-vowels, with the exception of 'phoneme', since there is no potential phonemic contrast in the back of the vowel space. The regression model for F_1 returned only one significant independent variable, 'syllable type' ($p < 0.01$): vowels in final closed syllables (/CvC#/) and medial open syllables (/vCV(C)#/) were shown to have significantly higher F_1 values. In the regression model for F_2, no independent variables were returned as significant predictors of the variation observed.

French Mid-vowels

...ken counts for the four French mid-vowels, /e/, /ɛ/, /o/, and /ɔ/, are presented ...Table 4.4 for male and female speakers. The non-normalised data (means and ...ard deviations) for the French mid-vowels is provided in Appendix 2 (Tables ...A2.6 for the front mid-vowels; Tables A2.7–A2.8 for the back mid-vowels).

Sex	/e/	/ɛ/	/o/	/ɔ/
Male	111	114	119	95
Female	85	132	151	67

TABLE 4.4. Token counts for French mid-vowels

...sed F_1 and F_2 values and their respective standard deviations for these ...ented in Figure 4.2; there is some overlap between the normalised .../ and /ɛ/, although mean values suggest that these vowels are ...the basis of vowel height; the distributions of /o/ and /ɔ/ overlap

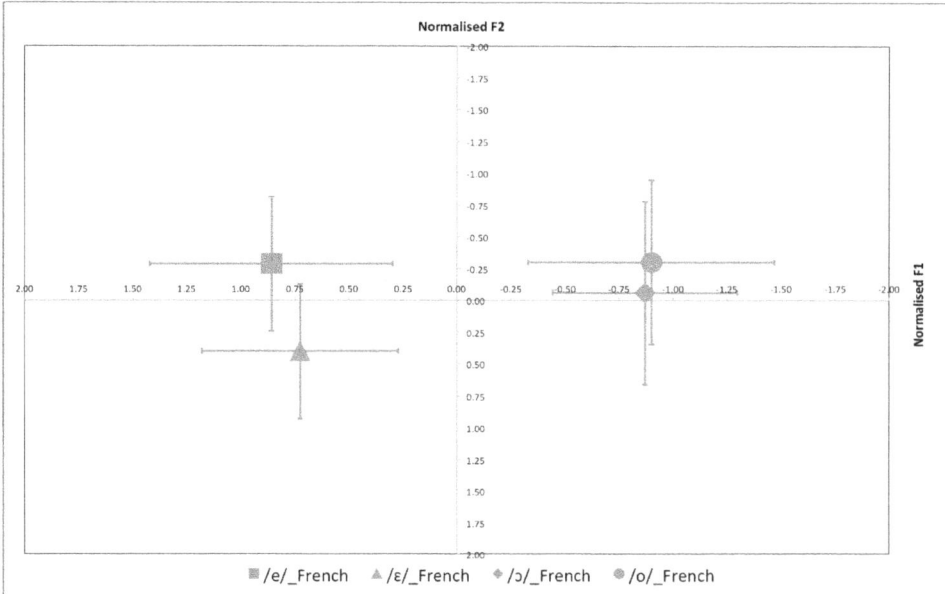

FIG. 4.2. Mean normalised F1 and F2 values for French mid-vowels (all speakers)

on the F1 and F2 dimensions, suggesting that these vowels are not distinguished phonetically.

For the front mid-vowels, the regression analysis for F1 returned two significant independent variables: syllable type ($p \approx 0$); phoneme ($p < 0.01$). The very highly significant correlation between syllable type and the value of F1 shows that open vowels are present in closed syllables and that close vowels are present in open syllables; in other words, the *loi de position* is used by older speakers. The significant effect for phoneme indicates that /ɛ/ favours high F1 values while /e/ favours lower F1 values; despite the tendency for quality to vary with syllable type, a phonemic distinction is maintained. The effect of 'syllable' is stronger than that of 'phoneme' and, since the *loi de position* entails the neutralisation of phonemic contrast in open final syllables, there is evidence to suggest that these vowels are in complementary distribution. The regression model for F2 included syllable type as the only significant independent variable ($p \approx 0$): open syllables favour fronter vowels than closed syllables. A non-significant effect for 'phoneme' ($p = 0.906$) showed that the older speakers do not distinguish significantly between the front mid-vowels on the basis of F2. That 'phoneme' is not returned as a significant predictor of F2 suggests that while phonemic distinctions, such as *j'irai* /e/ ~ *j'irais* /ɛ/, are not made on the basis of F2, phonetic distinctions, such as *j'irai/j'irais* [e] — *arrête* [ɛ], are realised in open and closed syllables respectively.

For the back mid-vowels, the regression analyses for F1 and F2 returned only syllable type ($p \approx 0$, in both cases) as a highly significant independent variable: the *loi de position* is used by all speakers; medial syllables favour centralised vowels while final syllables favour back vowels. The non-significant result for 'phoneme' confirms that neither male nor female speakers make a significant vowel height or vowel frontness distinction between /o/ and /ɔ/, consistent with the overlapping distributions for these vowels in Figure 4.2.

Phonological Transfer

The section examines unilateral linguistic transfer from the mid-vowel system of Béarnais into the structurally related system of French. We have previously noted that a large majority of research has focused on the effect of the L1 on L2 performance but that there has been growing evidence to suggest that the influence may be bi-directional (see Flege, 2007). The analysis of transfer presented here will not explicitly address this L2-to-L1 transfer. We must, however, bear in mind that the baseline Béarnais norm presented here for older speakers may diverge somewhat from the language used in their infancy and from any hypothetical monolingual Béarnais norm posited.

In examining phonological and phonetic transfer, evidence from the Béarnais and French data sets will be used to test the hypotheses advanced by Flege's Speech Learning Model (SLM) (see Section 3.1). This analysis aims explicitly to assess the linguistic mechanisms active during the emergence of RF from language contact and to examine the status of RF as 'substrate residue'. Evidence for equivalence classification is investigated by examining the parallels between the phonemic categories of Béarnais and French. Evidence for phonological transfer must be based on evidence for equivalence classification, that is that structurally related phonemes in Béarnais and French are linked as 'cognates' and exist in a common phonological space. For each analysis, the specific hypothesis derived from the SLM is advanced, and acoustic data and statistical analyses are used to test this hypothesis.

Based on the traditional accounts of Béarnais and French, the specific hypothesis derived from the SLM is that the existence of the phonemes /e/ and /ɛ/ in Béarnais will be equated with French /e/ and /ɛ/ in common phonological space. In Béarnais, speakers make a statistically significant phonetic distinction between /e/ and /ɛ/ on the basis of F1 ($\pm$0.115; $p \approx$0) but do not distinguish the phonemes on the basis of F2. In French, speakers also distinguish between /e/ and /ɛ/ on the basis of F1 ($\pm$0.342; $p <$ 0.01) and make no significant front/back (F2) distinction between the phonemes. Therefore, the bilingual speakers make a comparably significant phonetic distinction between the front mid-vowels on the basis of vowel height in both languages: /e/ is closer than /ɛ/. The existence of phonemic categories for /e/ and /ɛ/ in both of the bilinguals' languages lends weight to the hypothesis that they would be equated in a common abstract phonological representation and that they would thus be stored in common phonetic categories, [e] and [ɛ]. It has been noted that the existence of /e/ **and** /ɛ/ in Béarnais (or, more generally, in *langue d'oc* varieties) may facilitate the maintenance of this contrast, which is subject to varying degrees of neutralisation in supralocal French, in the French of bilingual speakers (Morin, 2005; Moreux, 2006; Durand, 2009).

For the back mid-vowels, the SLM-derived hypothesis predicts that the existence of one back mid-vowel phonemic category in Béarnais /ɔ/ will lead to the establishment of a single phonemic category in French (conflating /o/ and /ɔ/).

Put another way, equivalence classification will equate the two French sounds with the single sound in Béarnais as the phonetic height distinction between French /o/ and /ɔ/ is not meaningful in Béarnais. The statistical analyses of F1 and F2 in French confirmed this hypothesis to be true: no significant effect was returned for 'phoneme' in either analysis. In French, the bilingual speakers do not make a significant phonetic distinction between /o/ and /ɔ/, demonstrating that these sounds occupy a single phonemic category, which is, in SLM terms, equated with Béarnais /ɔ/ in a common abstract phonological representation. The symbol /O/ shall henceforth be used to designate the common phonemic category for French /o/ and /ɔ/, following the usage of Durand: 'les symboles E, Ø, O ne représentent pas des archiphonèmes au sens de Martinet mais des voyelles sous-spécifiées pour l'aperture [...] ou des classes de sons pour rester théoriquement plus neutre' (2009: 6). We can thus conclude that, based on this analysis, Béarnais /ɔ/ and French /O/ are cognate phonemic categories for the bilingual speakers.

Durand notes the existence of many southern varieties of French that maintain a phonetic distinction between the front mid-vowels /e/ and /ɛ/ while neutralising the distinction between /o/ and /ɔ/ (and also between /ø/ and /œ/) (2009: 6). Martinet views such neutralisation as a consequence of articulatory asymmetry between the possible degrees of vowel height in the front and back of the vowel space (1955: 99). While there may exist some articulatory bias favouring the existence of a single back vowel category in French, this asymmetry is not present in many other varieties of metropolitan French and, in the case of the supralocal norm, there is partial assimilation of phonological contrast in the front and back of the mid-vowel space with a range of partly structured phonetic realisations. It is most likely therefore that this is language contact effect. Flege notes that this type of transfer at the phonemic category level occurs when L2 learners fail to perceive phonetic differences that distinguish contrastive sound units of the L2, or which distinguish L2 sounds from sounds in the L1 (1995: 99).

In sum, three potential equivalence classes exist for the bilingual speakers in the language contact study: Béarnais /e/ and French /e/; Béarnais /ɛ/ and French /ɛ/; Béarnais /ɔ/ and French /O/. In each case, the Béarnais and French sounds should, via the process of cross-language phonetic category assimilation, resemble each other phonetically.

Phonetic Transfer

The SLM predicts that equivalence classification of L1 and L2 phonemes will lead to phonetic category assimilation: the L1 and L2 sounds will be pronounced in the same way. Each of the equivalence classes identified above were examined separately in order to test this hypothesis: the Béarnais and French data sets for each class were combined, and mixed-effect regression analyses including 'language' [Béarnais; French] as the only fixed independent variable were used to establish significant variations in F1 and F2 that are related to cognate sounds being realised in one language or the other.

We have seen that Béarnais /e/ and /ɛ/ and French /e/ and /ɛ/ are hypothesised to be cognate phonemes in the bilinguals' common phonological space. According to the SLM, these equivalence classifications should realised as members of the same phonetic category: French /e/ should be phonetically identical to Béarnais /e/, and French /ɛ/ should be phonetically identical to Béarnais /ɛ/. In acoustic terms, the F1 and F2 values would not be significantly different in each of the languages for each of the vowels. Beginning with /e/, the regression analysis returned 'language' as a non-significant independent variable for vowel height (p = 0.44) and vowel frontness/backness (p = 0.07). This confirms that, on the basis of F1 and F2, Béarnais and French /e/ are not significantly different and do resemble each other phonetically.

The regression analyses for F1 and F2 in /ɛ/ returned 'language' as a non-significant independent variable, confirming that, as for /e/, no significant phonetic distinction is made between /ɛ/ in French and /ɛ/ in Béarnais for vowel height (p = 0.95) or vowel frontness/backness (p = 0.054). From the perspective of the SLM, the equivalence classification of Béarnais and French /ɛ/ means that they are present in a single phonetic category which is used to process and produce the perceptually linked L1 and L2 diaphones which also, as predicted, resemble each other phonetically.

For the back mid-vowels, the regression analysis for F1 returned 'language' as a highly significant predictor of the variation observed (p < 0.01; see Table 4.5): Béarnais /ɔ/ has significantly higher F1 values than French /O/ which favours lower F1 values. This shows that the Béarnais vowel is significantly more open than the French vowel. Similar regression analyses comparing (i) Béarnais /ɔ/ and French /ɔ/ and (ii) Béarnais /ɔ/ and French /o/ revealed the same pattern to be true in each case: Béarnais /ɔ/ is significantly more open than all French back mid-vowels. The equivalent regression model for F2 returned 'language' as a significant predictor of vowel frontness/backness (±0.101; p < 0.01): Béarnais /ɔ/ was further back in the vowel space than French /O/.

Dependent variable = F1				
N = 576		Deviance: 1093		
Grand mean = 0.067		Degrees of freedom: 6		
Factor Group	Factor	Coeff.	N	p-value
Language	Béarnais	0.208	144	0.00016
	French	-0.208	432	
Non-significant factor groups were Speaker sex (p=0.2).				

TABLE 4.5. All speakers: Mixed-effects regression for F1 values
from Béarnais (/ɔ/) and French (/O/).

These statistical analyses reveal Béarnais /ɔ/ to be phonetically distinct from French /O/ on the basis of both F1 and F2: French /O/ is closer and more centralised than Béarnais /ɔ/. This shows that Béarnais /ɔ/ and French /O/ are not members of the same phonetic category. From this, we must infer that a new phonetic category has been established for French /O/.

It was previously demonstrated that French /ɔ/ and /o/ were merged into a single phonemic category, /O/, by analogy with the single back mid-vowel phoneme in Béarnais, and because the French phonetic contrast was not meaningful in the L1. This is an instance of phonological transfer, but the findings above have shown phonetic transfer to be absent. The establishment of a new phonetic category for French /O/ appears to have activated the linguistic mechanism of 'phonetic category dissimilation', whereby a newly established L2 category disperses in the bilingual vowel space and dissimilates from neighbouring L1 and/or L2 sounds to preserve phonetic contrast. In this case, the single French /O/ category has moved away from Béarnais /ɔ/ by raising and centralising. The new French /O/ phonetic category was perhaps also 'attracted' to the gap in the asymmetrical L1 vowel space between Béarnais /ɔ/ and Béarnais /u/. It is also a possibility that the low position of the Béarnais /ɔ/ vowel is a result of the L1 phonetic category also dissimilating, moving low in the vowel space to maximise phonetic contrast with the newly established L2 category for French /O/.

The mean normalised F1 and F2 values used in the statistical analyses for the Béarnais and French mid-vowels are plotted in Figure 4.3: the distributions of /e/ and /ɛ/ in each language overlap; Béarnais /ɔ/ is more open than (merged) French /o/ and /ɔ/.

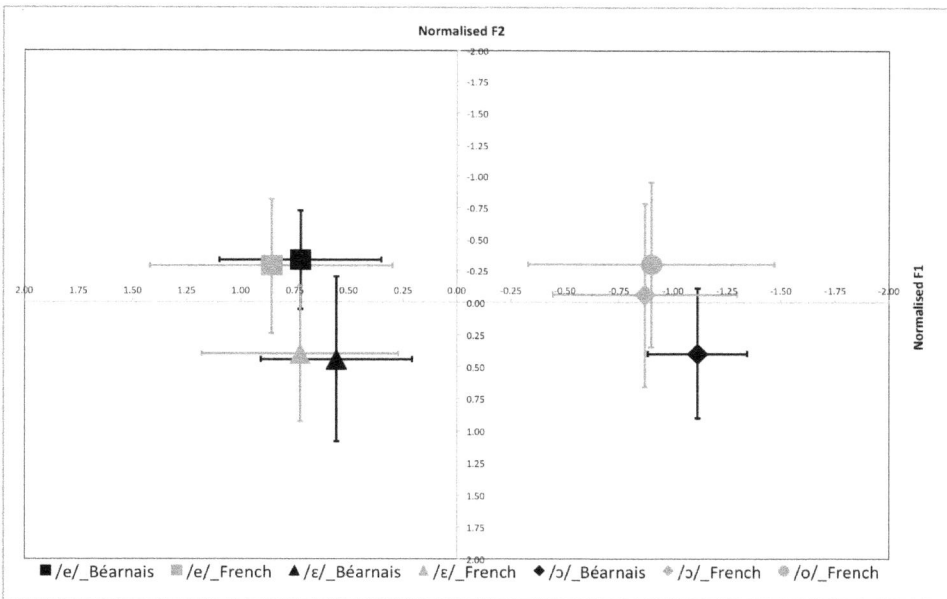

FIG. 4.3. Mean normalised F1 and F2 values for Béarnais and French mid-vowels (all speakers)

We can also examine the phonetic realisation rules that act on French /O/. For F1, the *loi de position* was shown to be active as a phonetic realisation rule: final closed syllables favour more open vowels than open syllables, which favour close vowels. The phonetic realisation rules, or *loi de position*, act on one L2 phonemic category, French /O/, which occupies the close-mid area of the bilingual vowel space. This means that the open-close alternations in French /O/, linked to the *loi de position*, occur within a restricted area of the vowel space and do not utilise the entire range (because the open-mid area of the vowel space is occupied by Béarnais

/ɔ/). The contextual open and close variants of French /O/ will thus necessarily differ from monolingual (and particularly northern) French norms. We may note that this concurs with Carton et al.'s observation which describes the open [ɔ] variant in Gascony as not being *as open* as the /ɔ/ of SF but somewhere between [o] and [ɔ] (1983: 61).

Overall, phonemic transfer has not resulted in phonetic transfer for the majority of older bilingual speakers. The majority pattern showed the establishment of a new phonetic category for French /O/ which dissimilated phonetically from Béarnais /ɔ/ by raising and centralising. Simonet (2011) found that Spanish-dominant Spanish-Catalan bilinguals who had merged Catalan /o/ and /ɔ/ into a single merged back vowel by analogy with Spanish /o/, had nonetheless also developed a separate phonetic category for this merged Catalan vowel, which was significantly more open and slightly more fronted than their Spanish /o/. This finding parallels the results presented above for the Béarnais-French bilinguals. In both cases, the neutralisation of an L2 phonological contrast not present in the speakers' L1, as a result of equivalence classification, did not lead to phonetic category assimilation, as predicted by the SLM. It seems that phonological L1-to-L2 transfer may occur when there is no one-to-one correspondence between the L1 and L2 phonologies but that the SLM hypothesis that equivalence classification leads to phonetic category assimilation must be modified to take account of these structural divergences when advancing predictions about phonetic category assimilation. This is because phonemic divergences between the languages in contact have been shown here to inhibit the production of an L2 sound as an instance of an L1 phonetic category, even when they appear to have been equated as cognates from a phonological perspective.

4.2. Transfer in the Nasal Vowels

Béarnais Nasal Units

The main purpose of this section is to examine the relative position of the vowels in the Béarnais nasal units, /ĩN ỹN ẽN ãN ũN/. The reader is, however, reminded that the nasal units involve complex non-linear interactions between at least three parameters: vowel quality; vowel nasalisation; nasal consonant presence/absence.

The presence of a nasal consonant is governed by both contextual and lexical constraints (see Section 2.1) and the analysis examines vowel quality in each phonetic environment separately: sequential [ṽN] and non-sequential [ṽ]. The potential effect of consonant presence on nasalisation and on the vowel formant frequencies precludes an analysis which considers the phonetic environments together even if the methodology adopted assumes them to realise phonologically the same unit.

The discussion will examine the quality of vowels in nasal units, first comparing the front vowels /ĩN ỹN ẽN/ (F1, F2), followed by an individual analysis of the open and close vowels /ãN ũN/ (F1, F2). F3 is also analysed for the vocalic elements in /ĩN ỹN ũN/ (close vowels) due to lip-rounding contrasts present in the close front area of the vowel space. Table 4.6 presents the token counts included in the analysis for male and female Béarnais speakers; the non-normalised data (means and standard deviations) may be consulted in Appendix 2 (Tables A2.9–A2.12 for F1 and F2; Tables A2.13–A2.16 for F3).

Sex	/ĩN/		/ỹN/		/ẽN/		/ãN/		/ũN/	
	[ĩN]	[ĩ]	[ỹN]	[ỹ]	[ẽN]	[ẽ]	[ãN]	[ã]	[ũN]	[ũ]
M	26	44	30	34	63	9	40	30	37	33
F	26	46	31	36	60	12	43	26	37	32

TABLE 4.6. Token counts for Béarnais (sequential and non-sequential) nasal units

For the front vowels, /ĩN ỹN ẽN/, regression analyses of the first three formant frequencies were undertaken, including 'speaker' and 'word' as random effects and as well as 'nasal unit' and 'speaker sex' as independent variables. In sequential nasal units, F1 was significantly predicted by the phonemic identity of the nasal unit but not by speaker sex (see Table 4.7). This result shows that the vowels in the [ẽN] nasal unit are substantially more open than vowels in the [ỹN] and [ĩN] units, the expected pattern.

Nasal Unit = [ĩN ỹN ẽN]			Deviance: 147		
Dependent variable = F1			Degrees of freedom: 7		
N = 236					
Grand mean = -0.235					

Factor Group	Factor	Coeff.	N	p-value
Nasal Unit	[ẽN]	0.453	123	3.37e-13
	[ỹN]	-0.160	61	
	[ĩN]	-0.293	52	

Non-significant factor groups were Speaker sex (p=0.736)

TABLE 4.7. All speakers: Mixed-effects regression for
F1 values from Béarnais [ĩN ỹN ẽN].

In non-sequential nasal units, on the other hand, both independent variables are included as significant predictors of F1: a highly significant result for nasal unit shows that [ẽ] favours relatively high F1 values while [ỹ] and [ĩ] favour lower F1 values (p < 0.001). The significant result for speaker sex indicates that male and female speakers differ in their linguistic behaviour for the front vowels when no nasal consonant is present in the nasal unit (p < 0.05). Regression models considering the sexes separately revealed, for male speakers, a highly significant effect of nasal unit identity on the value of F1 ($p < 0.01$): [ẽ] favours more open vowels than [ĩ] and [ỹ]. For female speakers, the effect of nasal unit identity was not returned as significant in the regression analysis ($p = 0.289$). This means that female speakers do not distinguish significantly between these vowels in terms of height when no nasal consonant is present, perhaps suggesting that non-sequential units favour neutralisation of the phonetic distinction between these vowels on the height dimension.

Table 4.8 presents the regression analysis for F2 in the close front vowels in sequential nasal units. The effect of nasal unit identity is highly significant across speakers: [ĩN] favours higher F2 values while [ỹN] favours lower F2 values. The [ẽN] vowels occupy an intermediate space on the F2 continuum between these two close vowels; in non-sequential units, the same pattern was observed across speakers (p < 0.01).

Nasal Unit = [ĩN ỹN ẽN]				
Dependent variable = F2			Deviance: 135	
N = 236			Degrees of freedom: 7	
Grand mean = 0.572				

Factor Group	Factor	Coeff.	N	p-value
Nasal Unit	[ĩN]	0.540	52	1.16e-12
	[ẽN]	-0.071	123	
	[ỹN]	-0.470	61	

Non-significant factor groups were Speaker sex (p=0.776).

TABLE 4.8. All speakers: Mixed-effects regression for
F2 values from Béarnais [ĩN ỹN ẽN]

The analysis of F3 considers only the three close vowels: the correlation between lip-rounding and F3 was examined as well as the use of this correlation in distinguishing between the vocalic elements of the /ĩN/ and /ỹN/ nasal units whereby the feature [+round] distinguishes the latter from the former. The discussion presented here includes data for F3 in the close back rounded vowels of the /ũN/ nasal unit for comparison. In sequential nasal units, 'nasal unit' was returned as a significant predictor of F3 values (p ≈ 0) (see Table 4.9). This result shows that the feature [+round] significantly predicts the value of F3 across speakers. The [ĩN] unit favours high F3 values while both [ỹN] and [ũN] favour low F3 values. Rounded segments thus have substantially lower F3 values than the unrounded segments, the expected acoustic correlate of lip-rounding.

Nasal Unit = [ĩN ỹN ũN]				
Dependent variable = F3			Deviance: 360	
N = 187			Degrees of freedom: 9	
Grand mean = -0.206				

Factor Group	Factor	Coeff.	N	p-value
Nasal Unit	[ĩN]	1.293	52	2.57e-17
	[ỹN]	-0.374	61	
	[ũN]	-0.920	74	

Non-significant effects were Speaker sex*Nasal unit (p=0.984) and Speaker sex (p=0.108).

TABLE 4.9. All speakers: Mixed-effects regression for
F3 values from Béarnais [ĩN ỹN ũN]

In non-sequential units, the same pattern was evident: rounded vowels [ỹ] and [ũ] favour lower F3 values while the unrounded vowel [ĩ] favours high F3 values (p ≈ 0). Overall, in both sequential and non-sequential nasal units, speakers distinguish between the vowels /ĩN/, /ỹN/, and /ũN/ in Béarnais on the basis of F3.

The individual regression models for F1 and F2 in the /ãN/ and /ũN/ nasal units included 'speaker' and 'word' as random effects and the following independent variables: speaker sex; lexical frequency; syllable type. No significant independent variables were returned by the regression analyses of F1 and F2 when /ãN/ occurred in sequential nasal units, [ãN]. In non-sequential nasal units, on the other hand, 'speaker sex' was a significant predictor of vowel height in non-sequential units, [ã] (p < 0.05): male speakers make use of more open [ã] vowels (+0.179) than female speakers (−0.179). For F2 in non-sequential units 'speaker sex' ($p < 0.05$) and 'syllable type' ($p < 0.05$) were returned as significant independent variables: [ã] vowels in closed syllables are significantly fronted relative to [ã] vowels in open syllables; separate regression analyses for male and female speakers revealed the 'syllable type' effect to be significant for male speakers ($p < 0.01$) but not for female speakers ($p = 0.73$).

The regression models for /ũN/ in sequential and non-sequential nasal units showed that no independent variables considered were significant predictors of F1 or F2. Therefore, vowel height and vowel frontness/**backness** in /ũN/ did not appear to be influenced by syllable type, speaker sex, or lexical frequency.

French Nasal Vowels

The French nasal vowels /ɛ̃ œ̃ ã ɔ̃/ are examined here in phonetically sequential and non-sequential contexts. The discussion of vowel quality focuses on the extent to which the /ɛ̃/~/œ̃/ and /ã/~/ɔ̃/ pairs are distinguished on the basis of F1, F2, and F3. Table 4.10 presents the token counts of the French nasal units; overall, there is a strong tendency among the older speakers to realise the nasal units with nasal consonant codas. The lower number of token counts for /œ̃/ is due to the low type frequency of the nasal vowel, occurring primarily in the high frequency word *un* and derivatives thereof, e.g,. *quelqu'un*, *chacun* etc., as well as the fact that is it restricted phonotactically, occurring primarily in word final open syllables; /œ̃/ may also occur in open medial syllables (/ṽCV(C)#/), e.g. *lundi*, and in final closed syllables (/CṽC#/), e.g. *j'emprunte*, but these occurrences are extremely rare. The data (means and standard deviations) for the French nasal vowels may be consulted in Appendix 2 (Tables A2.17–A2.20 for F1 and F2; Tables A2.21–A2.28 for F3).

Sex	/ɛ̃/		/œ̃/		/ã/		/ɔ̃/	
	[ɛ̃N]	[ɛ̃]	[œ̃N]	[œ̃]	[ãN]	[ã]	[ɔ̃N]	[ɔ̃]
M	127	42	69	7	187	26	40	18
F	138	44	55	23	155	52	43	64

TABLE 4.10. Token counts for French (sequential and non-sequential) nasal units

Beginning with the front nasal vowels, a mixed-effects linear regression analysis was undertaken in order to model the phonetic realisation (F1, F2, F3) of the traditional /ɛ̃/~/œ̃/ phonemic contrast. Each model contained 'speaker' and 'word' as random effects and included the following independent variables: 'phoneme', and 'speaker sex'. Table 4.11 presents the results of the regression analysis of F1 in sequential nasal units [ṽN]: speaker sex is the only significant independent variable returned by the analysis; the phonemes /ɛ̃/ and /œ̃/ do not appear, perhaps unsurprisingly, to be distinguished in terms of vowel height. Separate models considering male and female speakers separately showed that 'phoneme' was in fact a significant predictor of vowel height for male speakers (±0.218; $p < 0.05$) but not for female speakers ($p = 0.831$); male speakers distinguish between the front nasal vowels on the height dimension while female speakers do not.

Nasal Unit = [ɛ̃N œ̃N]				
Dependent variable = F1		Deviance: 893		
N = 389		Degrees of freedom: 7		
Grand mean = -0.408				

Factor Group	Factor	Coeff.	N	*p*-value
Sex	Female	0.122	193	0.0114
	Male	-0.122	196	

Non-significant factor groups were Phoneme (p=0.34).

TABLE 4.11. All speakers: Mixed-effects regression for
F1 values from French [ɛ̃N œ̃N]

In non-sequential nasal units [ṽ], /ɛ̃/ and /œ̃/ were not distinguished phonetically on the basis of F1 (*p* = 0.721) and no effect of speaker sex was returned by the analysis (*p* = 0.197). We may also note that while male speakers distinguished between /ɛ̃/ and /œ̃/ when a nasal consonant coda was present, they do not make a significant F1 distinction between the vowels when no nasal consonant occurs in the unit.

Table 4.12 presents the regression model of F2 values for the front nasal vowels in sequential nasal units [ṽN]. Since F2 lowering is a common acoustic consequence of lip-rounding, we would expect F2 to be significantly different for /ɛ̃/ and /œ̃/ if they are not merged. 'Phoneme' is indeed returned by the analysis as a highly significant predictor of F2: /ɛ̃/ favours relatively higher F2 values while /œ̃/ favours lower F2 values. The magnitude of this effect is large, meaning that [ɛ̃N] is significantly fronter in acoustic space than [œ̃N]. This is most likely due to F2 lowering as a result of lip-rounding rather than lingual configuration. In the regression model for F2 in non-sequential units [ṽ], 'phoneme' is also returned as a highly significant predictor of F2 (*p* < 0.01): /ɛ̃/ favours high F2 values while /œ̃/ favours lower F2 values. This confirms that in both phonetic contexts, /ɛ̃/ and /œ̃/ are discriminated significantly on the basis of their F2 values.

Nasal Unit = [ɛ̃N œ̃N]				
Dependent variable = F2		Deviance: 837		
N = 389		Degrees of freedom: 7		
Grand mean = 0.763				

Factor Group	Factor	Coeff.	N	*p*-value
Phoneme	/ɛ̃/	0.425	265	0.000176
	/œ̃/	-0.425	124	

Non-significant factor groups were Speaker sex (p=0.244).

TABLE 4.12. All speakers: Mixed-effects regression for F2 values from French [ɛ̃N œ̃N]

Table 4.13 presents the mixed-effects regression model for F3 in the front nasal vowels in sequential units. 'Phoneme' is returned as a significant predictor of F3: /ɛ̃/ favours significantly higher F3 values than /œ̃/. As F3 lowering is a common acoustic correlate of lip-rounding, this result suggests that the contrastive rounding distinction, indicated in the F2 analyses, is retained between the front nasal vowels, when all speakers are considered.

Nasal Unit = [ɛ̃N œ̃N]
Dependent variable = F3
N = 389
Grand mean = 0.126

Deviance: 1039
Degrees of freedom: 7

Factor Group	Factor	Coeff.	N	p-value
Phoneme	/ɛ̃/	0.252	265	0.039
	/œ̃/	-0.252	124	

Non-significant factor groups were Speaker sex (p=0.0768).

TABLE 4.13. All speakers: Mixed-effects regression for F3 values from French [ɛ̃N œ̃N]

In the regression analysis of F3 in non-sequential units, 'phoneme' was not returned as a significant independent variable: [ɛ̃] and [œ̃] are not distinguished significantly on the basis of F3 when they occur in nasal units with no nasal consonant coda. This contrasts with the situation for sequential nasal units, where the phonemes are distinguished on the basis of F3 when they occur in nasal units where a nasal consonant coda is present. Such sequential units are non-standard in that nasal consonant codas do not occur in supralocal French, and it is precisely in this context that the /ɛ̃/~/œ̃/ distinction is maintained. In the non-sequential context, when no nasal consonant coda is present, speakers appear to use a supralocal three-term nasal vowel system (at least for F3).

Table 4.14 examines the relationship between the phonemic identity of /ɑ̃/ and /ɔ̃/ and F1 values. The model shows the F1 distinction between [ɑ̃N] and [ɔ̃N] to be highly significant, with [ɑ̃N] favouring higher F1 values and [ɔ̃N] favouring low F1 values. This ties in with the expected placement of these vowels in articulatory space: /ɑ̃/ is realised as a significantly more open vowel than /ɔ̃/ in sequential nasal units. In non-sequential units, 'phoneme' was also returned as a highly significant predictor of F1 ($p \approx 0$): [ɑ̃] favours high F1 values while [ɔ̃] favours low F1 values. This confirms that, in non-sequential units, /ɑ̃/ and /ɔ̃/ are distinguished significantly on the basis of F1 when all speakers are considered together: [ɑ̃] is a more open vowel than [ɔ̃].

Nasal Unit = [ɑ̃N ɔ̃N]
Dependent variable = F1
N = 659
Grand mean = 0.24

Deviance: 1581
Degrees of freedom: 6

Factor Group	Factor	Coeff.	N	p-value
Phoneme	/ɑ̃/	0.603	342	1.05e-38
	/ɔ̃/	-0.603	317	

Non-significant factor groups were Speaker sex (p=0.0829).

TABLE 4.14. All speakers: Mixed-effects regression for F1 values from French [ɑ̃N ɔ̃N]

The relationship between F2 values and the phonemic identity of /ɑ̃/ and /ɔ̃/ in sequential nasal units is modelled in Table 4.15. 'Phoneme' is a highly significant predictor of F2: [ɑ̃N] favours significantly higher F2 values than [ɔ̃N]. This shows that the vowels in [ɑ̃N] nasal units are both more open and fronter than the vowels in [ɔ̃N] nasal units, when a consonantal coda is present: the potential supralocal merger of /ɑ̃/ and /ɔ̃/ does not appear to be taking place in the older speakers' regional variety of French. The equivalent model for non-sequential nasal units also returned 'phoneme' as a highly significant independent variable ($p \approx 0$): [ɑ̃] was shown to favour higher F2 values (fronter vowels) than [ɔ̃]. Therefore, in both sequential and non-sequential nasal units, /ɑ̃/ is significantly different from /ɔ̃/ on the basis of F1 and F2: /ɑ̃/ is more open and fronter than /ɔ̃/.

Nasal Unit = [ɑ̃N ɔ̃N]				
Dependent variable = F2			Deviance: 1145	
N = 659			Degrees of freedom: 7	
Grand mean = -0.483				
Factor Group	**Factor**	**Coeff.**	**N**	***p*-value**
Phoneme	/ɑ̃/	0.485	342	7.65e-55
	/ɔ̃/	-0.485	317	
Non-significant factor groups were Speaker sex (p=0.056).				

TABLE 4.15. All speakers: Mixed-effects regression for F2 values from French [ɑ̃N ɔ̃N]

The regression analyses for F3 revealed 'phoneme' to be a non-significant independent variable in sequential and non-sequential nasal units. This result shows that /ɑ̃/ and /ɔ̃/ are not distinguished significantly on the basis of F3 ($p = 0.966$ for sequential units; $p = 0.228$ for non-sequential units). We saw previously, however, that the back nasal vowels were distinguished significantly on the basis of F1 and F2 in both phonetic contexts.

Finally, we can examine the factors conditioning the presence of a nasal consonant coda in the RF nasal vowels. The frequency distribution for nasal consonant presence and absence is presented in Table 4.16 for each of the four nasal units. The frequency of nasal consonant presence is comparably similar for all nasal vowels ranging from 75% for /œ̃/ to 81% for /ɛ̃/ and /ɑ̃/. This suggests that the identity of the historically appropriate phonemes does not have any substantial effect on the distribution of nasal consonants.

	Consonant presence/absence		
Nasal Unit	*N*	*% Sequential*	*% Non-sequential*
/ɛ̃/	420	81	19
/œ̃/	351	75	25
/ɑ̃/	154	81	19
/ɔ̃/	399	79	21

TABLE 4.16. All speakers: The relationship between nasal consonant presence/absence and nasal unit in French.

Table 4.17 considers the relationship between syllable type and nasal consonant presence for each nasal vowel separately and across all nasal vowels. /œ̃/ does not occur in closed final syllables (/CṽC#/) in the data set and is extremely infrequent in open medial syllables (/ṽCV(C)#/). The three non-final tokens of /œ̃/ included in the table all occur, with nasal consonant coda, in the word *lundi* /lœ̃di/. For these reasons, it is not possible to discuss the effect of syllable type on consonant absence/presence for /œ̃/ and we can simply say that in open final syllables (/Cṽ#/), where it occurs with the highest frequency, 80% of tokens are realised with a nasal consonant coda. For all of the other vowels, the overall pattern suggests that final closed and medial open syllables favour consonant presence while final open syllables favour consonant absence.

		Consonant presence/absence		
Nasal Unit	N	Syllable type	% Sequential	% Non-sequential
/ɛ̃/	70	/CṽC#/	93	17
	140	/ṽCV(C)#/	73	27
	141	/Cṽ#/	70	30
/œ̃/	0	/CṽC#/	ND	ND
	3	/ṽCV(C)#/	100	0
	151	/Cṽ#/	80	20
/ɑ̃/	133	/CṽC#/	82	18
	147	/ṽCV(C)#/	90	10
	140	/Cṽ#/	72	28
/ɔ̃/	101	/CṽC#/	86	14
	147	/ṽCV(C)#/	84	16
	151	/Cṽ#/	70	30
Total	304	/CṽC#/	86	14
	437	/ṽCV(C)#/	83	17
	583	/Cṽ#/	73	27

TABLE 4.17. The relationship between nasal consonant presence/absence and syllable type sequential nasal units in French.

A mixed-effects logistic regression analysis was used to model the binary variable of consonant presence/absence across nasal units. The response variable was 'presence', 'speaker' and 'word' were included as random effects, and the following independent variables were included in the analysis: phoneme, syllable type, speaker sex, lexical frequency. The descriptive analysis presented in Tables 4.16 and 4.17 suggested that the phonemic identity of the nasal unit did not appear to affect the frequency of sequential nasal units. Syllable type, on the other hand, appeared to condition the variation observed: final closed (/CṽC#/) and open medial (/ṽCV(C)#/) syllables favour consonant presence; open final (/Cṽ#/) syllables favour consonant absence.

Table 4.18 presents the regression analysis for male and female speakers considered together. 'Lexical frequency' and 'phoneme' are returned as non-significant independent variables, the latter confirming the hypothesis that phoneme was not important in predicting consonant presence. Syllable type, however, is returned as a very highly significant independent variable ($p < 0.01$) of the variation observed: final closed and medial open syllables are shown to favour the presence of a nasal consonant coda while final open syllables favour non-sequential units, with no consonantal coda. The magnitude of this effect is large and follows the expected pattern, based on the frequency data. Speaker sex is also returned as a significant predictor of consonant presence ($p \leq 0.05$), with male speakers using significantly more nasal consonantal codas than female speakers.

				Nasal Unit = /ɛ̃ œ̃ ɑ̃ ɔ̃/

Nasal Unit = /ɛ̃ œ̃ ɑ̃ ɔ̃/
Dependent variable = Consonant absence/presence   Deviance: 1189
Response variable = Consonant presence   Degrees of freedom: 10
N = 1324
Grand mean = 0.792

Factor Group	Factor	Log Odds	N	p-value
Syllable type	/CṼC#/	0.582	304	8.8e-08
	/ṼCV(C)#/	0.391	437	
	/CṼ#/	-0.973	583	
Speaker sex	Male	0.558	658	0.017
	Female	-0.558	666	

Non-significant factor groups were Lexical frequency (p=0.146) and Phoneme (p=0.401).

TABLE 4.18. All speakers: Results of mixed-effects logistic regression
for consonant absence/presence.

Separate regression models for male and female speakers revealed both 'syllable type' and 'phoneme' to be significant independent variables for male speakers but only 'syllable type' was significant for female speakers. The significant results for syllable type mirror the pattern shown in the composite model (Table 4.18). For male speakers separately, phonemic identity ($p < 0.001$) was more important than syllable type ($p < 0.05$) in predicting nasal consonant presence. The occurrence of a sequential unit is favoured by the back nasal vowels /ɔ̃/ and /ɑ̃/, with the open-mid vowel phoneme showing the largest regression coefficient (+0.807): nasal consonants occur significantly more in /ɔ̃/ than in other nasal units. The front nasal vowels, /ɛ̃/ and /œ̃/, disfavour the occurrence of a nasal consonant in the nasal unit, with /ɛ̃/ exhibiting the highest magnitude negative coefficient (−0.748). These results show that not only do male and female speakers realise nasal consonant codas at different rates but that there are different constraints on the variation observed between the sexes.

Phonological Transfer

An analysis of phonological and phonetic transfer between the Béarnais nasal unit system, /ĩN ỹN ẽN ãN ũN/, and the nasal vowel system of French, /ɛ̃ œ̃ ɑ̃ ɔ̃/, is problematic from the outset because there is no one-to-one phonetic or phonological correspondence between all of the elements of the respective systems. The discussion of transfer presented here will necessarily adopt a more complex approach than that presented for the mid-vowels in Section 4.1. Firstly, the analysis of phonological transfer examines the (various) ways in which the Béarnais and French systems may, in the absence of obvious candidates for equivalence classification, be equated structurally and phonetically. This discussion outlines the predictions of the SLM for each of the possible scenarios in turn: underlying phonemic category association; under-differentiation; new category formation. Secondly, lexical and contextual constraints on nasal consonant coda presence in Béarnais and French are discussed, assessing evidence for the replication of the contextually and lexically constrained system of the former in the latter.

Flege's SLM would assume the Béarnais and French nasal units to exist in a common phonological space. Based on these assumptions, and on the predictions of the SLM, we can identify (at least) three possible mechanisms via which the Béarnais and French systems may be related:

(1) Equivalence classification: components of the L1 and L2 systems are associated based on their equivalent representations in their respective phonologies.

(2) Under-differentiation: for a given pair of phonemic cognates in the L2 and the L1, if the perceptual dissimilarity between their realisations is great, the L2 phoneme may be assigned to the phonetic category of a L1 phoneme with which it has no structural relation.

(3) New category formation: perceptual dissimilarity between L2 and L1 phonetic categories will block equivalence classification and cause the formation of new L2 phonetic categories.

'Equivalence classification', is the most abstract mechanism by which the components of the Béarnais and French systems may be equated. The typological similarity between Béarnais and French facilitates the direct association of equivalent phonemes or sequences of phonemes: in lexical cognates with common Latin etyma, phonemic units may be equated in common phonological space. This process, which acts between all elements of the lexicon on a large scale, provides the bilingual speaker with a latent awareness of the structural correspondences between phonological and phonetic components of each of their languages. For example, Béarnais *bén* /bẽN/ would be associated with French *vent* /vɑ̃/ leading to the association of Béarnais /b/ and /ẽN/ with French /v/ and /ɑ̃/ respectively. This process may involve more complex associations involving sequences of phonemes such as the association of Béarnais *hê* /hẽN/ with French *foin* /fwẽ/: Béarnais /h/ and /ẽN/ are equated with French /f/ and /wẽ/ respectively.

From a phonological perspective, the following nasal phonemic cognate pairs are possible between Béarnais and French, noting again that there is no one-to-one correspondence between all components of the phonological systems:

French	Béarnais
/ɛ̃/	/ĩN/
/ɛ̃/	/ẽN/
/ɛ̃/	/ãN/
/œ̃/	/ỹN/
/ɑ̃/	/ẽN/
/ɑ̃/	/ãN/
/ɔ̃/	/ũN/

From a phonetic perspective, the situation is of course much more complex, involving multiple permutations of the primary variable parameters (vowel quality, nasalisation, nasal consonant codas) present in each language.

We know that the French nasal vowels are regularly found in allomorphic alternations with vowel plus nasal consonant (VN) sequences (from Latin open syllables), e.g. *plein* /plẽ/ and *pleine* /plɛn/. The following allomorphic alternations are possible in (conservative standard) French:

Ṽ	VN
/ɛ̃/	/iN/
/ɛ̃/	/ɛN/
/ɛ̃/	/eN/*
/ɛ̃/	/aN/
/ɛ̃/	/əN/*
/œ̃/	/yN/
/œ̃/	/øN/*
/ɑ̃/	/ɛN/
/ɑ̃/	/aN/
/ɑ̃/	/əN/*
/ɔ̃/	/ɔN/

vn sequences marked with (*) were not attested in the French data set for the bilingual speakers. If we consider only words containing nasal vowels for which an allomorphic alternation is known to exist (e.g., *fin* /fɛ̃/ and *fine* /fin/), the French data can be reclassified into five alternating categories: /iN/, /yN/, /ɛN/, /aN/, and /ɔN/. While this would involve excluding potentially large portions of the data, to include such forms would be theoretically problematic given that it is not possible to state unambiguously the correspondences between the allomorphic pairs on the basis of surface phonology alone (Ayres-Bennett et al., 2001: 83). The resultant alternating categories reveal, more clearly, the structural correspondences between the Béarnais and French systems, as represented graphically in Figure 4.4.

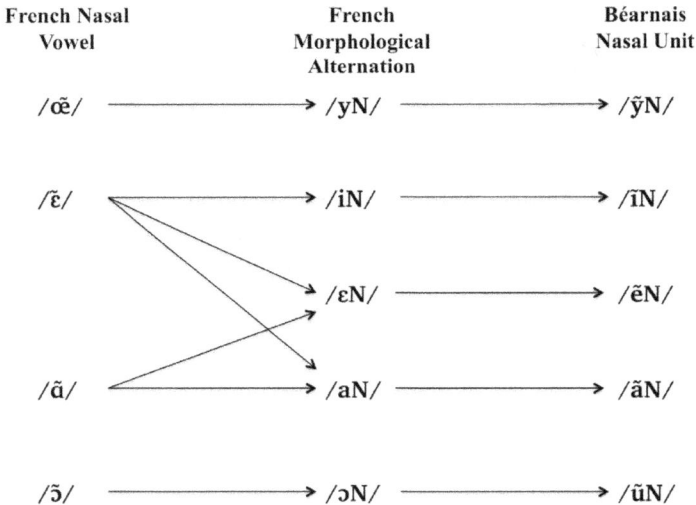

Fig. 4.4. Underlying 'phonemic cognate' relationship between the Béarnais nasal units and the French nasal vowels

Figure 4.4 shows that French /œ̃/ and /ɔ̃/ alternate exclusively with the vn sequences /yN/ and /ɔN/ which, in turn, map directly onto the Béarnais nasal units /ỹN/ and /ũN/ respectively. This means that there is a one-to-one correspondence between French /œ̃/ and Béarnais /ỹN/ and between French /ɔ̃/ and Béarnais /ũN/: they are unambiguous phonemic cognates from a structural perspective. French /ɛ̃/ can map onto Béarnais /ĩN/, /ẽN/ or /ãN/ depending on the allomorphic alternation involved. Similarly French /ɑ̃/ can map onto Béarnais /ẽN/ or /ãN/. If /ɛ̃/ and /ɑ̃/ are derived from the alternating VN forms, their structural association with the corresponding Béarnais nasal units may be unproblematic for the bilingual. Based on Figure 4.4, we can group the nasal units into sub-categories, based on their structural associations: 'unambiguous phonemic cognates' and 'ambiguous phonemic cognates'.

Prediction two, under-differentiation, is perhaps a more likely scenario for the ambiguous phonemic cognates. According to this principle, the L2 sounds (French /ɛ̃/ and /ɑ̃/) would be dissociated from their underlying structural equivalents in the L1 (/ĩN/, /ẽN/, and /ãN/ for French /ɛ̃/; /ẽN/ and /ãN/ for French /ɑ̃/) and assigned to the nearest perceptually similar phonetic category in the L1. If under-differentiation is the mechanism governing transfer for the ambiguous nasal units, we might expect French /ɛ̃/ to be processed and produced as an instance of the Béarnais [ẽN] phonetic category given their 'perceptual' similarity. Likewise, we might expect French /ɑ̃/ to be realised as an instance of the Béarnais [ãN] phonetic category. It is also possible that French /ɛ̃/ and /ɑ̃/ will form new phonetic categories in the bilingual vowel space either because they are judged to be sufficiently phonetically different from any L1 phonetic categories or because of the opacity of the complex structural relationship between the French and Béarnais systems for these nasal units. This relationship may inhibit equivalence classification and instigate new category formation.

We have previously noted that nasal consonant presence and absence in Béarnais nasal units are in complementary distribution with both contextual and lexical constraints: nasal consonants are present in medial syllables, e.g. *crampe* /ˈkrãmpɔ/, and final closed syllables, *téms* /ˈtẽms/; nasal consonants are lexically constrained in final open syllables, e.g. *plâ* /plã/ and *poun* /pun/. In French, on the other hand, the appearance of a nasal consonant following a phonemically nasal vowel is variable synchronically. The statistical analysis of this variability revealed that the presence of a nasal consonant was the majority form for all syllable types with the following constraints on variation: nasal consonant presence is favoured by medial open syllables, e.g. *chantait* /ʃɑ̃tɛ/ [ʃɑ̃nte], and final closed syllables, e.g. *cinq* /sɛ̃k/ [sɛ̃ŋk]; the absence of a nasal consonant is favoured in final open syllables, e.g. *bonbon* /bɔ̃bɔ̃/ [bɔ̃mbɔ̃]. It appears that the historical constraints of the Béarnais system are, to a certain extent, replicated in RF but this is by no means categorical. The tendency for nasal consonants to occur as the majority variant in all positions is, however, modified significantly by constraints in the L2 that resemble the pattern present in the L1.

The existence of lexical cognates between French and Béarnais may cause the appearance of the Béarnais lexical distribution for nasal consonant codas, /ṽN/ or /ṽ/, in equivalent French words as [ṽN] or [ṽ]. In the absence of one-to-one lexical equivalents in the Béarnais and French data sets, it is not possible to test transfer of the lexical distribution empirically. Therefore, the phonetic analysis of transfer in the following sections will examine transfer of vowel quality from Béarnais [ṽN] (sequential units) to French [ṽN] (sequential units) and from Béarnais [ṽ] (non-sequential units) to French [ṽ] (non-sequential units). This assumes the underlying representation for all French and Béarnais lexical items to be /ṽN/ even though there are cases in both languages where there is no surface evidence for underlying vowel + nasal consonant sequences. Since, however, the division of the Béarnais and French data sets into sequential and non-sequential units aimed to control for the effect of consonant presence on formant frequencies, an investigation of transfer in vowel quality is not problematic in this respect as the phonetic environment is held constant. Additionally, the constraints on variation in consonant presence have been shown to be different in French, suggesting that there is no one-to-one transfer for equated lexemes in both of the languages.

Phonetic Transfer

The analysis of phonetic transfer investigated empirically the (possible) phonological relationships outlined above between the Béarnais and French systems and modelled statistically the complex links between the phonetic and phonological components of the bilingual system. The phonetic analyses focused on F1, F2, and (where necessary) F3 in both sequential and non-sequential nasal units. As was the case for the mid-vowels, regression models using 'language' as an independent variable (and controlling for 'speaker' and 'word' as random effects) were used to determine if a French phonetic category was realised as an instance of a (structurally related or perceptually similar) Béarnais phonetic category: this aimed to determine whether the pronunciations in each of the languages were significantly different for pairs of sounds that we expect to be structurally or phonetically correlated, according to the SLM.

Beginning with the unambiguous phonemic cognates, the French nasal vowels /œ̃/ and /ɔ̃/ have been shown to exhibit a one-to-one correspondence with the Béarnais nasal units /ỹN/ and /ũN/, respectively, from a structural perspective. The SLM would predict the following outcomes for transfer:

(1) Phonetic category assimilation: If phonetic category assimilation has taken place, then the F1, F2 and F3 values for Béarnais /ỹN/ and French /œ̃/and for Béarnais /ũN/ and French /ɔ̃/ respectively will not be significantly different.

or

(2) New category formation: If new category formation has taken place, then the F1, F2 and F3 values for Béarnais /ỹN/ and French /œ̃/ and for Béarnais /ũN/ and French /ɔ̃/ respectively will be significantly different.

French /œ̃/ and Béarnais /ỹN/

In sequential nasal units, the regression models could not distinguish significantly between F1 and F2 values based on the information about the language a token was realised in alone ($p = 0.015$ and $p = 0.634$, respectively). This provides evidence for phonetic category assimilation, which supports prediction (1), above: in sequential nasal units, French /œ̃/ and Béarnais /ỹN/ are not significantly different in terms of vowel height or vowel frontness/backness. Their association as an equivalence class appears to have facilitated their resemblance phonetically. The regression model for F3 did, however, return 'language' as a highly significant independent variable (p < 0.01): Béarnais is shown to favour lower F3 values than French. The magnitude of this effect is relatively large (±0.132), indicating perhaps that more rounding is present for Béarnais /ỹN/ than for French /œ̃/. Overall, we can conclude that, in sequential nasal units, French /œ̃/ and Béarnais /ỹN/ are not completely the same phonetically because they differ in their F3 values.

In non-sequential nasal units, 'language' was returned as a significant predictor of F1 and F3 for the phonemic cognates (p < 0.05), but 'language' was not found to be a significant predictor of F2 (p = 0.567). These results provide evidence for prediction (2), new category formation. For F1, Béarnais favours significantly lower values than French: /ỹN/ is significantly more close than /œ̃/ in the vowel space. This finding coincides with their impressionistic representations as close and open-mid vowels respectively. F2 was found to be 'the same' for French /œ̃/ and Béarnais /ỹN/ but this does not provide substantial evidence for phonetic category assimilation, given that they are both front vowels and we would expect them to be similar on the basis of F2. The F3 distinction presented above for sequential nasal units is again returned as significant for non-sequential units: Béarnais favours lower F3 values than French, perhaps indicating more rounding for Béarnais /ỹN/ than for French /œ̃/.

Overall, the statistical analysis presented here provides evidence to suggest that equivalence classification of Béarnais /ỹN/ with French /œ̃/ has led to a certain degree of phonetic category assimilation in sequential units (although F3 is significantly different in each of the languages). In non-sequential nasal units, on the other hand, new category formation appears to have taken place: French /œ̃/ is significantly phonetically different from Béarnais /ỹN/. Thus, nasal consonant codas appear to favour phonetic category assimilation while their absence favours new category formation for L2 sounds. This means that when a French /œ̃/ is realised with a nasal consonant coda, it is phonetically much more similar to Béarnais /ỹN/ than when it is not: [œ̃N] is more phonetically similar to [ỹN] than [œ̃] is to [ỹ].

French /ɔ̃/ and Béarnais /ũN/

For the second unambiguous phonemic cognate pair, French /ɔ̃/ and Béarnais /ũN/, the regression models for the first three formant frequencies returned 'language' as a non-significant predictor of F1 but as a significant predictor of both F2 and F3, for both sequential and non-sequential units. For F1, information about whether a F1 token was from French /ɔ̃/ or Béarnais /ũN/ was insufficient to predict the values observed (p = 0.693 for sequential units; p = 0.16 for non-sequential units). We would expect vowel height to be the primary phonetic distinction between these sounds given that they are both back rounded vowels. The F1 phonetic assimilation of French /ɔ̃/ and Béarnais /ũN/ may be due to equivalence classification at a structural level: raising of French /ɔ̃/ and lowering of Béarnais /ũN/ would be facilitated by the mechanism of cross-language phonetic category assimilation.

In both phonetic contexts, 'language' is shown to be highly significant predictor of vowel frontness/backness (p ≈ 0 for sequential and non-sequential units):

Béarnais /ũN/ is significantly more back (has significantly lower F2 values) than French /ɔ̃/. The results for F3 display a similar pattern with significantly lower F3 values for Béarnais /ũN/ across the board ($p \approx 0$ for sequential units; $p < 0.05$ for non-sequential units). It is possible that the lower F2 and F3 values in Béarnais are an acoustic consequence of increased lip-rounding relative to French /ɔ̃/. In any case, the phonetic categories for each of the phonemic cognates are distinct for both F2 and F3.

These results support prediction (2) for the most part: a new phonetic category has been established for French /ɔ̃/. There is however some evidence to suggest that the mechanism of cross-language phonetic category assimilation is active because no significant phonetic difference is made between the cognate phonemes on the basis of vowel height. This finding supports the hypothesis that Béarnais /ũN/ and French /ɔ̃/ are equated structurally, even if evidence for equivalence classification leading to complete phonetic category assimilation is lacking. The patterns presented here also appear to be equally true for the phonemic cognates when they occur with or without a nasal consonant coda.

For the phonemic cognates that exhibit complex structural relations at a pho-nemic category level, French /ɛ̃/ and /ã/ and the Béarnais nasal units /ĩN/, /ẽN/ and /ãN/, the SLM predicts (at least) two different outcomes at the phonetic category level:

(1) Under-differentiation: If under-differentiation has taken place, then the F1 and F2 values for Béarnais /ẽN/ and French /ɛ̃/ and for Béarnais /ãN/ and French /ã/ respectively will not be significantly different.

or

(2) New category formation: If new category formation has taken place then the F1 and F2 values for Béarnais /ẽN/ and French /ɛ̃/ and for Béarnais /ãN/ and French /ã/ respectively will be significantly different.

Each of these possible language contact outcomes were considered separately below for French /ɛ̃/ and its nearest perceptual L1 category, Béarnais /ẽN/, and for French /ã/ and its nearest perceptual L1 category, Béarnais /ãN/.

French /ɛ̃/ and Béarnais /ẽN/

For sequential nasal units, the French and Béarnais F1 and F2 values are highly significantly different (p ≈ 0 for both F1 and F2): Béarnais /ẽN/ vowels are more open and more centralised than French /ɛ̃/ vowels. The results suggest that the L2 sound has formed a new phonetic category as a result of perceptual dissimilarity with its nearest phonetically similar L1 category. In non-sequential units, on the other hand, regression models for F1 and F2 returned 'language' as a non-significant predictor of the variation observed ($p = 0.871$ for F1; $p = 0.279$ for F2). This result shows that there is no significant vowel height or vowel frontness/backness difference between Béarnais /ẽN/ and French /ɛ̃/. This provides evidence for the mechanism of under-differentiation in non-sequential units: French /ɛ̃/ does not appear to be equated structurally with Béarnais /ĩN/, /ẽN/, and /ãN/, but instead with its nearest perceptually similar phonetic category, Béarnais [ẽ]. This under-differentiation has subsequently lead to phonetic category assimilation whereby French [ɛ̃] and Béarnais [ẽ] now resemble each other phonetically.

Differing phonetic structures (presence/absence of a nasal consonant) appear to condition transfer in separate ways leading to both new category formation and under-differentiation. This means that French [ɛ̃N] is different from Béarnais [ẽN] while French [ɛ̃] and Béarnais [ẽ] were not shown to be significantly different. The opposite pattern, phonetic category assimilation in sequential nasal units and new category formation in non-sequential units, was observed above for French /œ̃/ and Béarnais /ỹN/.

French /ɑ̃/ and Béarnais /ãN/

For both phonetic environments, French /ɑ̃/ and Béarnais /ãN/ were significantly different in terms of both F1 and F2. In both phonetic structures, Béarnais /ãN/ is highly significantly more open in the vowel space than French /ɑ̃/ ($p \approx 0$ for sequential and non-sequential units). For F2, 'language' was a significant independent variable in both phonetic environments ($p \approx 0$ for sequential units; $p < 0.05$ for non-sequential units): Béarnais /ãN/ is significantly further back in the vowel space than French /ɑ̃/. The evidence presented here suggests that French /ɑ̃/ has formed a new phonetic category, distinct from Béarnais /ãN/ by being more open on the height dimension and further forward in the vowel space. There is no evidence to suggest that under-differentiation has led to the equation of French /ɑ̃/ and Béarnais /ãN/ and these results are consistently significant for both phonetic structures.

Overall, there is no unambiguous-ambiguous split governing the SLM mechanism which facilitates transfer (phonetic category assimilation) or blocks transfer (new category formation). The majority pattern established by the statistical analyses was new category formation for L2 (French) sounds. This is not surprising given the difference between the surface phonologies of the Béarnais and French systems. Two instances of transfer were, however, identified. Firstly, French /œ̃/ and Béarnais /ỹN/ are phonetically 'the same', or are realised as variants of a single bilingual phonetic category, only when they occur with a nasal consonant coda. These phonemic cognates exhibit a one-to-one structural correspondence. Secondly, French /ɛ̃/ and Béarnais /ẽN/ are realised as instances of a single phonetic category when they occur with no nasal consonant coda. The existence of /ɛ̃/ and /ẽN/ as an equivalence class is a case of under-differentiation. Finally, we may note that for the French /ɔ̃/ and Béarnais /ũN/ phonemic cognates, which exhibit one-to-one structural correspondence, the L2 and L1 sounds were phonetically assimilated for F1, the primary dimension for distinguishing them in impressionistic terms. F2 and F3 values were, however, significantly different for the cognates and thus complete phonetic category assimilation cannot be said to have taken place.

4.3 Evidence for Substrate Influence in Regional French

Examining the applicability of the SLM to the situation of language contact between Béarnais and French has allowed this study to test the 'residue' hypothesis by providing a new perspective on L1-to-L2 linguistic transfer, considering 'speech learning' in a situation of long-term territorial language contact. In addition to raising questions about previous analyses of the mid-vowels and nasal units, the language contact study produced key findings regarding the linguistic mechanisms active during the emergence of RF from language contact:

(I)   Structural disaccord between the languages in contact results in the establishment of an analogical L2 (phonemic) category, based on the phonemic category of the L1.

Finding (I) provides evidence that the phonological categories of emergent RF are, at least in the early stages of contact, based on phonemic categories present in Béarnais. The RF of the older, bilingual speakers was shown to make a distinction between /e/ and /ɛ/ but the distinction between conservative French /o/ and /ɔ/ was not maintained, both French sounds being equated in RF in the same category, /O/. These three emergent RF categories, /e/, /ɛ/ and /O/ appeared to be equated with the Béarnais phonemic categories, /e/, /ɛ/ and /ɔ/ by equivalence classification. The surface phonologies of Béarnais and French nasal units were shown to exhibit complex structural correspondences and French /œ̃/ and /ɔ̃/ were shown to be unambiguous phonemic cognates of Béarnais /ỹN/ and /ũN/, respectively. The relationships between the other elements of the French nasal vowel system, /ɛ̃/ and /ɑ̃/, and the remaining Béarnais units, /ĩN, ẽN, ãN/, were found to be opaque or ambiguous, from an analysis of their surface realisations alone.

(II) Equivalence classification led to cross-linguistic phonetic category assimilation when the phonemic categories of the L1 and L2 were in one-to-one structural correspondence.

Finding (II) shows that the phonetic categories of Béarnais (the actual pronunciations) were transferred into RF if and only if there existed an isomorphic relationship between L1 and L2 structural cognates. This was true primarily of RF /e/ and /ɛ/, which were pronounced in the same way in both Béarnais and RF. For the unambiguous phonemic cognates of the RF nasal vowels, or those that exhibited a one-to-one structural correspondence with historically related Béarnais nasal units, equivalence classification led to varying levels of phonetic category assimilation in RF. For example, RF /œ̃/ was realised as an instance of the Béarnais [ỹN] phonetic category in sequential units alone: RF [œ̃N] and Béarnais [ỹN] were pronounced the same (in Flege's terms they are realisations of the same phonetic category), while RF [œ̃] and Béarnais [ỹ] were pronounced differently. In this case, it appeared that nasal consonant presence was a complicating factor in the transfer analysis. Additionally, vowel quality in RF /ɔ̃/ was not distinguished phonetically from Béarnais /ũN/ in terms of vowel height, the primary dimension which distinguishes these vowels in impressionistic terms, but there was also evidence to suggest that these vowels are phonetically distinct on other (F2 and F3) dimensions.

(III) Phonological transfer did not necessarily entail phonetic transfer: the establishment of one L2 phonemic category in RF (which conflates two monolingual
L2 categories) by analogy with a single L1 category did not always lead to
phonetic category assimilation via equivalence classification.

Finding (III) derives from the analysis of RF /O/ which, as indicated by Finding (I),
was established as a phonological category by analogy with Béarnais /ɔ/. The status
of Béarnais /ɔ/ and French /O/ as a structural equivalence class did not, as predicted
by the SLM, lead to phonetic category assimilation: the RF vowel was, in fact,
phonetically distinct from Béarnais [ɔ]. It appeared that, while the establishment
of a single L2 category for RF was a clear case of phonological transfer, this /O/
category has dispersed in the vowel space, via the linguistic mechanism of phonetic
category dissimilation, in order to preserve phonetic contrast with Béarnais [ɔ].

(IV) New category formation led to the establishment of new L2 phonetic categories in RF when there was structural disaccord or overly complex structural relationships between the corresponding elements of the L1 and L2
phonologies.

Finding (IV) shows that distinct phonetic categories were established for RF
sounds when no one-to-one structural correspondences existed between the L1
and L2 surface phonologies. Such new category formation can, as for French
/O/, lead to phonetic category dissimilation whereby RF sounds subsequently
disperse in the bilingual vowel space to maximise phonetic contrast with Béarnais
phonetic categories. For the RF nasal vowels, the analysis demonstrated that new
L2 phonetic categories were established for /ɛ̃/ and /ɑ̃/: on the whole, these sounds
were realised as phonetically distinct from Béarnais [ẽN] and [ãN] (their closest
'perceptual' cognates). RF /ɛ̃/ occurring in phonetically non-sequential units, [ɛ̃],
was realised as an instance of the non-sequential Béarnais /ẽN/ phonetic category,
[ẽ]: the RF and Béarnais vowels were phonetically identical. This is a case of under-
differentiation, where an L2 sound is equated with the nearest phonetically similar
L1 phonetic category but where no one-to-one isomorphic relationship exists
between the L1 and L2 sounds from a surface phonological perspective. Again, the
presence of a nasal consonant in the Béarnais and the French nasal units was argued
to be a complicating factor in the analysis of L1-to-L2 transfer.

The findings of the language contact study shed light on the 'residue' hypothesis,
that RF is a result of the transfer of substrate features, from obsolescent Béarnais,
into French. There is some evidence to support this hypothesis but, crucially, the
account of emergent RF phonology presented in the language contact study dem-
onstrates that the mechanisms of linguistic transfer involved in the formation of the
post-contact variety are far more complex than might be presumed. Indeed, the
genesis of RF appears to involve an array of phonetic and phonological assimilation
and dissimilation, comprising both what might be termed linguistic 'residue' and
linguistic innovation.

Phonemic cognates which bear a one-to-one isomorphic relationship in Béarnais
and French were prime candidates for L1-to-L2 transfer: the analysis of vowel
quality provided strong evidence to suggest that RF /e/, /ɛ/, /œ̃/ and /ɔ̃/ are realised

phonetically as instances of their structurally corresponding Béarnais phonetic categories, [e], [ɛ], [ỹN] and [ũN], respectively. This equivalence classification of L2 sounds with L1 phonemic categories, leading to phonetic category assimilation, is clearly a case of phonetic (and phonological) transfer from Béarnais into RF and, thus, constitutes, in very crude terms, 'ce qui reste du dialecte quand le dialecte a disparu' (Tuaillon, 1974: 576).

There was ample evidence to suggest, however, that RF sounds have formed new phonetic categories in the bilingual vowel space, thus contradicting the 'residue' hypothesis. Transfer from Béarnais into French was shown to be disfavoured when structural correspondences between their respective phonologies were overly complex or when there was no one-to-one correspondence between the elements of their surface phonologies: RF /ɛ̃/ and /ɑ̃/ were shown to have formed new phonetic categories, distinct from their (ambiguous) structural cognates in Béarnais, /ĩN ẽN ãN/, and from their nearest 'perceptually similar' L1 phonetic categories, [ẽN] and [ãN], respectively. The phonetic category assimilation of Béarnais [ẽ] and French [ɛ̃], via under-differentiation, however, provided additional evidence for 'residue' from Béarnais in RF.

Finally, the case of RF /O/ constitutes an example of both phonological 'residue' from Béarnais and of genuine phonetic innovation in RF. The conflation of French /o/ and /ɔ/ into one phonemic category, /O/, in RF was an instance of phonological transfer, calqued on Béarnais /ɔ/. The subsequent phonetic category dissimilation of RF [O] from Béarnais [ɔ] means that the RF phonetic category diverges from both the Béarnais pronunciation and from the (hypothetical) monolingual French norm. Therefore, RF /O/ established a previously non-occurring phonetic category which was neither 'residue' from Béarnais nor an approximation of the 'standard' variety of French: RF [O] is an innovation.

Based on the evidence presented in this study, we can conclude that, while RF phonology contains clear cases of 'residue' from Béarnais, the formation of RF combines many linguistic transfer mechanisms which depend importantly on the existence of structural correspondences between the underlying and surface phonologies of the languages in contact. The idea of RF as 'substrate residue' is not entirely incorrect, as the concrete phonetic evidence has shown, but this over-simplification fails to acknowledge equally robust evidence for phonetic and phonological separation between Béarnais and RF and, indeed, evidence for the use of innovative regional variants that have emerged from contact but which did not involve linguistic transfer in the traditional sense.

CHAPTER 5

❖

Dialect Contact:
Evidence for Supralocalisation

Le meilleur des mondes sera-t-il celui de la discipline et de la parfaite mono-
tonie? Puissent survivre encore longtemps tous ces régionalismes du français,
ces heureuses, ces savoureuses désobéissances.
GASTON TUAILLON, *Le français régional*, 1988

Over the course of the twentieth century, Béarnais was gradually ousted from
all domains by the dominant French language. This reduction in domains was
accompanied by rapid language shift and an abrupt cessation in intergenerational
transmission during the aftermath of the Second World War. Consequently, those
born in Béarn after 1955–60 to Béarnais families are almost exclusively French-
speaking monolinguals. The subsequent rise of industrialisation, social mobility and
in-migration to the region has led to another type of contact situation: the RF that
had emerged from language contact has been in contact with incoming varieties of
French for some time, the most notable of which is the supralocal northern norm.
This contact between RF and incoming supralocal French in Béarn has thus led to
a situation of dialect contact in that the varieties in contact are dialects of the same
language.

We have seen, in Chapter 4, that some characteristics of the mid- and nasal
vowels in the French of the older generation can be ascribed to language contact
with Béarnais, leading to phonetic transfer, whereas in other cases new phonetic
categories have emerged for these L2 speakers. In this chapter, an apparent-time
contrast of these speakers with two younger generations is used to investigate
subsequent changes in the phonological categories and quality of the same vowels
(see 'Informant Selection' in Section 3.3; see Appendix 1). These changes are interpreted with reference to Kerswill's (2003) model, with the aim of explaining why
some features are retained by younger generations while others are lost from RF. In
some cases the complex phonetic and phonological parallels and differences mean
that different outcomes would be expected from the different mechanisms of change
operating in the alternative RDL model (levelling and diffusion); in others it will be
seen that differentiating between these mechanisms is less straightforward.

The results presented in this chapter derive from an analysis of fine-grained
acoustic phonetic data making it possible to investigate the exact levels of convergence, among younger generations, to the supralocal northern norm. This analysis

has the aim of examining the evolution of RF as time goes by and after the 'dust of contact' has settled, of identifying the linguistic mechanisms responsible for these changes, and of addressing explicitly the question of whether it is accurate to characterise RF as ephemeral, that is, that local features are lost in favour of northern supralocal forms over time.

5.1. Change in the Mid-vowels

The analysis of the mid-vowels first examines evidence for phonological and phonetic variation in each of the three generations under investigation; the specific variables and hypotheses for this analysis are presented in Section 3.1. The variability present between the generations is then compared qualitatively in order to examine the changing nature of the mid-vowel system in RF over time. Finally, the phonetic evolution of the mid-vowels is examined statistically and these findings are interpreted within the context of Kerswill's RDL model. These analyses have the aim of examining convergence towards and divergence from the standard, supralocal and majority southern norms. Changes identified in the RF of Béarn are interpreted relative to the RF system presented for the oldest generation of speakers. The outcomes of language contact established in Chapter 4 are thus taken as the baseline norm, a baseline that deviates somewhat from traditional descriptions of southwestern RF (see Section 2.3).

	/e/	/ɛ/	/o/	/ɔ/
Old	196	246	277	155
Middle	226	225	248	186
Young	208	230	263	179

TABLE 5.1. Token counts for French mid-vowels

The analyses presented here focus on normalised F1/F2 acoustic data obtained for the quality of the mid-vowels in each generation; the non-normalised data (means and standard deviations) can be consulted for the old generation in Appendix 2 (Tables A2.5–A2.8), and for the middle and young generations in Appendix 3 (Tables A3.1–A3.8). The token counts for the apparent-time mid-vowel analysis are presented in Table 5.1. In each case, normalised F1 and F2 data were submitted to a statistical analysis in order to establish the extent to which the mid-vowel phonemes were distinguished phonetically on the basis of the first two formant frequencies, and to investigate the constraints on variation present for the mid-vowel pairs.

Front Mid-vowels

All older speakers distinguish significantly between the front mid-vowel phonemes (/e/ and /ɛ/) on the basis of F1 ($p < 0.01$), but not F2 ($p = 0.906$): both male and female speakers thus make the traditional vowel height distinction between the vowels but the vowels are not distinguished in terms of frontness/backness (see Tables A2.5 and A2.6 for raw data). The system used by the older speakers appears to be an instance of standardisation when compared with the traditional southwestern system which uses [ɛ] in all contexts (see Section 2.3): older speakers make a vowel height distinction between the front mid-vowels, characteristic of the prescriptive norm (see Section 2.2). Older speakers were, however, also shown to use allophonic variants: close front vowels in open syllables; open centralised vowels in closed syllables. The phonetic distinction between /e/ and /ɛ/ is apparently contradicted by this finding which indicates the neutralisation of contrast in final open syllables. While the *loi de position* was not present in traditional accounts of southwestern RF, we may note that Moreux found evidence for gradual change in the direction of the DSP in the 1980s and that this is consistent with the data presented here for the older generation which appears to show some influence of the DSP, where close variants in open syllables and open variants in closed syllables are the majority form.

The middle generation of speakers, on the other hand, did not make any consistent phonetic distinction between the front mid-vowels (see Tables A3.1 and A3.2 for non-normalised data) on the F1 ($p = 0.491$) or F2 ($p = 0.06$) dimensions. The neutralisation of contrast between /e/ and /ɛ/ shows the middle generation to make use of a system common to the DSP and supralocal French: the use of a single phonemic category, /E/, could thus be a result of levelling 'proper' (adopting a pan-regional feature) or of geographical diffusion (adopting a supralocal feature), or of both acting in tandem. In the middle generation, speakers realise the *loi de position* on the basis of vowel height alone ($p \approx 0$): close vowels [e] in open syllables; open vowels [ɛ] in closed syllables which is, again, consistent with dominant southern and dominant northern, rather than standard, norms. In standard French, only /ɛ/ occurs in closed syllables, /e/ and /ɛ/ are in contrastive distribution in final open syllables, and in non-final syllables the *loi de position* applies.

The young generation distinguish between the front mid-vowels on the basis of F2 alone ($p < 0.01$): younger speakers use neither the system of their parents nor their grandparents (see Tables A3.5 and A3.6 for raw data). The young generation do not distinguish between the front mid-vowels on the basis of vowel height ($p = 0.316$) but they do significantly centralise /ɛ/ relative to /e/. Therefore, the traditional phonemic distinction, made on the basis of vowel height, is not maintained in RF for young speakers. Analyses that have examined the mid-vowels in terms of a tense-lax distinction (e.g., Scullen, 1997) have similarly noted that /ɛ/ is somewhat lowered and retracted when compared to /e/. It appears that younger speakers are implementing the front mid-vowel contrast phonetically in a new way: older speakers use only the open-close (F1) distinction while younger speakers use only the front-centralised (F2) distinction. Younger speakers in Béarn have not adopted the single phonemic category, /E/, present in the speech of their parents' generation, and therefore their system cannot be said to represent the cumulative effect of an apparent-time change. The young generation were shown, however, to use both height ($p \approx 0$) and frontness/backness ($p \approx 0$) to make a three-way allophonic distinction: close front vowels in final open syllables; close central vowels in medial open syllables; open central vowels in final closed syllables. Again, this contextual conditioning appears to contradict the phonetic distinction between /e/ **and** /ɛ/ made on the basis of a front-centralised (F2) distinction. It appears that young speakers may have adopted the *loi de position* for vowel height, neutralising contrasts between /e/ and /ɛ/ in final open syllables on this dimension, while distinguishing phonetically between these vowels on the front/back dimension. The pattern for young speakers appears to be based on, but to be distinct from, the two-way allophonic distinction in the system of their grandparents' generation.

Since some generations distinguish phonetically between the close-mid /e/ and open-mid /ɛ/ mid-vowels, while others do not, the conservative SF categories (/e/ and /ɛ/) are used here to examine diachronic changes in vowel quality: these categories indicate maximal phonetic separation between the mid-vowels. This analysis aims to track linguistic changes in vowel quality for each vowel between the generations. In each case, a mixed-effects regression model is used to analyse change in apparent time, including the following independent variables: speaker age; speaker sex; the interaction between age and sex.

For both F1 and F2, the regression analyses for /e/ returned 'age' as a non-significant predictor of vowel height or vowel frontness. This shows that the normalised F1 and F2 values do not differ significantly between the generations and that no change in progress is evident for the close-mid front vowel: /e/ occupies a similar position in the normalised vowel space for all speakers.

The analysis of /ɛ/ also shows vowel height (F1) to be relatively stable across the generations in the normalised vowel space. For F2, on the other hand, speaker sex ($p < 0.05$) and age ($p < 0.01$) are returned by the analysis as significant predictors of vowel frontness (see Table 5.2).

Dependent variable = F2				
N = 701		Deviance: 916		
Grand mean = 0.653		Degrees of freedom: 9		
Factor Group	Factor	Coeff.	N	*p*-value
Sex	Male	+0.035	341	0.045
	Female	−0.035	360	
Age	Old	+0.079	246	0.00969
	Young	−0.032	230	
	Middle	−0.046	225	
Non-significant factor groups were Age*Sex (p = 0.65).				

TABLE 5.2. Three generations: regression model for F2 (/ɛ/)

The significant effect for speaker sex reveals male speakers (positive coefficient) to favour fronter vowels than female speakers who favour more centralised realisations of /ɛ/. The significant effect for age shows vowel frontness to vary between the generations: old speakers favour fronter realisations of /ɛ/ (positive coefficient) than both middle and young generations (negative coefficients), who favour centralised variants. This backing of /ɛ/ may contribute, for the younger generation, to the significant phonetic distinction between /e/ and /ɛ/ made on the basis of F2. On the other hand, the favouring effects for centralisation of /ɛ/ are of similar magnitude (-0.032 and -0.046) for middle and young speakers, suggesting perhaps that this is a change that has come to completion. In fact, a supplementary regression analysis, comparing the middle and young speakers, showed that there is no significant F2 difference between the generations (p = 0.765) for /ɛ/. There was, however, a significant difference between middle and young speakers (grouped together) and the older generation (p = 0.00245), supporting the claim that this is a change that is no longer in progress.

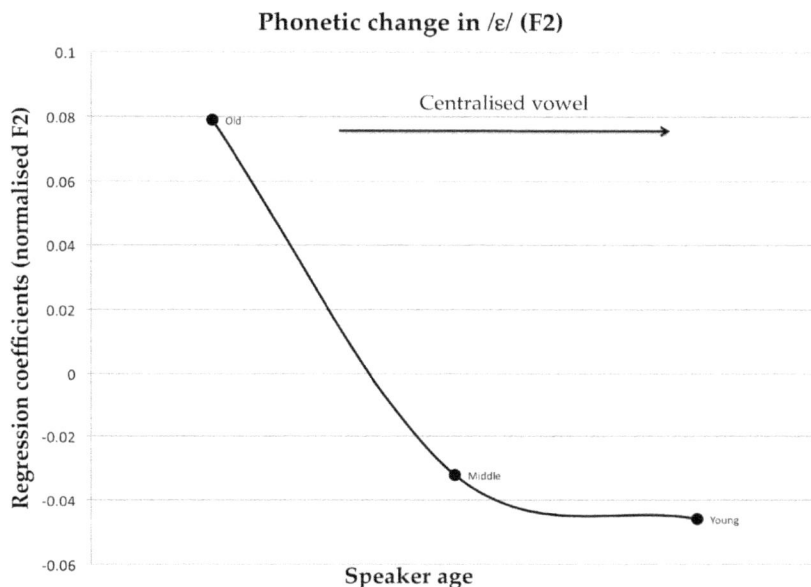

Phonetic change in /ɛ/ (F2)

FIG. 5.1. Phonetic change in /ɛ/ (F2) (© Damien Mooney)

The graph in Figure 5.1 demonstrates this visually: there is a steep drop in the value of F2 between the old and middle generations, with this slope indicating a period of 'selection and propogation' in the spread of this change. The centralisation change appears, however, to have come to completion ('fixation') in the younger generations, given the relative similarity of the middle and young generations' F2 values.

In the front of the vowel space, old and young speakers make a phonetic distinction between /e/ and /ɛ/. For the former, this involves using variations in vowel height (F1) and for the latter, variations in vowel frontness (F2). The middle generation use a single phonemic category for the front mid-vowels, /E/. The evidence for phonetic change presented here, when the vowels are considered individually, can shed some light on the linguistic mechanisms that have resulted in these different phonological patterns: the significant centralisation of /ɛ/, for example, by the younger generation allows younger speakers to differentiate it from /e/ (since they do not make a significant vowel height distinction between the vowels).

Back Mid-vowels

Older speakers do not distinguish phonetically between /o/ and /ɔ/ on the basis of F1 (p = 0.729) or F2 (p = 0.404), indicating that the historical phonemic height distinction between the back vowels was not present in their variety of French (see

Tables A2.7 and A2.8). The *loi de position* was, however, used significantly in the speech of the old speakers ($p \approx 0$): open variants [ɔ] occurred in closed syllables and close variants [o] in open syllables. The use of a single phonetic category mirrors the system reported in accounts of southwestern RF, where [ɔ] was used in all positions (see Section 2.3); I have argued that this is a language contact effect rather than an effect of supralocalisation (see Section 4.1) and we may note that the single phonemic category /O/ of these speakers is a close-mid and centralised rather than an open-mid vowel. Three allophonic variants were distinguished phonetically for /O/: close back variants in final open syllables; close central variants in medial open syllables; open back variants in final closed syllables. The divergence between the baseline norm for the older speakers and the traditional southwestern system is consistent with the levelling 'proper' which appears to have favoured the adoption of the DSP system in which the *loi de position* neutralises the SF /o/~/ɔ/ contrast in final closed syllables. Again, Moreux provided evidence to suggest that this change was under way from as early as the 1980s.

For the middle generation of speakers, a significant vowel height distinction was made between the back mid-vowels ($p < 0.001$), with /o/ positioned significantly closer in the vowel space than /ɔ/ (see Tables A3.3 and A3.4 for non-normalised data). Speakers in the middle generation were shown, however, to distinguish phonetically between close variants [o] in open syllables and open variants [ɔ] in closed syllables ($p \approx 0$). While the use of the *loi de position* by the middle speakers is in line with the baseline norm (and with the DSP), the phonetic distinction made between the back mid-vowels in different phonological contexts is inconsistent with the phonetic distinction made between /o/ and /ɔ/. The higher significance value for the use of the *loi de position* may, therefore, indicate a gradual reduction in the phonetic distinction between the /o/ and /ɔ/ in final open syllables.

For the youngest generation, there was evidence to suggest that young speakers distinguish phonetically between the /o/ and /ɔ/ on the basis of F1 ($p < 0.05$; /o/ is closer in the vowel space than /ɔ/) but additional models comparing only 'syllable type' and 'phoneme' as fixed effects showed 'syllable type' to be the most significant predictor of the variation observed, thus neutralising the phonemic distinction between the back mid-vowels on the basis of F1 ($p \approx 0$). The young generation use a similar system to the older generation and do not make a consistent phonetic distinction between /o/ and /ɔ/ in terms of vowel height or vowel frontness/backness (see Tables A3.7 and A3.8 for non-normalised data). They use a three-way pattern of allophonic variation which mirrors that of the front mid-vowels: close back vowels in final open syllables, close central vowels in medial open syllables; open central vowels in final closed syllables. The only difference between the young speakers' system and that of the older speakers is that the variant used in closed final syllables is open and central for young speakers but open and back for old speakers. The use of a more symmetrical system of allophonic variation in the young generation, for the front and back mid-vowels, may be viewed as a (perhaps innovative) continuum with at least three terms and with final open and final closed allophones as the end-points of such a continuum. Trudgill (1986) stipulates that simplification involves the regularisation of allophonic categories, which appears to be the case for younger speakers. We may note, however, that the system used by the middle generation of speakers (the *loi de position* on the basis of FI alone) is also regular and, indeed, contains fewer allophonic variants.

The diachronic analysis of apparent-time change for /o/ revealed age to be a non-significant predictor of variation for both FI ($p = 0.157$) and F2 ($p = 0.319$). We can conclude from this that, in the normalised vowel space, /o/ occupies a similar relative position for male and female speakers in all age groups, for both vowel height and vowel frontness/**backness**. For /ɔ/, on the other hand, while vowel height was relatively stable across the generations, the F2 model revealed significant change in apparent time to be taking place (see Table 5.3).

Dependent variable = F2				
N = 520		Deviance: 541		
Grand mean = -0.855		Degrees of freedom: 9		
Factor Group	Factor	Coeff.	N	*p*-value
Age	Young	+0.072	179	0.0393
	Old	-0.018	155	
	Middle	-0.053	186	
Non-significant factor groups were Sex (p = 0.183) and Age★Sex (p = 0.314).				

TABLE 5.3. Three generations: regression model for F2 (/ɔ/)

The significant effect for age shows young speakers to have the most centralised /ɔ/ vowel, e.g., *sotte* [sœt], the middle generation of speakers to have the most 'back' vowel and the older speakers to be intermediate to the two other generations with a tendency to favour back realisations.

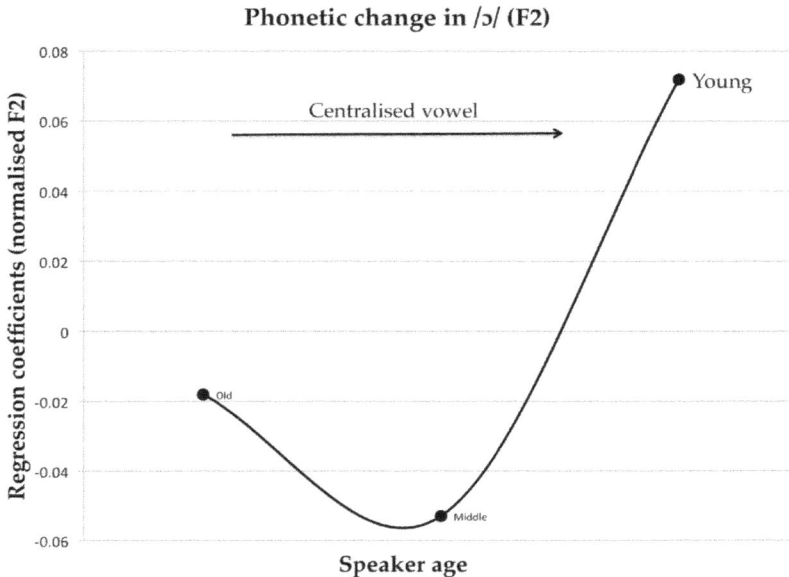

FIG. 5.2. Phonetic change in /ɔ/ (F2) (© Damien Mooney)

The centralisation of /ɔ/ may therefore be seen as a characteristic of the younger generation, as indicated by the steep rise in F2 values for the younger generation in Figure 5.2. A regression analysis comparing young speakers to all other speakers (middle and old generations grouped together) reveals this difference to be statistically significant ($p < 0.05$). On the other hand, a regression analysis comparing only the middle and old generations showed that there is not a significant difference between the two generations ($p = 0.465$). This confirms that /ɔ/-centralisation is characteristic of younger speakers, a well-known phenomenon in supralocal French (cf. Martinet 1945, 1958; Armstrong and Low 2008)[1]. This change cannot be said to be the end-point of linear apparent-time change in that the older and middle speakers do not appear to be taking part in its adoption. Armstrong and Low (2008), working in Roanne, central-eastern France, consider this feature to be diffusing from Paris, having a relatively non-standard status which carries covert, rather than overt, prestige: 'In the case of overt prestige, the social valuation lies in a unified, widely accepted set of social norms, whereas with covert prestige the positive social significance lies in the local culture of social relations. It is therefore possible for a socially stigmatized variant in one setting to have covert prestige in another' (Wolfram, 2004: 71). Armstrong and Low argue that speakers in older generations have not adopted /ɔ/-fronting because they appear to favour the adoption of more well-established supralocal features that carry more overt prestige. The social capital of /ɔ/-fronting appears to have changed, however, from the perspective of younger speakers who engage in this supralocal change via geographical diffusion. The spread of /ɔ/-fronting, and indeed other more widely distributed (but not overtly prestigious) forms, in the speech of younger generations throughout France, implies 'not linguistic homogenisation, but greater linguistic diversity, at least from an intermediate perspective' (Armstrong and Low 2008: 452).

5.2. Change in the Nasal Vowels

The analysis of the French nasal vowels examines variations in vowel quality and nasal consonant occurrence in each generation. The former is primarily discussed in relation to evidence for the supralocal merger of the front nasal vowels, /ɛ̃/ and /œ̃/, to /ɛ̃/. The synchronic models for each parameter in each of the three generations are compared qualitatively to investigate possible change in the nasal vowel system in apparent time; the specific variables and hypotheses for this analysis are presented in Section 3.2. Following this, phonetic change over time in each of the nasal vowels is modelled statistically, focusing on the effects of age and speaker sex and the interaction of these independent variables on vowel quality and consonant absence/presence.

The analysis of the nasal vowels focuses on acoustic measurements of F1, F2 and F3, the latter being a well-known acoustic correlate of lip-rounding which traditionally distinguishes the front nasal vowel phonemes; the non-normalised data (means and standard deviations for F1, F2, and F3) can be consulted for the old generation in Appendix 2 (Tables A2.17–A2.28), and for the middle and young generations in Appendix 3 (Tables A3.9–A3.24). The token counts for these analyses are presented in Table 5.4.

	/ɛ̃/	/œ̃/	/ɑ̃/	/ɔ̃/
Old	372	154	420	399
Middle	371	155	438	449
Young	307	155	442	401

TABLE 5.4. Token counts for French nasal vowels

The normalised formant data was submitted to a statistical analysis in order to establish the extent to which the nasal vowel phonemes were distinguished and to track phonetic change taking place in apparent time. The analysis of each nasal vowel considers, however, phonetically sequential [ṼN] and non-sequential [Ṽ] nasal units separately to account for the potential effect of nasal consonant presence on vowel quality.

Phonological Change

The examination of phonological contrast between the nasal vowels in the older generation focused on phonetic contrasts between the front nasal vowels (/ɛ̃/ and /œ̃/) and between the back nasal vowels (/ɑ̃/ and /ɔ̃/). For the front vowels, the variation conformed to the traditional pattern: /œ̃/ had significantly lower F2 than /ɛ̃/ ($p < 0.001$ for [ṼN]; $p < 0.01$ for [Ṽ]). In sequential nasal units, /œ̃/ exhibited significantly lower F3 than /ɛ̃/ ($p < 0.05$), indicating that the vowels may be distinguished on the basis of lip-rounding. Older male speakers were also found, however, to use F1 to distinguish the vowel height of /ɛ̃/ and /œ̃/ in sequential units, with /ɛ̃/ significantly more open than /œ̃/ ($p < 0.05$). These low F1 values for /œ̃/, relative to /ɛ̃/, for male speakers may constitute a contact effect: /œ̃/ was shown to be significantly correlated to Béarnais /ỹN/, and thus phonetically raised, in the language contact study (see Section 4.2). In non-sequential nasal units, older speakers did not distinguish phonetically on the basis of F3 between /ɛ̃/ and /œ̃/ ($p = 0.506$). The presence of a nasal consonant appeared to be linked to the degree of merger evident for the front nasal vowels on this dimension: consonant presence appeared to favour phonetic separation (in terms of F3) between the traditional phonemes; consonant absence appeared to favour an increasingly merged category. For the back nasal vowels, phonemic contrast was evident in both sequential and non-sequential units: /ɑ̃/ and /ɔ̃/ were distinguished on the basis of F1 ($p \approx 0$ for [ṼN]; $p \approx 0$ for [Ṽ]) and F2 ($p \approx 0$ for [ṼN]; $p \approx 0$ for [Ṽ]), /ɑ̃/ being more open and more centralised than /ɔ̃/. For F3, by contrast, no significant distinction was made between /ɑ̃/ and /ɔ̃/ in sequential ($p = 0.966$) or non-sequential nasal units ($p = 0.228$), indicating that lip-rounding for /ɔ̃/ vowel does not appear to have depressed F3.

For the middle generation, the phonological contrast between the front nasal vowels was maintained in the same way in sequential ($p \approx 0$) and non-sequential nasal units ($p < 0.001$): speakers distinguished between /ɛ̃/ and /œ̃/ on the basis of F2, but not F1 or F3. For the back nasal vowels, /ɑ̃/ and /ɔ̃/ were distinguished significantly on the basis of both F1 ($p \approx 0$ for [ṼN]; $p \approx 0$ for [Ṽ]) and F2 ($p \approx 0$ for [ṼN]; $p \approx 0$ for [Ṽ]): /ɑ̃/ was significantly more open and more central than /ɔ̃/ in both sequential and non-sequential units. For F3, no significant distinction was made between the back nasal vowels in non-sequential nasal units ($p = 0.567$) or by male speakers in sequential nasal units ($p = 0.303$). Only female speakers made a phonetic distinction between /ã/ and /ɔ̃/ in sequential units ($p < 0.01$), with /ɔ̃/ favouring lower F3 values, thus indicating, as expected, more rounding of /ɔ̃/ relative to /ã/.

In the youngest generation, the potential phonological contrast between /ɛ̃/ and /œ̃/ was maintained: the vowels were distinguished in the same way in both phonetic environments. No height distinction was found for F1 ($p = 0.386$ for [ṽN]; $p = 0.0993$ for [ṽ]) but there were significant differences in F2 ($p < 0.05$ for [ṽN]; $p < 0.05$ for [ṽ]) and F3 ($p < 0.01$ for [ṽN]; $p < 0.05$ for [ṽ]), with /œ̃/ favouring lower F2 and F3 values overall. This indicates that young speakers realise the traditional phonetic distinction on the basis of lip-rounding (and possibly frontness/backness). For the back nasal vowels, different patterns were evident in sequential and non-sequential nasal units. In both cases, /ã/ was distinguished from /ɔ̃/ on the basis of F1, or vowel height ($p \approx 0$ for [ṽN]; $p \approx 0$ for [ṽ]), with /ã/ being consistently more open in the vowel space. In sequential nasal units, the back vowels were distinguished on the basis of F2 ($p < 0.01$), but not F3 ($p = 0.139$). In non-sequential nasal units, on the other hand, the reverse was the case: the back vowels were distinguished on the basis of F3 ($p < 0.001$), but not F2 ($p = 0.117$).

The presence of a nasal coda following the nasal vowel is conditioned, in the system of the older generation, by syllable type ($p \approx 0$): closed final and medial open syllables favour consonant presence, e.g. *(je) chante* /ʃãt/, *chanter* /ʃã.te/; open final syllables favour consonant absence, e.g. *bon* /bɔ̃/. Male speakers were also shown to use more consonantal codas than female speakers ($p < 0.05$) and the phonemic identity of the nasal unit was shown to condition consonant absence/presence for male speakers ($p < 0.001$) but not for female speakers ($p = 0.666$): /ɔ̃/ favoured consonant presence, followed by /ã/, while /œ̃/ and /ɛ̃/ contained significantly fewer nasal consonant codas in the nasal units. The same syllabic conditioning was evident in the middle ($p \approx 0$) and young ($p \approx 0$) generations, though no sex effect was returned as significant by the synchronic analyses ($p = 0.361$ for the middle generation; $p = 0.89$ for the young generation). The youngest generation did not show any effect of phonemic identity on nasal consonant presence ($p = 0.142$) but, in the middle generation, /œ̃/ favoured consonant presence the most, followed by /ɛ̃/, and then /ɔ̃/ and /ã/ ($p < 0.01$).

In summary, all speakers in all generations were shown to make a phonetic distinction between /ɛ̃/ and /œ̃/ on the basis of F2: /œ̃/ values were significantly lower than /ɛ̃/ values in both sequential and non-sequential nasal units and the younger generations do not appear to have adopted the supralocal merger. None of the generations made a consistent vowel height (F1) distinction between the front nasal vowels and F3 was used variably to distinguish the vowels phonetically: 'phoneme' was a significant predictor of F3 for old speakers in sequential nasal units and for young speakers in both phonetic contexts. The distinction between /ɛ̃/ and /œ̃/ on the basis of F2 alone contradicts the traditional assumption that /ɛ̃/ is raised to [ẽ] in southwestern RF. If the traditional accounts were correct, the change from a close-mid [ẽ] to an open-mid [ɛ̃] vowel may indicate diffusion of the standard or supralocal norm, [ɛ̃]. For the back nasal vowels, all three generations distinguish significantly between /ɑ̃/ and /ɔ̃/ on the basis of F1 and F2: /ɑ̃/ is more open and more centralised than /ɔ̃/. The only exception to this is that younger speakers do not make a significant F2 distinction between non-sequential [ɑ̃] and [ɔ̃]. There was no regular F3 distinction made between the back nasal vowels in any of the three generations. Again, there is stability in the phonological system over time in that the phonemic contrast is maintained and is realised phonetically in a similar way by all generations, with no clear evidence for a supralocal change in progress, whereby /ɑ̃/ is becoming more similar to /ɔ̃/ with the primary distinction between them being made on the basis of lip-rounding of the latter. From a phonological perspective, the RF of Béarn is stable across the three generations examined in the apparent-time study. Each generation maintains a four-term nasal vowel system (/ɛ̃/, /œ̃/, /ɑ̃/, /ɔ̃/). This phonological stability over apparent time has most likely been favoured by levelling 'proper': the DSP traditionally maintains the /ɛ̃/~/œ̃/ distinction and contact with adjacent varieties would thus have resulted in the retention of the local system by virtue of its association with the pan-regional norm. The four-term system is also, of course, used in SF but these findings appear to be more consistent with levelling 'proper' in the direction of the DSP rather than diffusion of SF because the phonetic characteristics of the nasal vowels are more typically southern than standard.

Phonetic Change

Despite the phonological stability in the nasal vowel system of the RF of Béarn, the apparent-time study revealed various phonetic changes to be taking place in the nasal vowels. While /ɛ̃/ appears to be stable across the generations with no significant phonetic changes taking place, significant change in apparent time is, as we shall see, occurring in the other nasal vowels: /œ̃/-fronting; /ɑ̃/-backing; /ɔ̃/-centralisation.

All regression analyses for /ɛ̃/ return age as a non-significant independent variable for all three formant frequencies, suggesting that no apparent-time change is taking place for this vowel. For /œ̃/, on the other hand, the model for F2, presented in Table 5.5, includes 'age' as a significant independent variable: old speakers have lower F2 values than middle speakers who in turn have lower F2 values than young speakers.

Dependent variable = F2				
N = 464			Deviance: 809	
Grand mean = 0.384			Degrees of freedom: 6	
Factor Group	Factor	Coeff.	N	*p*-value
Age	Young	+0.153	155	0.00248
	Middle	+0.050	155	
	Old	-0.203	154	

TABLE 5.5. Three generations: regression model for F2 (/œ̃/)

This is evidence for change in apparent time: /œ̃/ is significantly fronter in the acoustic vowel space for each successive generation. There was, however, no parallel apparent-time change detected in the model for F3, suggesting perhaps that progressive unrounding was not underway for this vowel.

Phonetic change in /œ̃/ (F2)

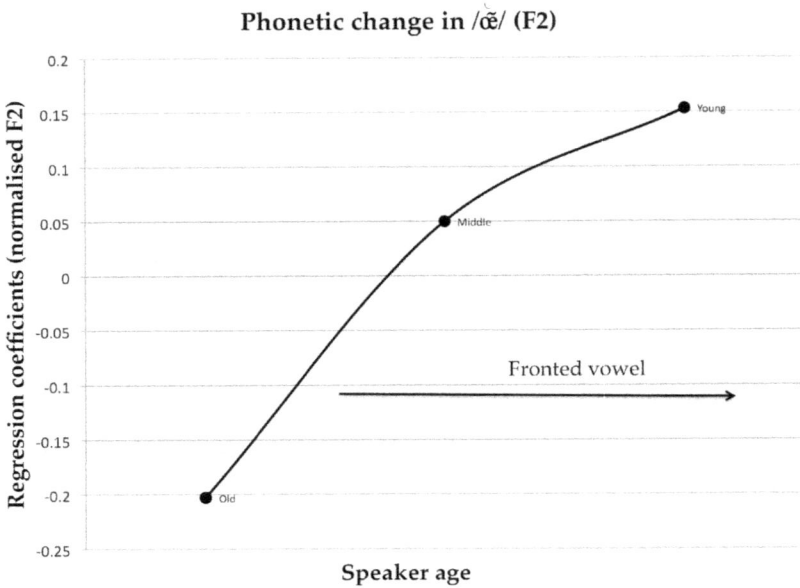

FIG. 5.3. Phonetic change in /œ̃/ (F2) (© Damien Mooney)

The gradual increase in F2 values between successive generations is illustrated in Figure 5.3: each age group advances the change in apparent time in an unbroken chain of intergenerational transmission. This significant fronting of /œ̃/ in apparent time may be interpreted as evidence for geographical diffusion in that the acoustic fronting of /œ̃/ would reduce the phonetic difference between (stable) /ɛ̃/ and /œ̃/. It seems plausible, therefore, that the supralocal /ɛ̃/~/œ̃/ merger is taking place gradually in the RF of Béarn. If this is the case, it is clear that this change has not yet come to completion and that any apparent diffusion of the supralocal norm constitutes a change in progress.

Dependent variable = F2				
N = 1300		Deviance: 2098		
Grand mean = -0.297		Degrees of freedom: 6		
Factor Group	Factor	Coeff.	N	*p*-value
Age	Old	+0.242	420	3.36e-07
	Middle	-0.075	438	
	Young	-0.167	442	

TABLE 5.6. Three generations: regression model for F2 (/ɑ̃/)

The /ɑ̃/ vowel is also undergoing change in apparent time on the F2 dimension, becoming significantly more back in the acoustic vowel space with each successive generation. Evidence for this is presented in Table 5.6 and illustrated in Figure 5.4, where the regression coefficients indicate gradual F2-lowering: older speakers produce the frontest variants of /ɑ̃/, followed by the middle generation, and the youngest speakers lead the change. The F3 analysis did not, however, return 'age' as a significant predictor of the observed vowel qualities.

Phonetic change in /ɑ̃/ (F2)

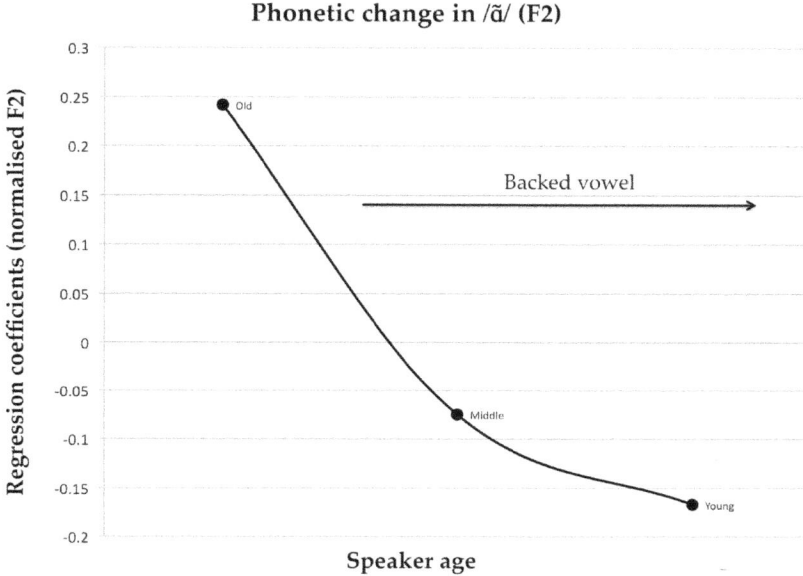

FIG. 5.4. Phonetic change in /ɑ̃/ (F2) (© Damien Mooney)

The /ɑ̃/-backing change may be interpreted as an instance of supralocalisation whereby the traditional centralised variant of the older generation (and of the traditional norm) has been replaced, in apparent time, by a open back variant (approximately [ɑ̃]) by the mechanism of geographical diffusion. There is no evidence for /ɑ̃/-raising on the F1 dimension: the supralocal merger in which /ɑ̃/ raises to merge with /ɔ̃/ does not appear to be taking place; the supralocal chain shift where /ɑ̃/ raises to [ɔ̃], causing /ɔ̃/ to raise to [õ], is not in evidence either.

Dependent variable = F2				
N = 1249			Deviance: 2712	
Grand mean = -0.758			Degrees of freedom: 6	

Factor Group	Factor	Coeff.	N	p-value
Age	Young	+0.220	401	0.00213
	Middle	-0.047	449	
	Old	-0.173	399	

TABLE 5.7. Three generations: regression model for F2 (/ɔ̃/)

The final apparent-time change taking place in Béarn is /ɔ̃/-centralisation. The regression analysis in Table 5.7 returned 'age' as a highly significant predictor of the value of F2: younger generations realise /ɔ̃/ as progressively more centralised than middle and old speakers. There was no evidence for apparent-time change on the F1 (height) or F3 (rounding) dimensions. The gradual progression of this change across the generations is illustrated in Figure 5.5: each successive generation advances the change via incrementation in apparent time.

Phonetic change in /ɔ̃/ (F2)

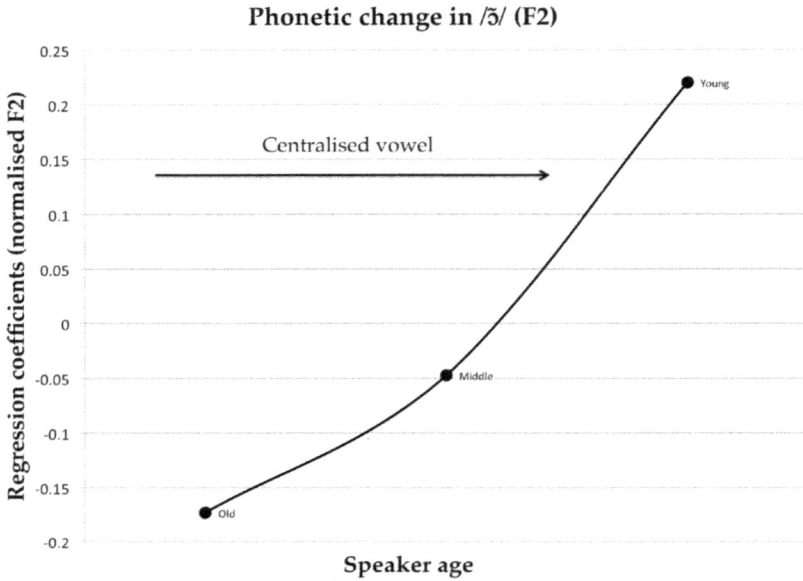

FIG. 5.5. Phonetic change in /ɔ̃/ (F2) (© Damien Mooney)

There is no evidence to suggest that this significant change in progress is the direct result of either levelling or geographical diffusion in that it is not attested in the DSP or in supralocal French. Martinet (1945, 1958) proposed a functional explanation for oral /ɔ/-fronting: the presence of /ɑ/ in the speech of northern informants was said to have caused crowding in the back of the vowel space leading to fronter realisations of /ɔ/. It is also possible, therefore, that /ɑ̃/-backing in the RF of Béarn has caused /ɔ̃/-centralisation to maximise the phonetic distinction between the phonemes and to maintain a four-term nasal vowel system. From a functional perspective, the significant /œ̃/-fronting discussed above may also be interpreted as part of a wider systemic change, or chain shift[2] (rather than a case of supralocalisation), as illustrated in Figure 5.6.

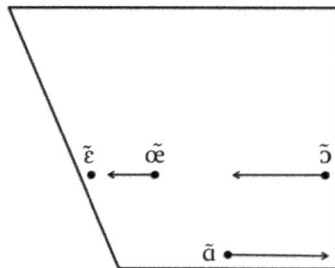

FIG. 5.6. Chain shift in the regional French of Béarn (© Damien Mooney)

Another explanation is that /ɔ̃/-centralisation is occurring by analogy with /ɔ/-fronting. In this case, /ɔ̃/-centralisation might be interpreted as an indirect consequence of supralocalisation (given that /ɔ/-fronting is a feature which has been adopted via geographical diffusion of the supralocal northern norm). We must note, however, that old and middle generations of speakers were not involved in the /ɔ/-fronting change, whereas /ɔ̃/-centralisation may accurately be described as a cumulative change in apparent time (see Table 5.7 and Figure 5.5): all generations participate in the change with young speakers using the most centralised vowels. This suggests that /ɔ̃/-centralisation cannot be occurring by analogy with oral /ɔ/-fronting, at least for the middle and older generations.

Finally, apparent-time change in the use of nasal consonant codas following nasal vowels is modelled in Table 5.8. Three independent variables are returned as significant: speaker age, syllable type, and the interaction between speaker age and phonemic identity. There is a clear apparent-time change taking place: older speakers use the most nasal consonants, followed by the middle generation of speakers, while young speakers use the fewest. The sequential nasal unit [ṽN] remains, however, the majority variant even in the speech of the young. The reduction in nasal coda use may be interpreted as a case of incipient supralocalisation as a result of the diffusion of the northern norm. The retention of nasal codas as majority variants, on the

Nasal Unit = /ɛ̃ œ̃ ɑ̃ ɔ̃/
Dependent variable = Consonant absence/presence   Deviance: 4080
Response variable = Consonant presence   Degrees of freedom: 23
N = 4042
Grand mean = 0.702

Factor Group	Factor	Log Odds	N	p-value
Age★Phoneme	Middle:/ɛ̃/	+0.485	371	1.31e-05
	Young:/ɑ̃/	+0.483	442	
	Young:/ɔ̃/	+0.383	401	
	Middle:/œ̃/	+0.350	155	
	Old:/ɛ̃/	+0.189	351	
	Old:/ɔ̃/	+0.178	399	
	Old:/œ̃/	-0.159	154	
	Young:/œ̃/	-0.191	155	
	Old:/ɑ̃/	-0.208	420	
	Middle:/ɑ̃/	-0.274	438	
	Middle:/ɔ̃/	-0.561	449	
	Young:/ɛ̃/	-0.675	307	
Syllable type	/CṽC#/	+0.507	996	5.59e-14
	/ṽCV(C)#/	+0.367	1268	
	/Cṽ#/	-0.874	1778	
Age	Old	+0.632	1324	0.00417
	Middle	-0.025	1413	
	Young	-0.607	1305	

Non-significant factor groups were Speaker sex (p = 0.0616), Phoneme (p = 0.298), Age★Syllable (p = 0.166), and Age★Sex (p = 0.214).

TABLE 5.8. Three generations: regression model for consonant absence/presence

other hand, appears to indicate pan-regionalisation as a result of levelling 'proper' which has favoured the retention of the DSP. Syllable type is shown to be a constant predictor of nasal consonant presence across all generations, as seen in the individual synchronic analyses for each generation. The occurrence of nasal consonant codas was shown to be favoured by certain syllable structures, /CṽC#/ and /ṽCV(C)#/, while /Cṽ#/ constituted a less favourable environment for nasal consonants.

The significant interaction effect between speaker age and phonemic identity reveals complex patterns of nasal consonant occurrence (as illustrated in Figure 5.7). For /ɛ̃/, the middle generation use the most nasal consonants, followed by old speakers whereas young speakers use nasal consonants extremely infrequently with this vowel. For /œ̃/, the middle generation again use more sequential nasal units, followed by older and younger speakers who show a similar magnitude negative correlation. For /ɑ̃/, young speakers use the most non-standard (sequential) variants, while both the old and middle generations show a negative effect of similar magnitude. Finally, for /ɔ̃/, young speakers also use the most nasal consonant codas, followed by older speakers, while the middle generation strongly disfavours consonant presence. Figure 5.7 shows that the youngest speakers use the opposite pattern of nasal consonant coda frequency to the middle generation: it is possible that the relative frequency of nasal codas within each phonemic category is used to signal membership of a particular age group, given the differential frequencies in particular between the two most recent generations.

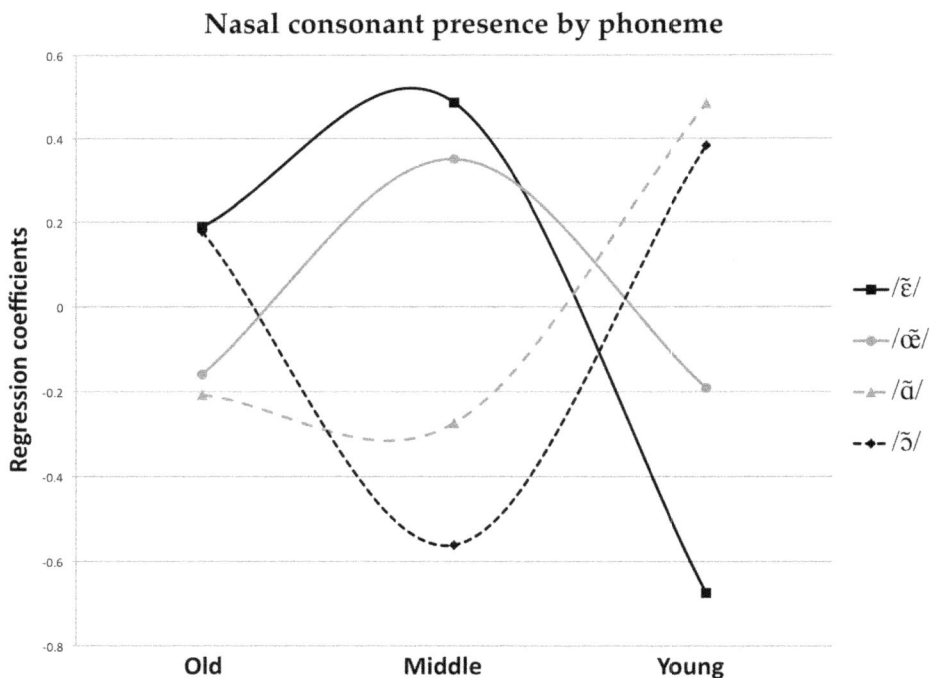

FIG. 5.7. Nasal consonant presence/absence by phoneme (© Damien Mooney)

5.3. The Outcomes of Dialect Contact for Regional French

When dialects of the same language come into contact, two primary linguistic mechanisms have been shown to favour linguistic change: levelling and geographical diffusion (Kerswill 2003). Levelling 'proper' acts over a relatively compact geographical space, favouring the retention of majority variants between the dialects in contact. Geographical diffusion, on the other hand, acts over a larger geographical space, favouring the adoption into regional varieties of supralocal variants from large, dominant urban centres.

The apparent–time study presented in this chapter provided a detailed phonetic and phonological account of the mid- and nasal vowels in the RF of Béarn, examining synchronic variation in each of three generations of speakers before investigating linguistic change diachronically. The interpretation of the synchronic and diachronic findings with reference to the RDL model allowed the investigation of linguistic variation and change to identify the outcomes for RF of contact with contiguous and incoming dialects of French in the speech of each generation and over time. This analysis had the aim of explaining the loss or retention of regional phonetic and phonological features by younger generations, set against the backdrop of the baseline norm for older speakers, established in Chapter 4. The findings presented also aimed to address explicitly the 'ephemeral' hypothesis, that RF is short-lived and transitory, and that it will eventually converge completely over time with the northern supralocal norm.

In the latter half of the twentieth century, large-scale in-migration to Béarn, primarily from the north of France has led to increased contact between RF speakers and migrants who make use of the northern supralocal norm. Dialect contact was shown to promote the adoption, into the RF of Béarn, of pan-regional southern features as well as non-local features of the supralocal northern norm. The linguistic mechanisms of levelling 'proper' and geographical diffusion were shown to be active in RF over time, indicating linguistic focusing in contemporary RF, rather than complete convergence towards the supralocal norm. Evidence for spontaneous local developments, which could not be explained directly by the process of RDL, were also presented, indicating innovation rather than obsolescence in RF. Indeed, the complex patterns of convergence towards and divergence from the northern norm indicate that the speech of young Béarn residents cannot be considered to be the result of wholesale dedialectalisation. Conversely, young speakers were shown, in some instances, to use more regional variants than speakers in the middle generation, contradicting the assumption that there is a 'manque de méridionalité' (Hornsby and Pooley, 2001: 510) in the speech of young southerners.

The patterns of linguistic change observed in the mid- and nasal vowels across three generations of speakers revealed marked differences in the speech of the young:

(I)   Young speakers clearly retain some regional features in their variety of French while abandoning others in favour of supralocal forms.

(II)   Young speakers have incorporated 'innovative' variants into their variety of French which cannot be explained by the process of regional dialect levelling.

The retention of regional features was evident in the RF of young speakers who distinguished between the front mid-vowels, did not make a phonetic distinction between the back mid-vowel phonemes, followed the *loi de position* for the mid-vowels, and used a four-term nasal vowel system with nasal consonant codas as a majority variant, particularly for /ã/ and /ɔ̃/. This retention of southern features has resulted, it was argued, from levelling 'proper', favouring majority southern (DSP) regional variants. By contrast, the adoption by young speakers of certain features associated with the northern statistical norm suggested that geographical diffusion was also taking place: /ã/-backing and a reduction in the frequency of usage of nasal consonant codas. These clear cases of supralocalisation are also, of course, instances of standardisation. Other supralocal changes were also identified, such as /ɔ/-fronting: this feature was argued to carry covert prestige and it was noted that the adoption of such forms increases linguistic diversity rather than reducing it (contrary to some narrow definitions of dialect levelling).

Some new variants in the speech of younger speakers may be classified as 'innovative', in the sense that they are spontaneous local developments as opposed to being the result of RDL. For example, young speakers were shown to make use of non-standard forms such as centralised /ɔ̃/ or a front-centralised distinction between /e/ and /ɛ/, rather than one of vowel height. Evidence was presented to suggest that these innovative variants may be internally motivated: from a functional perspective /ɔ̃/-centralisation may have been instigated by /ã/-backing; the front-centralised distinction between /e/ and /ɛ/ appears to be the generalisation of a tense-lax distinction, realised on the basis of both vowel height and vowel frontness, to use vowel frontness alone to distinguish the vowels phonetically.

Additionally, some linguistic features present in the RF of the youngest generation were not necessarily the result of cumulative apparent-time change. It became clear, particularly in the analysis of the mid-vowels, that:

(III) Speakers in the middle generation have adopted more supralocal variants than young speakers.

(IV) Speakers in the middle generation appear to favour the adoption of well-established northern supralocal features which carry overt, rather than covert, prestige.

From an apparent-time perspective, the adoption of some supralocal features in Béarn may be age-graded, 'that is correlated with a particular phase in life and repeated in successive generations' (Cukor-Avila and Bailey, 2013: 253). Adolescent speech is often characterised by linguistic innovation and by the use of non-standard (social and regional) forms while the transition from the teenage years to young adulthood is characterised by a rise in the use of standardised or overtly prestigious speech forms. The rise in the use of standard variants is thought to be a response to 'the pressures of the marketplace' (Cukor-Avila and Bailey, 2013: 253) in an effort to increase employability and to better meet the demands of their jobs. After young adulthood, vernaculars are considered to be generally stable with the caveat that, while adult speakers may participate in ongoing language change, older speakers seem to be influenced only 'slightly by the changes taking place around them' (Labov, 1994: 105). It is possible that when the youngest generation in the Béarn study leave second-level education (and consequently the semi-rural villages where they live), their social networks may become markedly more diffuse promoting the adoption of more supralocal variants, such as front mid /E/, as a response to the pressures of the linguistic marketplace. The finding that middle generation speakers have adopted more supralocal features than the young generation parallels the findings of Labov's (1963) Martha's Vineyard study: Labov considered the centralisation of (ay) and (aw) to be a reaction to threats to island identity such as the need to leave the island to work, but the youngest age group showed limited participation in this otherwise incremental change in progress. The younger speakers in Labov's study were not the leaders of change because, he argues, they had not yet been affected by the same external pressures as the adult speakers. The fact that younger speakers may adopt more standard or supralocal features as they move into adulthood points to the instability of teenage speech forms: 'the vernaculars of teenagers, even those of older teenagers, are not yet stable. In the early adult years we can reasonably assume that a vernacular is relatively stable, but apparent-time data for teenagers as one of the age cohorts must be viewed with some suspicion' (Cukor-Avila and Bailey, 2013: 253). Given that the youngest generation in the Béarn study are between 16 and 18 years of age, we must acknowledge the potential instability of their vernaculars as well as the possibility that they will abandon innovative and localised features in favour of supralocal norms as they move out into the world. Young speakers were shown, however, to have already adopted some supralocal features which, with the exception of /ɔ/-fronting, middle speakers were also using. This suggests that the youngest generation in Béarn have had ample exposure to the features of supralocal French as they have chosen to adopt some supralocal features while rejecting others. This evidence indicates that younger speakers are acutely aware of the prestige attached to the use of supralocal forms, favouring their adoption, but, nevertheless, the non-adoption of other supralocal forms suggests a deliberate (conscious or subconscious) rejection of wholesale supralocalisation in their speech. One could argue, however, that these young speakers may still adopt the remaining supralocal features examined in the coming years in response to societal adjustments associated with transitioning between life stages.

The findings of the apparent-time study provide important information on the evolution of RF as it moves through time and comes into contact with other con-temporary varieties of the language. The analysis of the mid- and nasal vowels identified the mechanisms of linguistic change active in the variety of French spoken in Béarn and demonstrated that the level of conformity to the supralocal norm was not sufficient to confirm Wanner's claim that 'déjà les jeunes parlent souvent un français parisien presque parfait' (1993: 81): a highly significant level of regional phonetic and phonological variants were attested in their speech. The assumption that 21st-century RF is ephemeral is grossly oversimplified. Indeed, Wanner's 'young' informants in Languedoc-Roussillon are now middle-aged and I have provided evidence to suggest that the youth of today use more regional variants in their speech than the youth of the 1990s (their parents). The combination of supralocal and regional elements in the speech of young Béarn residents dem-onstrates that they are using a system that is neither that of their grandparents nor of the supralocal norm. We can draw parallels here with Watt's young Newcastle speakers who were 'aiming to dispel the "cloth cap and clogs" image' and to 'sound like northerners but *modern* northerners' (1998: 7). These speakers are said to achieve this by avoiding variants which they perceive as stereotypically associated with their local roots, while simultaneously using non-standard variants that may be considered non-local from a traditional perspective.

As RF moves through time, the adoption of supralocal features is not surprising, given the increasing levels of contact between northern and southern populations in the latter half of the twentieth century. This approximation of northern norms cannot, however, be considered complete convergence. Linguistic homogeneity, motivated by centralising social pressures, appears, at least in the speech of the youngest generation, to be offset by (increasing) linguistic diversity: younger speakers combine innovative regional variants with traditional local and supralocal forms in a previously non-occurring combination of new and old features. In this way, younger generations in Béarn may negotiate conflicting regional and non-local identities by sounding like southerners, but *modern* southerners.

Notes to Chapter 5

1. See Mooney (2016) for a comprehensive literature review of the /ɔ/-fronting phenomenon in French in addition to a more detailed analysis of the linguistic and social constraints on this change in the Béarn data.
2. See Mooney (2015b) for a discussion of this chain shift within the framework of Labov's (2007) theoretical distinction between faithful linguistic 'transmission' from parent to child and the loss of structural constraints on variation and change during 'diffusion' between adult speakers over geographical space.

CHAPTER 6

❖

Rethinking Regional French

Si l'identité focalise sur elle tant de regards, c'est aussi parce qu'elle serait au
cœur de phénomènes sociaux dont la compréhension, voire la maîtrise, sont des
enjeux importants dans une société où les revendications pour la reconnaissance
des cultures régionales, locales, ethniques se font plus fortes.

DENIS CHEVALLIER and ALAIN MOREL,
Identité culturelle et appartenance régionale, 1985

Hornsby (2006) examined the genesis and evolution of RF in a situation of dialect
contact in Avion, northern France (see Introduction). In light of the findings of
the language and dialect contact studies in southern France, this chapter begins
with a comparison of the mechanisms of linguistic transfer and change in Avion
and Béarn. This comparative discussion sheds light on the differential outcomes of
language contact (in Béarn) and dialect contact (in Avion) during the formation
of RF, as well as permitting an examination of subsequent supralocalisation in
two areas with contrasting socio-demographic histories, at very different distances
from the Parisian centre. The second part of this chapter problematises further the
notion of 'modern southerners' (and Hornsby's (2006) 'modern northerners'): in
both Avion and Béarn, the speech of the youngest generations[1] was characterised by
a previously non-occurring mix of previously occurring (localised and supralocal)
features, with additional evidence, in Béarn, for 'innovative forms' or spontaneous
local developments. The RF of the youngest generations was interpreted as an
attempt to find a compromise between perhaps conflicting regional and national
identities, with the retention of traditional or new regional forms indexing a local
affiliation and the adoption of supralocal forms constituting an attempt to appear
more cosmopolitan and outward-looking. The changing nature of France's traditionally Jacobin socio-political climate, particularly in the postmodern era, is
presented as creating conditions favourable to the reconstruction, rather than the
reproduction, by younger generations of regional identities.

6.1. Northern and Southern Regional French

The widely held assumptions that French regionalisms are the result of transfer of
linguistic forms from local substrate varieties ('the residue hypothesis') and that
convergence in the direction of the supralocal norm will eventually lead to the
attrition of localised forms ('the ephemeral hypothesis') have been examined in
detail in southern regional French (in Béarn) and in northern regional French

(Hornsby, 2006). Hornsby examined variation and change in RF in a new industrial town while the Béarn study focuses on RF in a semi-rural area at some distance from Paris. This section compares and contrasts the linguistic mechanisms active during the formation of northern and southern RF and during their subsequent evolutions over time, addressing the residue and ephemeral hypotheses separately.

It is first necessary to contrast the contact situations in northern and southern France: the relative typological classifications of the varieties in contact during the genesis and evolution of RF are distinct in Avion and Béarn. Addressing the 'residue hypothesis', I have argued that the formation of RF in the south of France has resulted from *language* contact between two typologically dissimilar varieties of Gallo-Romance, one *langue d'oïl* (French) and one *langue d'oc* (Béarnais) (see Chapter 4). Hornsby (2006), on the other hand, examines the formation of RF from a *dialect* contact perspective: French and Picard are considered to be two dialects of the same language, the *langue d'oïl* (see Section 1.5). Examining the 'ephemeral hypothesis', the apparent-time study in Chapter 5 considered change in the RF of Béarn as it moves through time to be motivated by *dialect* contact with non-local varieties of French, in particular the northern supralocal norm. In this contact situation, the varieties in contact (southern RF and northern supralocal French) are considered to be dialects of the same language, 'French'. Hornsby's (2006) exploration of the evolution of RF in Avion also examines the effect on northern RF of *dialect* contact with other non-local varieties of French (primarily *français populaire* and supralocal French). It is important to note, at this point, that while the Béarn study considers the genesis of RF from a language contact perspective (between French and Béarnais) and the evolution of RF from a dialect contact perspective (between local and non-local French), Hornsby's Avion study examines two distinct situations of *dialect* contact: contact between two *dialectes d'oïl* is considered to have conditioned the emergence of RF in Avion; the evolution of RF over time is seen as the result of contact between RF and non-local French, as was the case in the Béarn study.

The formation of RF, which involves (at least partially) the transfer of linguistic features from the substrate into French ('residue hypothesis'), is motivated by dialect contact in the north and by language contact in the south of France. We may expect the linguistic outcomes of contact to be different in each case, on the basis that 'the degree of typological distance between specific subsystems of a source language and a receiving language helps to predict the kinds of interference that may occur (Thomason, 2010: 40), where 'typological distance' is 'a (very informal) measure of structural differences between two linguistic systems' (Thomason, 2010: 39). In general, we might expect more transfer between linguistic systems that are more typologically similar. Additionally, in situations of contact between typologically dissimilar languages, interference tends to be phonological or syntactic while increased similarity between linguistic subsystems may encourage transfer in inflectional (and derivational) morphology, which is rare in situations of language contact: 'minimal typological distance sometimes does facilitate otherwise rare types of contact-induced change in different languages' (Thomason, 2010: 40).

To examine the 'residue hypothesis', that French regionalisms result primarily from the transfer of substrate features, Hornsby applied Trudgill's (1986) 'koinéization' model to phonological and morphological data from Avion. During intense dialect contact, the process of koinéization facilitates the emergence of a new variety in which many of the irregularities from the contributory varieties have been removed (Trudgill, 1986: 98). This focusing is facilitated by two linguistic mechanisms: levelling 'proper',[2] or the retention of majority forms within a relatively compact geographical space; simplification, or an increase in morphophonemic regularity. The examination of the residue hypothesis in Béarn (Chapter 4) could not consider RF formation within the context of koinéization because the varieties in contact cannot be considered to be dialects of the same language, a prerequisite for koinéization (Siegel, 1993: 6). The language contact study adopted a novel approach to the analysis of substrate residue in the south of France using a well-established model of second language acquisition in the form of Flege's SLM. The findings for emergent RF in Béarn negated any strict confirmation of the residue hypothesis: RF was shown to be a combination of substrate residue, new phonetic categories, and genuinely innovative forms. While RF in Béarn contains clear cases of 'substrate residue' from Béarnais, its formation during language contact is better accounted for by a combination of linguistic transfer, divergence and innovation, with structural correspondences between the surface phonologies of the languages influencing the outcomes of contact in each case.

In Avion, levelling 'proper' appeared to be the best explanation for the survival of some Picard features in the RF of older speakers. Hornsby examined the relative vitality of non-standard features by investigating their attested geographical distribution in the *Atlas Linguistique de la France* (ALF) and the *Atlas Linguistique et Ethnographique Picard* (ALEP). These categorisations were then compared to the percentage scores for each variant in Avion RF on the assumption that, since most in-migrants to Avion came from the north of France, the variable distributions in the atlas data would be representative of the contributory varieties in the dialect mix. The 'elle' [al] variant was shown to enjoy a wide distribution in the linguistic atlases (in that it was present in much of the north of France), and this variant was, in fact, retained with the highest frequency in the RF of older speakers. For all other non-standard variants, however, the relationship between their area of distribution in linguistic atlases and their transfer into emergent RF was unclear. For example, the pattern that emerges from analysing the ALF distribution data is that forms such as unpalatalised /k/ and /g/ as in *vache* [vak] for [vaʃ] and *jardin* [gaʁdɛ̃] for [ʒaʁdɛ̃], which are attested throughout the Picard and Norman area, have only vestigial status in RF. These findings suggest that while levelling 'proper' may favour the adoption of some majority dialectal variants during koinéization, it is not an accurate predictor of the substrate features that are likely to be transferred (and retained) during the RF koinéization process (Hornsby, 2006: 97).

The transfer (and retention) of substrate features from Picard into RF was shown to be more accurately predicted by structural correspondences between the varieties in contact, Picard and French. Hornsby frames this transfer in terms of 'relative simplification' on the basis that a one-to-one isomorphic correspondence between the linguistic subsystems for a given feature facilitates its transfer from the speakers' L1 (Picard) into French: the substrate feature is considered to be 'simpler' from a

French perspective. Hornsby provides further evidence for 'relative' simplification in RF, showing that the most striking difference between obsolescent substrate features and those that exhibit vitality was that, for the latter, there existed a one-to-one isomorphic correspondence between the Picard variants and their French equivalents (Hornsby, 2006: 100). For the non-standard substrate variants, transfer in RF is said to be facilitated by a simple, exceptionless rule such as 'for [French] /A/, the rule is "velarize and round /A/ when it occurs word-finally"' (2006: 100), e.g. *pas* [po] or [pɔ] for SF [pɑ]. On the other hand, complex, unpredictable, or opaque structural correspondences between Picard and French were shown to discourage or inhibit the transfer of substrate features into RF. For example, if an outsider hears forms in northern RF such as *tellement* [tɛlmɛ̃] for [telmɑ̃] or *sentir* [sɛ̃tiʁ] for SF [sɑ̃tiʁ], they might deduce a RF rule such as 'replace [French] /ɑ̃/ by [ɛ̃]' but Picard [ɛ̃] also corresponds to French *on* /ɔ̃/ in the third-person indefinite pronoun, e.g. *in* [ɛ̃] *ravisse* for French *on* [ɔ̃] *regarde*, and another set of items require the same nasal vowel as in French [ɑ̃] (Hornsby, 2006: 100), e.g. *chanter* [kɑ̃te] for French [ʃɑ̃te]. There was some evidence to suggest, however, that frequently occurring lexically conditioned non-standard variants can also transfer into RF and exhibit greater resistance to dedialectalisation, at least in the short term, e.g. *dans* [dɛ̃] for SF [dɑ̃].

In the language contact study (Chapter 4), isomorphic structural correspondences, from a surface phonological perspective, between Béarnais and French were also shown to facilitate the transfer of substrate features from Béarnais into southern RF. For example, the distribution of Béarnais /ỹN/ and /ũN/ was shown to map directly onto French /œ̃/ and /ɔ̃/, leading to varying degrees of phonetic L1-to-L2 transfer in the older, bilingual speakers' variety of French. The same was true of Béarnais /e/ and /ɛ/ and French /e/ and /ɛ/ where phonemic cognates were not pronounced differently in the two languages. On the other hand, the Béarnais nasal units, /ĩN ẽN ãN/, which mapped onto their French phonemic cognates, /ɛ̃/ and /ɑ̃/, in a structurally complex way were less involved in phonological or phonetic transfer during the formation of RF. We can thus conclude that, as RF emerges from contact, during both bidialectalism and bilingualism, those features of the substrate (the speaker's L1) that bear a regular, predictable, and isomorphic relationship with French are most likely to transfer into emergent RF. The formation of RF during both dialect contact (in northern France) and language contact (in southern France) is characterised by the transfer of some substrate features when those features map directly onto French phonemic categories. In peripheral areas where French came into contact with typologically dissimilar non-Romance languages (Breton, Basque, etc.), the effects of structural isomorphism on linguistic transfer have not yet been examined: future studies in this area would further clarify the role that phonemic cognates have to play in the formation of RF more generally.

Hornsby's study of northern RF and the present study of southern RF provide evidence that both confirms and contradicts the residue hypothesis. The assertion that RF is 'ce qui reste du dialecte quand le dialecte a disparu' (Tuaillon, 1974: 576) is an oversimplified characterisation of RF. Substrate residue is certainly present in both northern and southern varieties of French but the mechanisms governing the transfer of substrate features into emergent RF were shown to be most likely to act when the subsystems of the varieties (languages or dialects) in contact are in one-to-one correspondence. On the other hand, non-standard forms occur in both northern and southern RF that have not previously occurred in the substrate or in French. In Béarn, bilingual speakers were shown, for example, to use a single back mid-vowel in French, /O/, which conflates French /o/ and /ɔ/ by analogy with Béarnais /ɔ/. This was a clearly a case of phonemic transfer, but the phonetic realisation of RF /O/ was raised and centralised relative to Béarnais /ɔ/: RF [O] is a new phonetic form that does not occur in Béarnais or in standard French. The formation of a new phonetic category for French [O] was initiated by (phonemic) transfer but it cannot be classified as 'residual' because it has not been directly transferred from Béarnais. Hornsby also notes the existence of 'interdialect forms' in northern RF as a result of linguistic convergence between Picard and French (2006: 87). These forms are said to be 'between the original [Picard] and target [French] dialects but present in neither' (Hornsby, 2006: 87) such as, for example, the use of a 'fudged' vowel, [ʌ̃]–[ɔ̃], which was phonetically intermediate between Picard /ɛ̃/ and French /ɑ̃/ (Hornsby, 2006: 88). This interdialect form was used primarily in lexical cognates where Picard /ɛ̃/ and French /ɑ̃/ are in one-to-one correspondence though, as we have seen, they are not isomorphic from a more general surface phonological perspective. In Béarn, RF /œ̃/ was shown to be significantly raised relative to /ɛ̃/ for bilingual male speakers (see Chapter 5) and it was argued that this was a contact effect since French /œ̃/ and Béarnais /ỹN/ were significantly correlated (see Chapter 4). As such, the raised pronunciation of southern RF [œ̃] appears to be intermediate between Béarnais [ỹN] and French [œ̃]. We cannot say that this regional pronunciation is an interdialect form since Béarnais and French are separate languages but their surface phonologies are in one-to-one correspondence for these vowels, which has perhaps facilitated convergence akin to the 'fudged' variant described by Hornsby in northern RF.

The hypothesis that RF forms are ephemeral or transitory and that they will be lost in favour of more standard or supralocal French forms as time goes by was examined using an apparent-time construct in both Avion and Béarn. Both studies examined the retention or loss of non-standard regional forms, some of which had been shown to have transferred from the local substrate language, by analysing the speech of younger generations in the regions. Changes from above taking place in northern or southern RF as a result of dialect contact with other non-local varieties of French were investigated to establish the level of convergence, in the speech of younger regional speakers, to dominant standard and non-standard varieties that have a wide geographical distribution in modern metropolitan French. In Béarn, the adoption by younger speakers of supralocal French features, carrying both overt and covert prestige, was shown to be facilitated by the process of RDL or supralocalisation. In Avion, Hornsby considered the adoption into northern RF of both supralocal and *français populaire* features diffusing from Paris.

Hornsby (2006) notes the large-scale loss of regional features (transferred from Picard via the linguistic mechanism of levelling 'proper') in the RF of younger Avionnais. He notes, however, that this loss of regional forms has not resulted in wholesale convergence towards the prestigious supralocal norm: younger generations were shown to have adopted many *français populaire* (Parisian working-class vernacular) variants as well as some supralocal variants diffusing hierarchically from Paris, such as word-final cluster simplification, e.g. *juste* [ʒys] for [ʒyst]. The changing nature of RF over time in Avion appears, therefore, to be a result of processes of supralocalisation or RDL (see Chapter 5), in that both levelling 'proper' and geographical diffusion are (consecutively) active during its formation and evolution. Hornsby notes, however, that while some non-standard RF variants, present in the speech of the oldest generation, have been completely lost from northern RF or reduced to vestigial status, others appeared to be quite stable in the speech of younger generations (2006: 92), e.g. the velarisation and rounding of /a/ or /ɑ/ as in *ça va* [sɔvɔ] for [sava]. This regional feature is strongly associated with northern RF but, as Hornsby notes, its retention may have been supported by the presence of this form in *français populaire*. Indeed, Hornsby notes that 'it was difficult to find any truly distinctive regional features in [northern RF] that had no association with geolinguistically unmarked *français populaire*' (2006: 137–38). Northern regional French is said, however, to be perceptually distinct from *français populaire* owing to differential relative frequencies of the variants used and because accent recognition is triggered by 'bundles of phonological features' (Hornsby, 2006: 138).

The dialect contact study in Béarn (see Chapter 5) refuted the claim that RF features are transitory: the results of the apparent-time study showed that the youngest generation in Béarn are not simply involved in the wholesale adoption of the supralocal norm over time. It was shown that the middle generation exhibited more evidence for supralocalisation in their speech, though they tended to disfavour the adoption of covertly prestigious supralocal forms, such as /ɔ/-fronting, which had been adopted by the youngest speakers. For the youngest speakers in Béarn, contemporary RF was shown to constitute a distinctive combination of local, supralocal and innovative features. For example, young speakers retained a four-term nasal vowel system with nasal consonant codas as a majority variant, while at the same time adopting supralocal forms such as /ɔ/-fronting; furthermore, an innovative counterclockwise chain shift of the nasal vowels was shown to be led by the youngest generation. The retention of local features was associated with the linguistic mechanism of levelling 'proper', favouring the retention of majority southern pan-regional forms, while the adoption of supralocal forms was argued to be due to geographical diffusion. Therefore, Kerswill's (2003) of RDL appeared to accurately account for the evolution of southern RF as it moves through time. The retention of distinctly regional features in southern RF is at odds with the situation described by Hornsby for northern RF, where regionality appeared to be signalled by the rate of adoption of supralocal or *français populaire* features. Hornsby suggests that 'in areas further removed from Paris [...] substrate features may be better placed to resist the diffusion of national norms' (2006: 137) which may provide an explanation for the differential retention of localised forms in northern and southern RF. On the other hand, Hornsby's 'young' speakers (0–29 years in 1988) were aged between 24 and 53 at the time of the Béarn study in 2012 making these speakers more directly comparable to the middle generation (30–50 years in 2012) in Béarn. Indeed, the middle generation in Béarn showed the least regionality in their pronunciation and high rates of adoption for forms diffusing from Paris. The increased regionality in the speech of the young Béarnais, relative to their parents' generation and to Hornsby's youngest generation in Avion, will be discussed in relation to socio-political changes affecting this generation in Section 6.2.

Overall, change in RF as it moves through time cannot simply be described as wholesale convergence towards overtly prestigious supralocal French and the findings in Avion and Béarn indicate that RF may be undergoing a new stage in its evolution, influenced by, but not a slave to, processes of supralocalisation. RF in both northern and southern France may increasingly be characterised by the retention of some local features, the adoption of overtly and covertly prestigious non-local forms, and, at least in Béarn, by the emergence of spontaneous, innovative localised variants. This combination of new, old, and standardised forms in contemporary RF may allow young Avionnais and Béarnais to retain a marked local or regional identity while at the same time avoiding social stigmatisation. These new developments during the evolution of RF may permit younger speakers to negotiate local and national identities by, on the one hand, signalling loyalty to their regional identity while, on the other hand, appearing 'modern' and cosmopolitan.

6.2 Regional Identity in 21st-Century France

Regional varieties of French have never been openly villified by the French state in the way that the regional languages of France were and they have never been the object of explicit language policy: 'owing to its linguistic affinity to the standard language, regional French has never been overtly persecuted either via legislation or in practice' (Jones, 2011: 54). The existence of regional variation in French, however, may be seen to challenge the deep-rooted ideology of standard French by introducing additional geographically-based variation into French, which the process of codification would normally aim to suppress during standardisation. L'Abbé Grégoire noted in 1794 that while the annihilation of the 'patois' should not take a very long time, regional accents would resist unification with standard French for longer, yet such unification was presented as inevitable if *la langue française* was to become the idealised symbol of national unity: 'l'accent n'est pas plus irréformable que les mots' (Grégoire, 1794 cited in Armstrong and Pooley, 2010: 23). Regional varieties of French have often been strongly associated with relatively well-defined geographical areas and, as such, may be used to index regional or local identities. Of course, these regional identities were traditionally more closely linked to the regional languages undergoing extensive language shift since the late eighteenth century but as French increasingly ousted these languages and dialects, RF progressively took on a symbolic role as a marker of regional origin. The reorganisation of the geographical and administrative divisions of France in the late eighteenth century replaced the provinces of the *Ancien Régime* with *départements*. This had the effect of removing the ethnolinguistic names of these provinces to be replaced with the names of natural geographical features such as rivers and mountains, which involved concomitant bleaching of local identities:

'these measures were intended to obliterate any related ethnolinguistic identity based on territoriality' (Armstrong and Pooley, 2010: 21). This form of institutional and linguistic identity is strongly linked to the ideals, principles and values of Jacobinism which have occupied a central position in French socio-political culture since at least the Revolution and which have, in many ways, persisted well into the modern period: 'the indivisibility of national sovereignty, the vocation of the State to transform society, governmental and administrative centralisation, the equality of citizens guaranteed by the uniformity of legislation, the regeneration of men by republican education, or merely a fastidious attachment to national independence' (Hazareesingh, 2002: 6). Jacobinism encouraged the denial of regional or localised identity by promoting the idea of the *citoyen*, or of individual citizenship, at the expense of any acknowledgement of particular communities, regional and otherwise (Schnapper, 2002: 198). Marley notes that, in the Early Modern and Modern periods, 'whole communities which had, for centuries, identified with a "petite patrie", in terms of a regional language and culture, within a couple of generations identified with a nation, in terms of its national language' (2007: 181). Thus, France emerged from the Early Modern period with a strong normative linguistic tradition which excluded RF from acquiring social prestige, on the basis that is was opposed to *le bon usage*, and discouraged *citoyens* from claiming affiliation to any localised identities which could be indexed by using geographically-based variation in their speech (Ayres-Bennett and Jones, 2007: 5).

Despite the Jacobin legacy, socio-political changes in the late twentieth century have led to a collective revision of its ideology. In the postmodern era, Western European societies have undergone a large-scale cultural shift in attitudes, often referred to as the *Zeitgeist*: 'traditional forms of authority — political, parental, religious — were called into question and remain so, and informality increased in a society that became, and has continued, measurably more equal and, in terms of public discourse at least, more egalitarian' (Armstrong and Pooley, 2010: 98). While Jacobin ideology is still present in French society, the cultural *Zeitgeist* has called into question the notion of a unified French identity: 'while the philosophy of Jacobinism was founded upon the point of convergence of political organization, economic practice, and national identity, these are becoming increasingly dissociated in the modern world' (Schnapper, 2002: 210). This revision of concepts traditionally used to construct societies and to understand the world led, to a certain extent, to a new form of acceptance for, or even celebration of, regional cultures: 'postmodernism rejects unity, totalization, transcendental concepts, or a belief in disinterested knowledge' (Pennycook, 2009: 62). Exposure to postmodernity, since the 1960s, and its related political issues has underlined, for the generations born from the late twentieth century onwards, the importance and cultural significance of 'regionalism, exaltation of identity and heritage' (Moreux, 2004: 53). Perrineau (1998) has even referred to these attitudinal changes which encourage a move away from the notion of a unified national identity as a *révolution invisible*. Increasing celebration of and respect for local cultural heritage has, I will argue, resulted in a reconstruction of regional identity in the postmodern period, notably by younger speakers for whom this identity reconstruction is characterised, at least partially, by their language use.

Jones takes the view that RF is relatively free of stigmatisation, at least when compared to the regional languages of France: 'it remains available as a stigma-free vehicle of regional identity as manifest through language' (2011: 514). It has been noted, however, that (traditional) southwestern accents and in particular those of older speakers are 'generally considered by ordinary French speakers as a "distorted" French created through bilingualism by the diglossic contact between standard French and the local language' (Armstrong and Blanchet, 2006: 265). This underlines the link, in the collective consciousness, between local languages and local varieties of French, the latter assumed to have been influenced by the former. Indeed, Armstrong and Blanchet note that in formal situations, it is not uncommon to hear speakers from southwestern France apologise for their accent (2006: 265). For example, Speaker D (aged 68 in 2012) in the language contact study said during her sociolinguistic interview: 'en plus avec l'accent que nous avons, quand on allait en région parisienne voir mon frère, je vous assure qu'il ne fallait pas dire d'où on était'. We have seen, however, that in both Avion and Béarn, the speech of the youngest generation was distinct from the traditional RF of older speakers but also from the supralocal norm. Hornsby describes the northern RF of young speakers to be a 'mix of regional forms associated with Nord-Pas-de-Calais urban centres and non-localized variants' (Hornsby, 2006: 122) and this is seen to allow younger Avionnais to signal a modern, rather than a traditional, *Ch'ti-mi* or *nordiste* identity comparable to that of Watt's (1998) 'modern northerners'. A similar situation was noted in Béarn (see Chapter 5) where the youngest generation appeared to be signalling loyalty to their local identity (by retaining local features in their speech) while concomitantly demonstrating their openness to the world outside of the region (via the use of supralocal pronunciations). The construction of modern regional identities through language by the 'modern northerners' in Avion and by the 'modern southerners' in Béarn is, I will argue, closely linked to the postmodern cultural *Zeitgeist* and to the removal of boundaries and traditional categories such as the ideology of 'standard' French and of national unity.

The speech of young RF speakers appears to be part and parcel of a more general process of identity construction on their part, which integrates multiple, competing identities. It is more accurate here to refer to identity *re*construction rather than identity construction since these younger speakers appear to base their 'modern' identities on pre-existing territorial identities tied to the Nord-Pas-de-Calais and to the region of Béarn. Indeed, the role of language in identity planning is 'centrally an agentive act, an act of reconstruction rather than of reproduction' (Pennycook, 2009: 70). Combining local, non-local, and new linguistic features in modern RF may allow young speakers to revise and reconstruct their regional and national identities in a single concept, contrary to the traditional assumption that such identities find themselves in opposition, or that regional identity threatens national identity. This process of identity reconstruction involves 'identity projecting synchronic ties operating both inwards and outwards, and reinforced where possible by (often resurrected) diachronic ties' (Ayres-Bennett and Jones, 2007: 7; cf. Anderson, 1991). In the case of modern RF, the projection of synchronic ties relates to the harmonious mixing of local (inward) and national (outward) affiliations while the resurrection of diachronic ties links this new identity to more traditional values, such as the local language and customs, reinforced by on-going relationships with and loyalty to older generations. This process of identity reconstruction appears to have been motivated by and to reflect social and socio-political changes in the postmodern era: 'the contemporary acknowledgement of mixture in origins and lineages indicates a sea change in subjectivities and consciousness that correlates, of course, with sea changes in social structures and practices' (Nederveen Pieterse, 2002: 227). It is possible that the influence of the cultural *Zeitgeist* is increasing as time advances, such that each subsequent generation is increasingly open to the redistribution of traditional societal constructs, perhaps explaining the increased level of supralocalisation evident in the speech of the middle generation in Béarn, when compared with the young 'modern southerners'. However, without demonstrating conclusively that there is an evidence-based correlation between these socio-cultural changes and the question of speaker attitudes to their regional identity, we cannot be sure that this apparent relationship is indeed causative.[3]

The expression of diachronic ties to local languages and cultures in the language of the dominant culture represents a strategy of being (modern) Xmen-via-Yish.[4] Fishman (1991) raises the question of whether it is even possible to maintain a distinct ethnic (or regional) identity when younger generations have stopped using a local language (such as Picard or Béarnais) on which this ethnic identity is based: 'as the spotlight turns on one identity, does another fade into the shadow?' (Nederveen Pieterse, 2002: 219). Fishman takes the view that language shift nearly always entails 'quite devastating and profound cultural change' (1991: 16), suggesting that the adoption by younger generations of French as their dominant language precludes the retention or reproduction of the ethnic or ethnolinguistic identity of older generations. Nevertheless, it is possible for younger generations to project an ethnic identity and to self-identify with this identity even when language shift has rendered the transmission and reproduction of the traditional ethnolinguistic identity impossible: 'while ethnocultural label-maintenance and self-concept-maintenance may long outlast language maintenance, the detailed pattern of culture, and any community's ability to maximize self-regulation of culture change and the regulation of culture contact, is invariably different when the historically associated language is present than when it is absent' (Fishman, 1991: 17). The concept of Xmen-via-Yish is overly simplistic, in the context of RF, in that it assumes the existence of two monolithic ethnolinguistic identities, linked to the obsolescent language (Xish) and the dominant language (Yish), respectively. Indeed, it emphasises the preservation of an unchanging Xish identity and ignores the possibility of (re)constructing an Xish identity in the light of social change, or of projecting both Xish and Yish identities at the same time; Fishman does acknowledge the possibility of being 'Xmen and Ymen simultaneously and entirely in Yish' (1991: 16) but this outcome is presented as undesirable in the context of language revitalisation because it negates the need to preserve Xish. Younger RF speakers cannot thus realise the idealistic vision of being strict Xmen-via-Yish but it seems that their reconstruction of the Xish identity involves varying degrees of ethnolinguistic and ethnocultural hybridity, which does not preclude the projection of an, albeit modified, local (Xish) identity.

It is generally unwise to consider the relationship between language and identity as a simple linear correlation. Pennycook notes that 'sociolinguistics has operated all too often with fixed and static categories of class, gender, and identity membership as if these were transparent givens onto which language can be mapped' (2009: 70; cf. Williams, 1992 and Cameron 1995, 1997). Identities cannot be interpreted as monolithic categories and the membership of multiple identities or the existence of hybrid identities must also be acknowledged: 'la problématique classique de l'identité [...] apparaît finalement difficilement tenable, car elle peine à rendre compte d'identités multiples, produits d'actes continuels de différentiations' (Gadet, 2007: 211). We have seen that French national ideology has been traditionally linked to the notion of linguistic homogenisation and any expression of regional identity (via language or otherwise) was seen to constitute a deviation from national norms: ideologies associated with regional and national identities were seen as mutually exclusive within the French context. The evolution of RF and the reconstruction of regional identities in the late twentieth and early twenty-first century appear to have been driven by profound cultural and societal change, indicating perhaps that the ideology of one (homogenised) language and one nation may no longer be tenable; as Schnapper wonders, 'to what extent can [...] particular identities, which [have] always existed alongside Jacobinism — more so than recognized by republican ideology — be accepted in the public domain without challenging everything that has constituted the history of this particular society?' (2002: 216). As a result of these changes, Marley (2007: 180) argues that 'French' identity is no longer 'clear-cut' and that the adoption of particular (regional, cultural, social) identities does not have to imply a rejection of French identity. There is nothing to suggest that young RF speakers are not using language to signal an XYish identity: they are no longer bound to the ideology that Xishness and Yishness are mutually exclusive.

The idea that modern RF indexes a hybrid or mixed identity is problematic in that the concept of hybrity is 'meaningless *without* the prior assumption of difference, purity, [and] fixed boundaries' (Nederveen Pieterse, 2002: 226). It is thus necessary to postulate that well-defined 'national' and 'local' identities exist in France and that the boundaries between these identities are easily delimited. From a traditional Jacobin perspective at least, national identity simply replaced regional identity. Modern RF and the reconstructed identities that it appears to index are involved in the removal of boundaries between previously competing identities and in challenging 'boundary fetishism' (Nederveen Pieterse, 2002: 224), where ideological distinctions are strictly maintained. Younger RF speakers realise this endeavour, at least partially, by 'crossing' (Rampton, 1995) or using the forms of speech of other groups, or by 'styling the Other': 'ways in which people use language and dialect in discursive practice to appropriate, explore, reproduce or challenge influential images and stereotypes of groups that they *don't* themselves (straightforwardly) belong to' (Rampton, 1999: 421). Modern RF identities may thus be considered as partially linked to ethnic, territorial, and national boundaries, but essentially the evolution of RF involves the crossing of these boundaries and the establishment of identifications across and beyond them (Pennycook, 2009: 71).

Such linguistic and identity-based hybridity may be seen to represent 'a new "elite" gaze [or] a new cosmopolitan elite' (Friedman, 1999: 237) where ties with pre-existing national and local identities are both loosened and strengthened by the reconstruction process.

Modern RF is thus a reaction to profound socio-political change and a means of blurring traditional boundaries between long-standing social constructs. It is part and parcel of a process where localised ethnocultural identity is reappropriated and modernised, integrating pre-existing identities and establishing new constructs in tandem. As such, modern RF reflects a desire to be at once the same and different, to be French and to be Xish. This new stage in the evolution of regional varieties of French will, quite possibly, be instrumental in the creation of an alternative future for modern France.

Notes to Chapter 6

1. We may note, however, that Hornsby's 'young' informants (aged 0–29 years in 1988) are today aged 28–57 and are not, therefore, directly comparable to the young speakers (aged 16–18 in 2012) presented in the Béarn study.

2. Hornsby (2006) calls this mechanism 'levelling', not levelling 'proper'. The term 'levelling' is not used here to avoid confusion between levelling 'proper' (the retention of majority forms during, relatively localised, dialect contact) and 'dialect levelling' in the RDL sense (which comprises both levelling 'proper' and geographical diffusion).

3. There are certainly parallels to be drawn with the resurrection of cultural practices in the postmodern era to recreate and modernize a traditional ethnic, rather than strictly ethnolinguistic, identity. For example, studies in the field of social psychology have shown that the traditional Maori practice of facial tattoos, *Ta Moko*, fell out of use in the 1950s as the Maori tried to assimilate to the norms of white New Zealand society (Te Awekotuku, 2002). This practice was subsequently revived by younger generations in the 1980s and 1990s; Nikora et al. argue that this revival of *Ta Moko* (in adapted forms) constitutes an effort to 'resist, modify, or renew "meanings" about [...] themselves' and that this reappropriated cultural practice is 'plainly associated with *broader political and ongoing engagement activities* towards realizing Maori autonomy and self-determination' (2007: 487; my emphasis).

4. Fishman (1991: 11) uses the term 'Xish' to designate any language, undergoing language shift, used by members of a given community (which he calls 'Xmen') with which that language has been historically associated. 'Yish', on the other hand, is used to refer to the dominant language, or the 'language of greater power and opportunity' (Fishman, 1991: 16), with which Xish finds itself in contact (and in competition). Fishman (1991: 16–17) raises the question of whether it is ever possible, during language shift, for speakers of the dominant language (Yish) to retain the ethnocultural identity of previous generations who spoke the endangered language (Xish) and thus if it is possible to be Xmen when speaking Yish, and not Xish, or to be Xmen-via-Yish.

CONCLUSION

❖

J'entens bien, dist Pantagruel; tu es Lymosin, pour tout potaige, et tu veulx
icy contrefaire le Parisian [...] A ceste heure parle tu naturellement.
FRANÇOIS RABELAIS, *Pantagruel*, 1532

This investigation of the genesis and evolution of RF considered phonetic and
phonological changes taking place in the RF of Béarn in two different contact
situations: language contact with Béarnais and dialect contact with other
contemporary varieties of French. The language and dialect contact studies have
examined two general hypotheses: that RF is a result of substrate 'residue' and that
this 'residue' is ephemeral and will therefore be lost as time advances.

The sociological and linguistic examination of all varieties of Gallo-Romance
spoken in the Béarn region showed Béarnais to be involved in a process of language
shift, whereby it has gradually been ousted from all domains by French. High levels
of active bilingualism were present in the region for a limited period dating from
the late nineteenth century until the decades following the Second World War,
but since then Béarnais has found itself in a situation of gradual obsolescence at the
hands of French. Importantly, I have argued that the typological distance between
Béarnais and French constitutes a language contact situation that is markedly
different from that examined in other theoretical analyses of emergent RF (e.g.,
Hornsby, 2006).

An examination of the phonological systems of Béarnais and French traced the
historical evolution of each language variety from Latin and identified structural
cognates in the contemporary Béarnais and French phonologies, that is, those sound
units that may transfer into French during language contact, potentially resulting
in the presence of substrate 'residue' in the RF of bilingual Béarnais-French
speakers. Comparisons were presented between southwestern regional patterns
and those common to all southern varieties of French (the DSP), and between the
regional patterns and the supralocal French system diffusing from the north. From
this comparison, the mid-vowels and nasal vowels emerged as candidates for close
analysis as they were shown to differ most dramatically between the southern and
northern systems.

The character of phonetic and phonological change during language contact
was discussed with explicit reference to L1-to-L2 linguistic transfer in bilingual
speech. The linguistic mechanisms by which transfer occurs were discussed in
relation to Flege's SLM, used hitherto in research on second language acquisition.
In this model, equivalence classification of cognate phonemes in a bilingual's
languages is said to promote 'phonetic category assimilation' whereby L1 and L2

sounds are stored in the same phonetic category and eventually come to resemble each other in production. The language contact study investigated unilateral L1-to-L2 transfer from Béarnais into French by examining the mid-vowels and nasal units of ten bilingual speakers from three fieldwork sites. This study used a combination of selected Labovian data collection techniques to construct corpora for French and Béarnais, and these data were subsequently analysed using acoustic phonetic techniques as well as some impressionistic analysis. The findings show that, while this variety of regional French contains clear cases of substrate 'residue' from Béarnais, its formation during language contact is better accounted for by a combination of linguistic transfer, divergence and innovation, with structural correspondences between the surface phonologies of the languages influencing the outcomes of contact in each case.

We saw that in the latter half of the twentieth century large-scale in-migration to Béarn, primarily from the north of France, has led to increased contact between RF speakers and migrants who make use of the northern supralocal norm. When dialects of the same language come into contact, two primary linguistic mechanisms were shown to favour linguistic change: levelling and geographical diffusion. These mechanisms were discussed in relation to Kerswill's (2003) model of 'regional dialect levelling' which comprises levelling 'proper' and geographical diffusion. Levelling 'proper' was shown to act over a relatively compact geographical space, favouring the retention of majority variants between the dialects in contact. Geographical diffusion, on the other hand, was seen to act over a larger geographical space, favouring the adoption into regional varieties of supralocal variants from large, dominant urban centres. The dialect contact study examined change over time in RF using an apparent-time methodology: linguistic mechanisms causing change in the mid- and nasal vowel systems were investigated by comparing three generations of speakers, native to the region of Béarn, including the generation of older bilinguals. The data consisted entirely of naturalistic speech collected during sociolinguistic interviews, and the analysis employed an acoustic phonetic methodology, as used in the language contact study. I have argued that changes taking place in RF over time are, at least partially, the result of dialect contact with other contiguous varieties of southern RF and, importantly, with incoming varieties of French from elsewhere. The assumption that regional French features are transitory was, however, refuted: the results of the apparent-time study showed that young speakers in Béarn are not simply involved in the wholesale adoption of the northern French norm over time, and contemporary regional French in Béarn was shown to constitute a distinctive combination of local, supralocal and innovative features.

This book has challenged two long-standing assumptions about RF by considering variation present in the RF of Béarn to be motivated by both language and dialect contact. The language contact study constituted a novel approach to the analysis of substrate 'residue', examining phonetic and phonological transfer by considering a long-term contact situation within the framework of a well-established model of second language acquisition. This study provides the only systematic and theoretical analysis of RF emerging from contact between French and a variety of southern Gallo-Romance: all variationist studies of the genesis or evolution of RF have thus far considered situations where French was in contact with northern *langue d'oïl* dialects (cf. Pooley, 1996; Hornsby, 2006; Hall, 2008). The dialect contact study explored convergence towards the supralocal northern norm in a southern region with distinctive socio-political characteristics, far-removed geographically from the 'hypercephalic' Parisian centre. The application of a variationist methodology in this context therefore contributes to current debates on the nature of RF but provides a fresh contextual and methodological framework within which to examine the formation and development of RF phonologies.

Modern RF was shown to constitute a distinctive mix of local, non-local and new features, suggesting an attempt on the part of the youngest generation to project a 'modern' or 'cosmopolitan' identity while at the same time signalling loyalty to their ethnocultural, or regional, roots. I have argued that this partial, rather than wholesale, supralocalisation facilitates the retention of local features, or rates of use of local features, that are not overtly stigmatised while replacing others with supralocal forms. These processes of 'crossing' or 'styling the Other' appear to be a reaction to large-scale socio-political changes that have taken place in France since the late twentieth century; the speech of young RF speakers indexes the long-standing national identity associated with Paris as well as local identities increasingly celebrated and legitimised by the postmodern *Zeitgeist*. Modern RF appears to be undergoing a new stage in its evolution rather than simple dedialectalisation: traditional and innovative geographically-based linguistic variation, offset by varying levels of supralocalisation, reflects social change on the one hand but also allows young generations in the regions to recreate their social reality and to reconstruct regional identity via the removal of traditional ideological boundaries.

BIBLIOGRAPHY

❖

ANDERSON, B. 1991. *Imagined Communities: Reflections on the Origin and Spread of Nationalism* (London & New York: Verso)

ARMSTRONG, N. 2001. *Social and Stylistic Variation in Spoken French* (Amsterdam: John Benjamins)

ARMSTRONG, N., and P. BLANCHET. 2006. 'The sociolinguistic situation of "contemporary dialects of French" in France today: an overview of recent contributions to the dialectalisation of Standard French', *Journal of French Language Studies*, 16: 251–75

ARMSTRONG, N., and J. LOW. 2008. 'C'est encoeur plus jeuli, le Mareuc: some evidence for the spread of /ɔ/-fronting in French', *Transactions of the Philological Society*, 106: 432–55

ARMSTRONG, N., and T. POOLEY. 2010. *Social and Linguistic Change in European French* (Basingstoke: Palgrave Macmillan)

AYRES-BENNETT, W., and J. CARRUTHERS, with R. M. TEMPLE. 2001. *Problems and Perspectives: Studies in the Modern French Language* (London: Longman)

AYRES-BENNETT, W., and M. C. JONES (eds). 2007. *The French language and questions of identity* (Oxford: Legenda)

BAUMAN, J. A. 1980. *A Guide to Issues in Indian Language Retention* (Washington D.C.: Center for Applied Linguistics)

BEC, P. 1963. *La Langue Occitane* (Paris: Presses Universitaires de France)

BENDEL, H. 1934. 'Beiträge zur Kenntnis der Mundart von Lescun (Bass.-Pyr.)' (unpublished doctoral thesis, Eberhard-Karls-Universität zu Tübingen)

BOERSMA, P. 2001. 'Praat: a System for doing Phonetics by Computer', *Glot International*, 5: 341–45

BOERSMA, P., and D. WEENINK. 2012. 'Praat: doing phonetics by computer' <http://www.praat.org/> [accessed 19 February 2016]

BORRELL, A., and M. BILLIÈRES. 1989. 'L'Évolution de la norme phonétique en français', *La Linguistique*, 25: 45–62

BOUZET, J. 1928. *Manuel de grammaire béarnaise* (Pau: Marrimpouey Jeune)

BOYER, H. 1986. '«Diglossie»: un concept à l'épreuve du terrain', *Lengas*, 20: 21–54

BRUN, A. 1923. *L'Introduction de la langue française en Béarn et en Roussillon* (Paris: Champion)

—— 1931. *Le français de Marseille* (Paris: Institut Historique de Provence)

CAMERON, D. 1995. *Verbal hygiene* (London: Routledge)

—— 1997. 'Performing gender identity: Young men's talk and the construction of heterosexual masculinity', in *Language and masculinity*, ed. by S. Johnson and U. H. Meinhof (Oxford: Blackwell), pp. 47–64

CARDAILLAC KELLY, R. 1973. *A Descriptive Analysis of Gascon* (The Hague and Paris: Mouton)

CARIGNAN, C., R. SHOSTED, M. FU, Z.-P. LIANG, and B. SUTTON. 2013. 'The Role of the Tongue and Pharynx in Enhancement of Vowel Nasalization: A Real-time MRI Investigation of French Nasal Vowels', *Proceedings of INTERSPEECH 2013*, 3042–46

CARTON, F. 1981. 'Les parlers ruraux de la région Nord-Picardie: situation sociolinguistique', *International Journal of the Sociology of Language*, 29: 15–28

CARTON, F., M. ROSSI, P. AUTESSERRE, and P. LÉON. 1983. *Les accents des Français* (Paris: Hachette)

CHAMBERS, J. K., and P. TRUDGILL. 1980. *Dialectology* (Cambridge: Cambridge University Press)

CHEVALLIER, D., and A. MOREL. 1985. 'Identité culturelle et appartenance régionale', *Terrain*, 5: 3–5

CLOPPER, C. G. 2011. 'Checking for Reliability', in *Sociophonetics: a Student's Guide*, ed. by M. Di Paolo and M. Yaeger-Dror (Abingdon: Routledge), pp. 188–97

COYOS, J.-B. 2004. *Politique linguistique: langue basque et langue occitane du Béarn et de Gascogne* (Donostia: Baiona Elkar)

COVENEY, A. 2001. *The Sounds of Contemporary French: Articulation and Diversity* (Exeter: Elm Bank)

CUKOR-AVILA, P., and G. BAILEY. 2013. 'Real Time and Apparent Time', in *The Handbook of Language Variation and Change*, ed. by J. K. Chambers and Nathalie Schilling (Oxford: Blackwell), pp. 239–62

DARRIGRAND, R. 2012. *Initiation au gascon* (Orthez: Per Noste)

DAUZAT, A. 1906. *Essai de méthodologie dans le domaine des langues et des patois romans* (Paris: Champion)

—— 1935. 'Français régional, français populaire, onomastique', in *Où en sont les études de français?*, ed. by A. Dauzat (Paris: D'Artrey), pp. 189–226

DAVIES, A. 2003. *The Native Speaker: Myth and Reality* (Clevedon: Multilingual Matters)

DE MAREÜIL, P. B., M. ADDA-DECKER, and C. WOEHRLING. 2007. 'Analysis of Oral and Nasal Vowel Realisation in Northern and Southern French Varieties', *16th International Congress of Phonetic Sciences*, 2221–24.

DESGROUAIS, J. 1801. *Les gasconismes corrigés, ouvrage utile à toutes les personnes qui veulent parler et écrire correctement, et principalement aux jeunes gens dont l'éducation n'est point encore formée* (Toulouse: Veuve Douladoure)

DERRIDA, J. 2001. 'La langue n'appartient pas — entretien avec Évelyne Grossman', *Europe*, 861/2: 81–91.

DI PAOLO, M., and M. YAEGER-DROR. 2011. 'Field Methods: Gathering Data, Creating a Corpus, and Reporting your Work', in *Sociophonetics: a Student's Guide*, ed. by M. Di Paolo and M. Yaeger-Dror (Abingdon: Routledge), pp. 7–23

DORIAN, N. 1981. *Language Death: The Life Cycle of a Scottish Gaelic Dialect* (Philadelphia: University of Pennsylvania Press)

DUBARAT, V.-P. 1900. *Documents et bibliographie sur la Réforme en Béarn et au pays basque* (Pau: Vignancour)

DURAND, J. 2009. 'Essai de panorama critique des accents du midi', in *Le français, d'un continent à l'autre: Mélanges offerts à Yves Charles Morin*, ed. by L. Baronian and F. Martineau (Québec: Presses de l'Université Laval), pp. 123–70

FANT, G. 1960. *Acoustic Theory of Speech Production* (The Hague: Mouton)

FLEGE, J. E. 1988. 'The Production and Perception of Speech Sounds in a Foreign Language', in *Human Communication and its Disorders: A Review 1988*, ed. by H. Winitz (Norwood, NJ: Ablex), pp. 224–401

—— 1990. 'The Intelligibility of English Vowels Spoken by British and Dutch Talkers', in *Intelligibility in Speech Disorders: Theory, Measurement, and Management*, ed. by R. Kent (Amsterdam: John Benjamins), pp. 157–232

—— 1991. 'Age Learning Effects the Authenticity of Voice-onset Time (VOT) in Stop Consonants produced in a Second Language', *Journal of the Acoustical Society of America*, 85: 395–411

—— 1995. 'The Phonetic Study of Bilingualism', in *European Studies in Phonetics and Speech Communication*, ed. by G. Bloothooft, V. Hazan, D. Huber, and J. Llisterri (Utrecht: OTS Publications), pp. 98–103

—— 1997. 'The Role of Category Formation in Second-language Speech Learning', in

New Sounds 97, Proceedings of the Third International Symposium on the Acquisition of Second-language Speech, ed. by J. Leather and A. James (Klagenfurt, Austria: University of Klagenfurt), pp. 79–89

———2005. 'The Origins and Development of the Speech Learning Model', Keynote Lecture at the 1st Acoustical Society of America Workshop on L2 Speech Learning (Vancouver, CA: Simon Fraser University), 14–15 April 2005

———2007. 'Language Contact in Bilingualism: Phonetic System Interactions', in *Laboratory Phonology 9*, ed. by J. Cole and J. Hualde (Berlin: Mouton de Gruyter), pp. 353–80

FLEGE, J. E., I. MACKAY, and D. MEADOR. 1999. 'Native Italian Speakers' Production and Perception of English Vowels', *Journal of the Acoustical Society of America*, 106: 2973–87

FOUGERON, C., and C. L. SMITH. 1999. 'Illustrations of the IPA: French', *Handbook of the International Phonetic Association* (Cambridge: Cambridge University Press), pp. 78–81

FOULKES, P., G. J. DOCHERTY, and M. J. JONES. 2011. 'Analyzing Stops', in *Sociophonetics: a Student's Guide*, ed. by M. Di Paolo and M. Yaeger-Dror (Abingdon: Routledge), pp. 58–71

FRIEDMAN, J. 1999. 'The Hybridization of Roots and the Abhorrence of the Bush', in *Spaces of Culture: City–Nation–World*, ed. by M. Featherstone and S. Lash (London: Sage), pp. 230–55

GADET, F. 'Identités françaises différentielles et linguistique du contact', in *The French language and questions of identity*, ed. by W. Ayres-Bennett and M. C. Jones (Oxford: Legenda), pp. 206–17

GARMADI, J. 1981. *La sociolinguistique* (Paris: Presses Universitaires de France)

GILLIÉRON, J. 1886. 'Mélanges gallo-romans', in École pratique des hautes-études (*Mélanges Renier*)

GILLIÉRON, J., and E. EDMONT. 1902–10. *Atlas linguistique de la France* (Paris: Champion)

GROSCLAUDE, M. 1986. *La langue béarnaise et son histoire: étude sur l'évolution de l'occitan du Béarn* (Orthez: Per Noste)

HALL, D. 2008. 'A Sociolinguistic Study of the Regional French of Normandy' (unpublished doctoral thesis, University of Pennsylvania)

HANSEN, A. B. 1998. *Les voyelles nasales du français parisien moderne* (Copenhagen: Mueum Tusculanum Press)

———2001. 'Lexical Diffusion as a Factor of Phonetic Change: The Case of Modern French Nasal Vowels', *Language Variation and Change*, 13: 209–52

HANSEN, A. B., and C. JUILLARD. 2011. 'La phonologie parisienne à trente ans d'intervalle: Les voyelles à double timbre', *Journal of French Language Studies*, 21: 313–60

HAWKINS, R. 1993. 'Regional variation in France', in *French Today: Language in its Social Context*, ed. by C. Sandars (Cambridge: Cambridge University Press), pp. 55–84

HAZAREESINGH, S. (ed.). 2002. *The Jacobin Legacy in Modern France* (Oxford: Oxford University Press)

HICKEY, R. (ed.). 2010. *The Handbook of Language Contact* (Oxford: Blackwell)

HOARE, R. 2003. *L'identité linguistique des jeunes en Bretagne* (Brest: Brud Nevez)

HOFFMAN, M. 2014. 'Sociolinguistic Interviews', in *Research Methods in Sociolinguistics: A Practical Guide*, ed. by J. Holmes and K. Hazen (Oxford: Blackwell), pp. 25–41

HORNSBY, D. 2006. *Redefining Regional French: Koinéization and Dialect Levelling in Northern France* (Oxford: Legenda)

HORNSBY, D., and T. POOLEY. 2001. 'La sociolinguistique et les accents de français d'Europe', in *French Accents: Phonological and Sociolinguistic Perspectives*, ed. by M.-A. Hintze, T. Pooley and A. Judge (London: AFLS/CILT), pp. 305–43

HOUDEBINE, A. M. 1995. 'Imaginaire linguistique et dynamique langagière: aspects théoriques et méthodologiques', *La Bretagne Linguistique*, 10: 239–55

INSEE. 2012. *Institut national de la statisitque et des études économiques* <www.insee.fr> [accessed February 2016]

JOHNSON, D. E. 2008. 'Rbrul' <http://www.ling.upenn.edu/~johnson4/Rbrul.R> [accessed July 2012]

——2009. 'Getting off the Goldvarb Standard: Introducing Rbrul for Mixed-Effects Variable Rule Analysis', *Language and Linguistics Compass*, 3: 359–83

JONES, M. C. 1998. *Language Obsolescence and Revitalisation: Linguistic Change in Two Sociolinguistically Contrasting Welsh Communities* (Oxford: Clarendon Press)

——2001. *Jersey Norman French: A Linguistic Study of an Obsolescent Dialect* (Oxford: Blackwell)

——2011. '*État présent*: Diatopic Variation and the Study of Regional French', *French Studies*, 4: 505–14

KELLER, J. 1985. 'Histoire de la langue béarnaise en Béarn', in *Drin de tot: Travaux de sociolinguistique et de dialectologie béarnaises*, ed. by A. M. Kristol and J. Th. Wüest (Bern: Peter Lang), pp. 63–74

KERSWILL, P. 2003. 'Dialect Levelling and Geographical Diffusion in British English', in *Social dialectology*, ed. by D. Britain and J. Cheshire (Amsterdam: John Benjamins), pp. 223–43

KERSWILL, P., and A. WILLIAMS. 2005. 'New Towns and Koinéization: Linguistic and Social Correlates', *Linguistics*, 43: 1023–48

KRISTOL, A. M., and J. Th. WÜEST (eds). 1985. *Drin de tot: Travaux de sociolinguistique et de dialectologie béarnaises* (Bern: Peter Lang)

KUIPER, L. 2005. 'Perception is Reality: Parisian and Provençal Perceptions of Regional Varieties of French', *Journal of Sociolinguistics*, 9: 28–52

LABOV, W. 1963. 'The social motivation of a sound change', *Word*, 19: 273–309

——1973. *Sample questionnaire used by the project on linguistic change and variation*, University of Pennsylvania, 1 March 1973.

——1983. 'Le changement linguistique. Entretien avec William Labov (participants: Pierre Bourdieu et Pierre Encrevé)', *Actes de la Recherche en Sciences Sociales*, 46: 67–72

——1984. 'Field Methods of the Project on Linguistic Change and Variation', in *Language in Use: Readings in Sociolinguistics*, ed. by J. Baugh and J. Sherzer (Englewood Cliffs, NJ: Prentice Hall), pp. 28–66

——1994. *Principles of Linguistic Change. Volume I: Internal Factors* (Oxford: Blackwell)

——2007. 'Transmission and diffusion', *Language*, 83: 344–87

LAFITTE, J. 1996. 'Le gascon, langue à part entière, et le béarnais, âme du gascon', *LiGam DiGam: Cadèrn de lingüistica e de lexicografia gasconas*, 4.

LANUSSE, M. 1891. *De l'influence du dialecte gascon sur la langue française* (Grenoble: Allier).

LAROUSSI, F., and J.-B. MARCELLESI. 1993. 'The Other Languages of France', in *French Today: Language in its Social Context*, ed. by C. Sanders (Cambridge: Cambridge University Press), pp. 85–104

LE PAGE, R. 1980. 'Projection, focussing, diffusion or steps towards a sociolinguistic theory of language', *York Papers in Linguistics*, 9: 9–31

LEROND, A. 1973. *Les parlers régionaux* (Paris: Larousse)

LOBANOV, B. M. 1971. 'Classification of Russian Vowels Spoken by Different Speakers', *Journal of the Acoustical Society of America*, 49: 606–08

LODGE, R. A. 1993. *French: From Dialect to Standard* (New York: Routledge)

LLAMAS, C. 2007. 'Field methods' in *The Routledge Companion to Sociolinguistics*, ed. by C. Llamas, L. Mullany and P. Stockwell (Abingdon: Routledge), pp. 12–18

LLAMAS, C., D. WATT, and D. E. JOHNSON. 2009. 'Linguistic Accommodation and Salience of National Identity Markers in a Border Town', *Journal of Language and Social Psychology*, 28: 381–407

MARLEY, D. 2007. 'Maghrebins via French', in *The French language and questions of identity*, ed. by W. Ayres-Bennett and M. C. Jones (Oxford: Legenda), pp. 180–91

MARTINET, A. 1945. *La prononciation du français contemporain: témoignages recueillis en 1941 dans un camp d'officiers prisonniers* (Paris: Droz)

——1955. *Économie des changements phonétiques* (Bern: A. Francke)

——1958. 'C'est jeuli, le Mareuc!', *Romance Philology*, 11: 345–55

MATISOFF, J. A. 1991. 'Endangered Languages of Mainland Southeast Asia', in *Endangered Languages*, ed. by E. M. Uhlenbeck and R. H. Robins (Oxford: Berg), pp. 189–228

MATRAS, Y. 2010. 'Contact, Convergence and Typology' in *The Handbook of Language Contact*, ed. by R. Hickey (Oxford: Blackwell), pp. 66–86

MEILLET, A. 1906. 'L'État actuel des études de linguistique générale: Leçon d'ouverture du Cours de Grammaire comparée au Collège de France lue le mardi 13 février 1906', *Revue des Idées* (Paris), 3: 296–308. Reprinted in Martinet, A. 1921. *Linguistique historique et linguistique générale*, Tome I (Paris: Champion), pp. 1–18

MILROY, L. 1980. *Language and Social Networks* (London: Basil Blackwell)

MILROY, J., and L. MILROY. 1985. *Authority in Language* (London: Routledge)

MILROY, J., L. MILROY, S. HARTLEY, and D. WALSHAW. 1994. 'Glottal Stops and Tyneside Glottalization: Competing Patterns of Variation and Change in British English', *Language Variation and Change*, 6: 327–58

MILROY, L., and M. GORDON. 2003. *Sociolinguistics: Method and Interpretation* (Oxford: Blackwell)

MOLARD, E. 1810. *Le mauvais langage corrigé, ou recueil par ordre alphabétique, d'expressions et de phrases vicieuses usitées en France, et notamment à Lyon* (Lyon: Yvernault et Cabin)

MOLYNEUX, R. G. 2002. *Grammar and Vocabulary for the Language of Béarn: for Beginners (Abridged and Translated from the works of Vastin Lespy)* (Monein: Éditions Pyrémonde)

MOONEY, D. 2014. 'Illustrations of the IPA: Béarnais (Gascon)', *Journal of the International Phonetic Association*, 44: 343–50

——2015a. 'Confrontation and language policy: non-militant perspectives on conflicting revitalisation strategies in Béarn, France' in *Policy and Planning for Endangered Languages*, ed. by M. C. Jones (Cambridge: Cambridge University Press), pp. 153–70.

——2015b. 'Transmission and diffusion: Linguistic change in the regional French of Béarn', *Journal of French Language Studies*, Advance online publication. doi.org/10.1017/S0959269515000290.

——2016. ''C'est jeuli, la Gasceugne!': L'antériorisation du phonème /ɔ/ dans le français régional du Béarn', *French Studies*, 70: 61–81.

MOREUX, B. 1985a. 'La "loi de position" en français du Midi, partie I: Sychronie (Béarn)', *Cahiers de grammaire*, 9: 45–138

——1985b. 'La "loi de position" en français du Midi, partie II: Diachronie (Béarn)', *Cahiers de grammaire*, 10: 95–174

——2004. '*Béarnais* and *Gascon* today: Language Behaviour and Perception', *International Journal of the Sociology of Language*, 169: 25–62

——2006. 'Les voyelles moyennes en français du Midi: une tentative de synthèse en 1985', *Cahiers de grammaire*, 30: 307–17

MOREUX, B., and C. MOREUX. 1989. 'La transmission du béarnais en milieu rural aujourd'hui', in *Langues en Béarn* ed. by B. Moreux (Toulouse: Presses Universitaires du Mirail), pp. 235–56

MOREUX, B., and J.-M. PUYAU. 2002. *Dictionnaire Français-Béarnais* (Monein: Éditions PyréMonde)

MOREUX, B., and J.-M. PUYAU. 2005. *Dictionnaire Béarnais-Français* (Monein: Éditions PyréMonde).

MORIN, Y. C. 2005. 'L'implantation du français à Marseille au XVIe siècle: les voyelles nasales et les semi-voyelles', in *Langues et contacts de langues dans l'aire méditerranéenne*, ed. by H. Boyer (Paris: L'Harmattan), pp. 225–37

—— 2009. 'Acquiring the Vowel System of a Cognate Language: The Role of Substrate and Spelling in the Development of the French Spoken in Marseilles during the Sixteenth Century', in *Romanística sin complejos*, ed. by F. Sànchez Miret (Bern: Peter Lang), pp. 409–54

MÜLLER, B. 1985. *Le français d'aujourd'hui* (Paris: Klincksieck)

MÜLLER, F., R. HUBER, B. NÜTZI, and D. NUSSBAUM. 1985. 'Enquête sociolinguistique dans trois communes du Béarn', in *Drin de tot: Travaux de sociolinguistique et de dialectologie béarnaises*, ed. by A. M. Kristol and J. Th. Wüest (Bern: Peter Lang), pp. 75–115

NEDERVEEN PIETERSE, J. 2002. 'Hybridity, So What? The Anti-hybridity Backlash and the Riddles of Recognition', in *Recognition and difference: Politics, identity, multiculture*, ed. by S. Lash and M. Featherstone (London: Sage), pp. 219–45

NEW, B., C. PALLIER, L. FERRAND, and R. MATOS. 2001. 'Une base de données lexicales du français contemporain sur internet: LEXIQUE', *L'Année Psychologique*, 101: 447–62: <http://www.lexique.org> [accessed February 2016]

NEW, B., M. BRYSBAERT, J. SEGUI, L. FERRAND, and K. RASTLE. 2004. 'The Processing of Singular and Plural Nouns in French and English', *Journal of Memory and Language*, 51: 568–85

NEW, B., M. BRYSBAERT, J. VERONIS, and C. PALLIER. 2007. 'The Use of Film Subtitles to Estimate Word Frequencies', *Applied Psycholinguistics*, 28: 661–77

NIKORA, L. W., RUA, M., and N. TE AWEKOTUKU. 2007. 'Renewal and Resistance: Moko in Contemporary New Zealand', *Journal of Community and Applied Social Psychology*, 17: 477–89

PALAY, S. 1980. *Dictionnaire du béarnais et du gascon modernes* (Pau: Marrimpouey Jeune)

PALTRIDGE, J., and H. GILES. 1984. 'Attitudes towards Speakers of Regional Accents of French: Effects of Regionality, Age and Sex of Listeners', *Linguistiche Berichte*, 90: 71–85

PANDHARIPANDE, R. V. 2002. 'Minority Matters: Issues in Minority Languages', *International Journal on Multicultural Studies*, 4: 213–34

PENNYCOOK, A. 2009. 'Postmodernism in Language Policy', in *Introduction to Language Policy: Theory and Method*, ed. by T. Ricento (Oxford: Blackwell)

PERRINEAU, P. 1998. 'La logique des clivages politiques', in *Les révolutions invisibles*, ed. by D. Cohen (Paris: Clamann-Lévy), pp. 289–300

POOLEY, T. 1996. *Ch'timi: the Urban Vernaculars of Northern France* (Clevedon: Multilingual Matters)

—— 2000. 'Sociolinguistics, Regional Varieties of French and Regional Languages in France', *Journal of French Language Studies*, 10: 117–57

—— 2006. 'On the Geographical Spread of Oïl French in France', *Journal of French Language Studies*, 16: 357–90

—— 2007. 'Dialect Levelling in Southern France', *Nottingham French Studies*, 46: 40–63

POTTIER, B. 1968. 'La situation linguistique en France', in *Le langage*, ed. by A. Martinet (Paris: Encyclopédie de la Pléiade), pp. 1144–61

PRICE, G. 2005. *An Introduction to French Pronunciation* (Oxford: Blackwell)

RABELAIS, F. 1964. *Pantagruel. 1532.* (Paris: Classiques de Poche)

RAMPTON, B. 1995. *Crossing: Language and ethnicity among adolescents* (London: Longman)

—— 1999. 'Styling the Other: Introduction', *Journal of Sociolinguistics*, 3: 421–27

RICKARD, P. 1974. *A History of the French Language* (Oxford: Routledge)

ROSNER, B. S., and J. B. PICKERING. 1994. *Vowel Perception and Production* (Oxford: Oxford University Press)

SANCIER, M. L., and C. A. FOWLER. 1997. 'Gestural Drift in a Bilingual Speaker of Brazilian Portuguese and English', *Journal of Phonetics*, 25: 421–36

SCHNAPPER, D. 2002. 'Making Citizens in an Increasingly Complex Society: Jacobinism Revisited', in *The Jacobin Legacy in Modern France*, ed. by S. Hazareesingh (Oxford: Oxford University Press), pp. 196–217

SCULLEN, M. E. 1997. *French Prosodic Morphology: A Unified Account*. (Bloomington: Indiana University Linguistics Club Publications)

SÉGUY, J. 1950. *Le français parlé à Toulouse* (Toulouse: Privat-Didier)

SÉGUY, J., and J. ALLIÈRES. 1954–73. *Atlas Linguistique et Ethnographique de la Gascogne* (Paris: CNRS)

SIEGEL, J. 1993. 'Introduction: Controversies in the Study of Koinés and Koinéization', *International Journal of the Sociology of Language*, 99: 5–8

SIMONET, M. 2011. 'Production of a Catalan-specific vowel contrast by early Spanish-Catalan bilinguals', *Phonetica*, 68: 88–110

TAGLIAMONTE, S. A. 2006. *Analysing Sociolinguistic Variation* (Cambridge: Cambridge University Press)

TAGLIAMONTE, S. A., and R. H. BAAYEN. 2012. 'Models, Forests and Trees of York English: *Was/were* Variation as a Case Study for Statistical Practice', *Language Variation and Change*, 24:2, 135–78.

TAYLOR, J. 1996. *Sound Evidence: Speech Communities and Social Accents in Aix-en-Provence* (Bern: Peter Lang)

TE AWEKOTUKU, N. 2002. 'More than Skin Deep: *Ta Moko* Today', in *Claiming the Stones, Naming the Bones: Cultural Property and the Negotiation of National and Ethnic Identity*, ed. by E. Barkan and R. Bush (Los Angeles: Getty Publications), pp. 243–58

THOMASON, S. 2010. 'Contact Explanations in Linguistics', in *The Handbook of Language Contact*, ed. by R. Hickey (Oxford: Blackwell), pp. 31–47

TRUDGILL, P. 1986. *Dialects in Contact* (Oxford: Blackwell)

TUAILLON, G. 1974. 'Compte-rendu de l'ALIFO', *Revue de Linguistique Romane*, 38: 576

—— 1988. 'Le français régional: formes de rencontre' in *Vingt-cinq communautés linguistiques de la France, I: Langues régionales et langues non territorialisées*, ed. by G. Vermes (Paris: L'Harmattan), pp. 291–300

TUCOO-CHALA, P. 1976. *Gaston Fébus: Un grand prince d'Occident au XVIᵉ siècle* (Pau: Marrimpouey Jeune)

—— 2009. *Petite histoire du Béarn du Moyen Âge au XXᵉ siècle* (Monein: Éditions Pyré-Monde)

VILLENEUVE, A.-J., and J. AUGER. 2013. '"Chtileu qu'i m'freumereu m'bouque i n'est point coér au monne': Grammatical Variation and Diglossia in Picardie', *Journal of French Language Studies*, 23: 109–33

WALTER, H. 1982. *Enquête phonologique et variétés régionales du français* (Paris: Presses Universitaires de France)

—— 1988. *Le français dans tous les sens* (Paris: Robert Laffont)

WANNER, A. 1993. 'Une enquête sociolinguistique comparative à Salses (Pyrénées-Orientales) et Sigean (Aude)', *Lengas*, 33: 7–124

WATT, D. 1998. 'Variation and Change in the Vowel System of Tyneside English' (unpublished doctoral thesis, University of Newcastle)

—— 2002. '"I don't speak with a Geordie accent, I speak, like, the Northern accent": Contact-induced Levelling in the Tyneside Vowel System', *Journal of Sociolinguistics*, 6: 44–63

WEBER, E. 1979. *Peasants into Frenchmen: The Modernization of Rural France 1870–1914* (London: Chatto and Windus)

WEINREICH, U. 1968. *Languages in Contact: Findings and Problems* (The Hague: Mouton)

WOLFRAM, W. 2004. 'Social varieties of American English', in *Language in the USA: Themes for the Twenty-first Century*, ed. by E. Finegan and J. R. Rickford (Cambridge: Cambridge University Press), pp. 58–75

—— 2011. 'Fieldwork Methods in Language Variation', in *The Sage Handbook of Sociolinguistics*, ed. by R. Wodak, B. Johnstone and P. Kerswill (London: Sage), pp. 296–312

YAEGER, M. 1973. 'On Style', *Pennsylvania Working Papers in Linguistics*, 1: 1

APPENDICES

❖

Appendix 1. Participants in the language and dialect contact studies

Speaker I.D	Sex	Age Group	Age	Site
A	F	65+	73	Gan
B	F	65+	78	Gan
C	F	65+	72	Nay
D	F	65+	68	Nay
E	F	65+	73	Gan
F	M	65+	89	Nousty
G	M	65+	71	Nousty
H	M	65+	72	Nay
I	M	65+	77	Gan
J	M	65+	86	Gan
K	F	30–50	47	Nousty
L	F	30–50	49	Nousty
M	F	30–50	39	Gan
N	F	30–50	47	Nay
O	F	30–50	39	Gan
P	M	30–50	48	Gan
Q	M	30–50	33	Nay
R	M	30–50	42	Gan
S	M	30–50	37	Gan
T	M	30–50	43	Nousty
U	F	16–18	17	Nay
V	F	16–18	18	Nay
W	F	16–18	16	Nay
X	F	16–18	18	Nay
Y	F	16–18	17	Nay
Z	M	16–18	16	Nay
@	M	16–18	17	Nay
$	M	16–18	16	Nay
£	M	16–18	16	Nay
€	M	16–18	16	Nay

Appendix 2. Means and Standard Deviation Data (Chapter 4)

Béarnais front mid-vowels

		/e/		/ɛ/	
		μ	σ	μ	σ
F1	Speaker F	521	(36)	614	(66)
	Speaker G	444	(35)	553	(83)
	Speaker H	425	(31)	536	(40)
	Speaker I	480	(47)	603	(90)
	Speaker J	404	(24)	507	(41)
		μ	σ	μ	σ
F2	Speaker F	1880	(175)	1932	(239)
	Speaker G	2208	(125)	1964	(105)
	Speaker H	1900	(140)	1937	(140)
	Speaker I	1963	(104)	1877	(142)
	Speaker J	2088	(153)	2028	(176)

Table A2.1. Old male speakers: Mean F1 and F2 values (Hz) and standard deviations for Béarnais front mid-vowels.

		/e/		/ɛ/	
		μ	σ	μ	σ
F1	Speaker A	575	(109)	697	(126)
	Speaker B	465	(23)	539	(112)
	Speaker C	463	(30)	541	(55)
	Speaker D	493	(44)	548	(130)
	Speaker E	442	(81)	531	(67)
		μ	σ	μ	σ
F2	Speaker A	2392	(180)	2213	(267)
	Speaker B	2105	(144)	2051	(107)
	Speaker C	2089	(161)	2015	(116)
	Speaker D	2289	(136)	2017	(105)
	Speaker E	2411	(353)	2081	(223)

Table A2.2. Old female speakers: Mean F1 and F2 values (Hz) with standard deviations for Béarnais front mid-vowels.

Béarnais back mid-vowel

		/ɔ/	
		μ	σ
FI	Speaker F	593	(41)
	Speaker G	562	(88)
	Speaker H	520	(41)
	Speaker I	588	(35)
	Speaker J	496	(40)
		μ	σ
F2	Speaker F	939	(53)
	Speaker G	1095	(86)
	Speaker H	959	(83)
	Speaker I	982	(99)
	Speaker J	910	(83)

Table A2.3. Old male speakers: Mean FI and F2 values (Hz) and standard deviations for Béarnais back mid-vowel.

		/ɔ/	
		μ	σ
FI	Speaker A	691	(95)
	Speaker B	548	(83)
	Speaker C	549	(32)
	Speaker D	612	(60)
	Speaker E	502	(56)
		μ	σ
F2	Speaker A	1060	(112)
	Speaker B	1153	(97)
	Speaker C	1063	(87)
	Speaker D	1237	(191)
	Speaker E	1099	(196)

Table A2.4. Old female speakers: Mean FI and F2 values (Hz) and standard deviations for Béarnais back mid-vowel.

French front mid-vowels

		/e/		/ɛ/	
		μ	σ	μ	σ
FI	Speaker F	497	(51)	620	(65)
	Speaker G	414	(45)	464	(81)
	Speaker H	400	(34)	471	(45)
	Speaker I	441	(45)	519	(65)
	Speaker J	405	(37)	458	(61)
		μ	σ	μ	σ
F2	Speaker F	1721	(208)	1700	(166)
	Speaker G	2137	(164)	1910	(234)
	Speaker H	1759	(167)	1664	(118)
	Speaker I	1880	(154)	1781	(162)
	Speaker J	1797	(155)	1876	(162)

Table A2.5. Old male Speakers: Mean FI and F2 values (Hz) and standard deviations for French front mid-vowels.

		/e/		/ɛ/	
		μ	σ	μ	σ
F1	Speaker A	501	(87)	618	(147)
	Speaker B	431	(43)	499	(91)
	Speaker C	469	(59)	522	(83)
	Speaker D	465	(49)	537	(112)
	Speaker E	388	(134)	493	(132)
		μ	σ	μ	σ
F2	Speaker A	2018	(331)	2037	(266)
	Speaker B	2065	(205)	1950	(199)
	Speaker C	2170	(220)	1964	(213)
	Speaker D	2215	(260)	2006	(220)
	Speaker E	2396	(340)	2216	(354)

Table A2.6. Old female Speakers: Mean F1 and F2 values (Hz) and standard deviations for French front mid-vowels.

French back mid-vowels

		/o/		/ɔ/	
		μ	σ	μ	σ
F1	Speaker F	556	(55)	547	(46)
	Speaker G	398	(51)	382	(86)
	Speaker H	391	(71)	444	(49)
	Speaker I	462	(51)	467	(59)
	Speaker J	407	(45)	482	(60)
		μ	σ	μ	σ
F2	Speaker F	928	(101)	1021	(172)
	Speaker G	987	(253)	1058	(124)
	Speaker H	880	(244)	911	(120)
	Speaker I	970	(166)	967	(149)
	Speaker J	854	(234)	981	(233)

Table A2.7. Old male speakers: Mean F1 and F2 values (Hz) and standard deviations for French back mid-vowels.

		/o/		/ɔ/	
		μ	σ	μ	σ
F1	Speaker A	498	(102)	642	(112)
	Speaker B	446	(49)	466	(62)
	Speaker C	461	(68)	496	(60)
	Speaker D	474	(106)	587	(97)
	Speaker E	421	(76)	459	(77)
		μ	σ	μ	σ
F2	Speaker A	1015	(186)	1121	(146)
	Speaker B	1110	(150)	1092	(83)
	Speaker C	1044	(249)	984	(152)
	Speaker D	1041	(239)	1176	(156)
	Speaker E	1278	(275)	1177	(270)

Table A2.8. Old female speakers: Mean F1 and F2 values (Hz) and standard deviations for French back mid-vowels.

Béarnais nasal units (F1 and F2)

		(ĩN)		(ỹN)		(ẽN)		(ãN)		(ũN)	
		[iN]	[ĩN]	[yN]	[ỹN]	[eN]	[ẽN]	[aN]	[ãN]	[uN]	[ũN]
		μ	μ	μ	μ	μ	μ	μ	μ	μ	μ
		σ	σ	σ	σ	σ	σ	σ	σ	σ	σ
F1	Speaker_F	376	511	402	350	529	538	758	ND	463	520
		78	—	64	—	24	20	53	—	50	—
	Speaker_G	347	326	362	ND	472	494	804	ND	368	435
		30	40	25	—	52	37	119	—	29	—
	Speaker_H	312	ND	328	349	437	463	659	573	373	ND
		13	—	21	17	30	11	36	—	51	—
	Speaker_I	364	346	378	ND	484	515	659	667	384	ND
		—	64	21	—	48	46	52	—	36	—
	Speaker_J	ND	331	330	ND	409	428	605	ND	348	ND
		—	12	16	—	30	48	26	—	26	—
F2	Speaker_F	2305	2485	1790	1734	1926	2086	1294	ND	868	853
		119	—	67	—	188	54	67	—	140	—
	Speaker_G	2562	2591	1834	ND	2126	2386	1462	ND	960	1189
		111	185	123	—	149	40	61	—	185	—
	Speaker_H	2119	ND	1806	1833	1822	1834	1149	1024	909	ND
		81	—	73	107	128	37	132	—	78	—
	Speaker_I	2121	2179	1596	ND	1935	1887	1480	1460	848	ND
		—	233	95	—	59	91	121	—	109	—
	Speaker_J	ND	2401	1689	ND	2001	2070	1492	ND	843	ND
		—	119	120	—	114	65	87	—	217	—

Table A2.9. Old male speakers: Mean F1 and F2 values (Hz) and standard deviations for Béarnais nasalised and non-nasalised vowels in sequential (ṽN) nasal units (ND = no data available).

		(ĩ)		(ỹ)		(ẽ)		(ã)		(ũ)	
		[i]	[ĩ]	[y]	[ỹ]	[e]	[ẽ]	[a]	[ã]	[u]	[ũ]
		μ	μ	μ	μ	μ	μ	μ	μ	μ	μ
		σ	σ	σ	σ	σ	σ	σ	σ	σ	σ
F1	Speaker_F	436	ND	382	277	ND	526	775	780	382	ND
		71	—	43	25	—	9	69	—	45	—
	Speaker_G	365	380	358	ND	379	475	878	907	352	360
		59	37	72	—	—	—	19	69	25	41
	Speaker_H	307	324	313	271	ND	385	742	634	300	302
		58	39	17	44	—	51	—	40	32	—
	Speaker_I	340	343	340	371	ND	430	690	678	395	ND
		31	26	25	35	—	5	—	17	13	—
	Speaker_J	364	326	300	291	ND	382	ND	611	326	303
		101	17	16	7	—	—	—	49	18	42
F2	Speaker_F	2302	ND	1812	1824	ND	2227	1172	1207	678	ND
		232	—	12	116	—	227	37	—	52	—
	Speaker_G	2769	2454	1822	ND	2399	2351	1391	1340	926	817
		67	42	108	—	—	—	124	68	78	209
	Speaker_H	2135	2230	1849	1848	ND	1883	1186	1242	752	635
		39	131	72	50	—	135	—	190	92	—
	Speaker_I	2346	2355	1714	1741	ND	2246	1297	1459	912	ND
		64	33	106	60	—	153	—	97	109	—
	Speaker_J	2465	2454	1667	1724	ND	2294	ND	1515	811	723
		129	67	113	69	—	—	—	161	196	12

Table A2.10. Old male speakers: Mean F1 and F2 values (Hz) and standard deviations for Béarnais nasalised and non-nasalised vowels in non-sequential (ṽ) nasal units (ND = no data available).

		(ĩN)		(ỹN)		(ẽN)		(ãN)		(ũN)	
		[iN]	[ĩN]	[yN]	[ỹN]	[eN]	[ẽN]	[aN]	[ãN]	[uN]	[ũN]
		μ σ	μ σ	μ σ	μ σ	μ σ	μ σ	μ σ	μ σ	μ σ	μ σ
F1	Speaker_A	391 16	433 36	479 112	389 —	565 70	ND —	892 81	884 —	391 28	591 —
	Speaker_B	331 86	400 33	422 27	470 —	479 86	517 —	780 60	823 27	401 12	382 17
	Speaker_C	387 25	377 81	402 25	358 62	483 42	515 —	752 62	ND —	389 69	ND —
	Speaker_D	437 9	446 66	441 16	383 —	528 70	482 109	722 42	ND —	339 22	ND —
	Speaker_E	330 41	325 —	371 52	ND —	386 39	408 12	711 137	ND —	362 49	ND —
F2	Speaker_A	2736 54	2697 549	2090 77	1762 —	2331 148	ND —	1644 93	1794 —	858 103	1196 —
	Speaker_B	2603 187	2577 47	1940 105	2057 —	2111 175	1973 —	1581 120	1534 76	1063 68	814 347
	Speaker_C	2139 180	2495 146	1712 106	1878 106	2160 134	2212 —	1525 86	ND —	1024 67	ND —
	Speaker_D	2360 175	2399 164	2012 116	1785 —	2168 62	2183 12	1721 106	ND —	743 59	ND —
	Speaker_E	2592 219	2601 —	1915 231	ND —	2246 59	2242 214	1580 156	ND —	724 155	ND —

Table A2.11. Old female speakers: Mean F1 and F2 values (Hz) and standard deviations for Béarnais nasalised and non-nasalised vowels in sequential (ṽN) nasal units (ND = no data available).

		(ĩ)		(ỹ)		(ẽ)		(ã)		(ũ)	
		[i]	[ĩ]	[y]	[ỹ]	[e]	[ẽ]	[a]	[ã]	[u]	[ũ]
		μ σ	μ σ	μ σ	μ σ	μ σ	μ σ	μ σ	μ σ	μ σ	μ σ
F1	Speaker_A	478 113	389 16	473 49	393 45	ND —	563 —	ND —	848 83	375 48	392 26
	Speaker_B	378 23	364 2	420 29	396 43	422 —	413 —	895 89	911 —	393 26	ND —
	Speaker_C	409 37	403 —	376 46	ND —	455 98	ND —	860 45	613 —	399 83	314 —
	Speaker_D	428 26	ND —	419 11	ND —	ND —	446 1	777 5	734 30	374 27	415 104
	Speaker_E	306 —	347 44	379 39	367 63	ND —	320 —	594 112	651 72	381 12	331 4
F2	Speaker_A	2792 117	2631 59	2278 200	2006 142	ND —	2323 —	ND —	1704 141	860 104	902 58
	Speaker_B	2729 163	2616 28	1872 61	1792 379	2418 —	2215 —	1584 120	1524 —	1002 165	ND —
	Speaker_C	2553 124	2418 —	1781 130	ND —	2179 165	ND —	1498 87	1350 —	929 116	933 —
	Speaker_D	2467 45	ND —	2011 127	ND —	ND —	2383 65	1709 58	1650 129	707 64	663 72
	Speaker_E	2530 —	2583 224	2053 252	2237 29	ND —	2270 —	1388 151	1612 76	824 162	657 29

Table A2.12. Old female speakers: Mean F1 and F2 values (Hz) and standard deviations for Béarnais nasalised and non-nasalised vowels in non-sequential (ṽ) nasal units (ND = no data available).

Béarnais nasal units (F3)

	[ĩN]	[ỹN]	[ũN]
	σ	σ	σ
	μ	μ	μ
F	3190	2305	2057
	75	86	176
G	3375	2634	2367
	256	93	359
H	3043	2980	2199
	48	116	254
I	2729	2382	2406
	71	196	204
J	3721	2229	2164
	252	66	163

Table A2.13. Old male speakers: Mean F3 means and standard deviations for Béarnais vowels in sequential nasal units.

	[ĩ]	[ỹ]	[ũ]
	σ	σ	σ
	μ	μ	μ
F	3093	2311	2326
	113	164	123
G	3426	2658	2443
	276	67	273
H	3087	3002	2089
	62	187	137
I	2903	2409	2506
	159	139	90
J	3506	2257	2225
	302	86	276

Table A2.14. Old male speakers: Mean F3 means and standard deviations for Béarnais vowels in non-sequential nasal units.

	[ĩN]	[ỹN]	[ũN]
	σ	σ	σ
	μ	μ	μ
A	3794	2950	2776
	401	58	371
B	3295	2682	2230
	126	116	191
C	3306	2420	2769
	257	112	278
D	3113	2510	2152
	58	77	221
E	3523	2802	1976
	218	202	238

Table A2.15. Old female speakers: Mean F3 means and standard deviations for Béarnais vowels in sequential nasal units.

	[ĩ]	[ỹ]	[ũ]
	σ	σ	σ
	μ	μ	μ
A	3957	2833	2731
	285	301	315
B	3800	2669	2822
	436	201	265
C	3231	2488	2732
	220	218	122
D	3334	2637	2315
	154	135	170
E	3418	2788	2189
	286	91	324

Table A2.16. Old female speakers: Mean F3 means and standard deviations for Béarnais vowels in non-sequential nasal units.

French nasal vowels (F1 and F2)

		[ɛ̃N]	[œ̃N]	[ɑ̃N]	[ɔ̃N]
		μ	μ	μ	μ
		σ	σ	σ	σ
F1	Speaker F	584	556	725	591
		60	46	75	54
	Speaker G	454	411	596	443
		43	45	113	42
	Speaker H	458	443	577	452
		47	45	54	45
	Speaker I	516	481	598	481
		47	46	50	55
	Speaker J	457	439	551	466
		31	62	41	35
F2	Speaker F	1672	1313	1287	959
		133	160	132	111
	Speaker G	1928	1417	1322	965
		260	346	147	124
	Speaker H	1566	1175	1292	957
		194	162	143	187
	Speaker I	1720	1284	1298	958
		146	180	220	165
	Speaker J	1669	1565	1358	936
		261	244	245	183

Table A2.17. Old male speakers: Mean F1 and F2 values (Hz)
and standard deviations for French vowels in sequential [ṽN] nasal units.

		[ɛ̃]	[œ̃]	[ɑ̃]	[ɔ̃]
		μ	μ	μ	μ
		σ	σ	σ	σ
F1	Speaker F	541	ND	675	560
		47	—	155	68
	Speaker G	451	474	580	427
		64	11	98	69
	Speaker H	481	ND	532	ND
		46	—	—	—
	Speaker I	512	424	523	544
		66	—	66	59
	Speaker J	449	407	533	ND
		42	—	—	—
F2	Speaker F	1714	ND	1254	955
		86	—	234	49
	Speaker G	1990	1573	1394	1021
		208	147	153	123
	Speaker H	1775	ND	1346	ND
		60	—	—	—
	Speaker I	1790	1479	1049	969
		109	—	119	257
	Speaker J	1870	1471	1513	ND
		105	—	—	—

Table A2.18. Old male speakers: Mean F1 and F2 values (Hz)
and standard deviations for French vowels in non-sequential [ṽ] nasal units
(ND = no data available).

		[ɛ̃ N]	[œ̃ N]	[ɑ̃ N]	[ɔ̃ N]
		μ	μ	μ	μ
		σ	σ	σ	σ
F1	Speaker A	651	565	771	598
		87	164	84	123
	Speaker B	436	450	602	502
		51	67	225	95
	Speaker C	575	572	725	578
		81	105	106	99
	Speaker D	561	553	686	518
		77	132	163	84
	Speaker E	463	417	586	430
		136	121	120	112
F2	Speaker A	1913	1848	1526	1106
		168	327	204	163
	Speaker B	1751	1479	1305	1126
		277	218	139	131
	Speaker C	1973	1551	1371	1053
		234	137	117	173
	Speaker D	2084	1782	1717	1142
		204	208	165	285
	Speaker E	2285	1835	1513	1318
		302	280	305	222

Table A2.19. Old female speakers: Mean F1 and F2 values (Hz) and standard deviations for French vowels in sequential [ṽN] nasal units.

		[ɛ̃]	[œ̃]	[ɑ̃]	[ɔ̃]
		μ	μ	μ	μ
		σ	σ	σ	σ
F1	Speaker A	720	677	791	705
		96	81	105	131
	Speaker B	461	403	570	499
		75	14	206	130
	Speaker C	561	597	652	526
		89	72	126	93
	Speaker D	555	502	707	543
		94	60	66	80
	Speaker E	609	445	602	430
		155	169	139	147
F2	Speaker A	1996	1618	1467	1158
		236	246	189	193
	Speaker B	1808	1358	1260	1194
		170	177	135	74
	Speaker C	1883	1577	1397	1178
		97	143	94	153
	Speaker D	2058	1814	1686	1208
		123	29	156	213
	Speaker E	2468	1739	1467	1257
		81	105	412	424

Table A2.20. Old female speakers: Mean F1 and F2 values (Hz) and standard deviations for French vowels in non-sequential [ṽ] nasal units.

French nasal vowels (F3)

	[ɛ̃N] μ σ	[œ̃N] μ σ
F	2604	2196
	364	287
G	2831	2615
	165	186
H	2384	2165
	258	243
I	2607	2443
	199	107
J	2461	2559
	401	507

Table A2.21. Old male speakers: Mean F3 values and standard deviations for French vowels in sequential nasal units.

	[ɛ̃] μ σ	[œ̃] μ σ
F	2662	ND
	159	—
G	2793	2876
	412	239
H	2581	2030
	360	—
I	2483	2382
	300	—
J	2739	2586
	363	—

Table A2.22. Old male speakers: Mean F3 values and standard deviations for French vowels in non-sequential nasal units.

	[ɛ̃N] μ σ	[œ̃N] μ σ
A	3142	3044
	434	226
B	3076	3086
	216	191
C	2833	2907
	205	139
D	2758	2567
	437	322
E	3331	3096
	364	303

Table A2.23. Old female speakers: Mean F3 values and standard deviations for French vowels in sequential nasal units.

	[ɛ̃]	[œ̃]
	μ	μ
	σ	σ
A	2975	3178
	579	178
B	3122	3144
	301	294
C	2881	2824
	263	232
D	2761	2396
	395	35
E	3382	3383
	275	—

Table A2.24. Old female speakers: Mean F3 values and standard deviations for French vowels in non-sequential nasal units.

	[ɑ̃N]	[ɔ̃N]
	μ	μ
	σ	σ
F	2322	2221
	254	312
G	2704	2704
	193	172
H	2304	2345
	313	343
I	2380	2435
	196	182
J	2487	2288
	526	206

Table A2.25. Old male speakers: Mean F3 values and standard deviations for French vowels in sequential nasal units.

	[ɑ̃]	[ɔ̃]
	μ	μ
	σ	σ
F	2204	1997
	266	235
G	2682	2612
	379	186
H	2147	ND
	—	—
I	2234	2410
	136	210
J	2297	ND
	—	—

Table A2.26. Old male speakers: Mean F3 values and standard deviations for French vowels in non-sequential nasal units.

	[ãN]	[õN]
	μ	μ
	σ	σ
A	3044	3068
	490	493
B	3133	3219
	383	309
C	2834	3034
	504	222
D	2582	2520
	407	206
E	3257	3151
	275	498

Table A2.27. Old female speakers: Mean F_3 values and standard deviations for French vowels in sequential nasal units.

	[ã]	[õ]
	μ	μ
	σ	σ
A	3302	2955
	335	495
B	3220	3335
	293	257
C	3021	2897
	273	288
D	2742	2509
	233	318
E	3224	2934
	424	447

Table A2.28. Old female speakers: Mean F_3 values and standard deviations for French vowels in non–sequential nasal units.

Appendix 3. Means and Standard Deviation Data (Chapter 5)

Middle speakers: mid-vowels

		/e/		/ɛ/	
		μ	σ	μ	σ
F1	Speaker_P	358	(44)	403	(52)
	Speaker_Q	374	(40)	446	(74)
	Speaker_R	380	(42)	459	(60)
	Speaker_S	386	(77)	478	(111)
	Speaker_T	412	(43)	470	(68)
F2	Speaker_P	1866	(195)	1706	(122)
	Speaker_Q	1924	(150)	1732	(174)
	Speaker_R	1857	(164)	1788	(152)
	Speaker_S	1946	(216)	1851	(201)
	Speaker_T	1867	(145)	1651	(155)

Table A3.1. Middle male speakers: Mean F1 and F2 values (Hz) for front mid-vowels.

		/e/		/ɛ/	
		μ	σ	μ	σ
F1	Speaker_K	476	(77)	659	(141)
	Speaker_L	409	(36)	498	(84)
	Speaker_M	470	(70)	639	(163)
	Speaker_N	400	(63)	564	(142)
	Speaker_O	426	(31)	585	(112)
F2	Speaker_K	2228	(206)	2042	(200)
	Speaker_L	2106	(121)	2001	(154)
	Speaker_M	2312	(248)	2082	(247)
	Speaker_N	2200	(175)	1958	(201)
	Speaker_O	2119	(194)	1882	(148)

Table A3.2. Middle female speakers: Mean F1 and F2 values (Hz) for front mid-vowels.

		/o/		/ɔ/	
		μ	σ	μ	σ
F1	Speaker_P	377	(49)	373	(52)
	Speaker_Q	388	(41)	398	(44)
	Speaker_R	444	(51)	445	(52)
	Speaker_S	382	(62)	414	(71)
	Speaker_T	418	(62)	445	(50)
F2	Speaker_P	947	(148)	969	(107)
	Speaker_Q	912	(174)	986	(139)
	Speaker_R	897	(158)	886	(107)
	Speaker_S	872	(174)	853	(119)
	Speaker_T	1026	(180)	1053	(102)

Table A3.3. Middle male speakers: Mean F1 and F2 values (Hz) for back mid-vowels.

		/o/ μ	/o/ σ	/ɔ/ μ	/ɔ/ σ
F1	Speaker_K	469	(53)	474	(84)
	Speaker_L	466	(81)	497	(70)
	Speaker_M	502	(82)	523	(85)
	Speaker_N	418	(55)	495	(86)
	Speaker_O	438	(60)	516	(102)
F2	Speaker_K	1063	(214)	1126	(163)
	Speaker_L	1009	(249)	978	(260)
	Speaker_M	1027	(172)	1114	(171)
	Speaker_N	1104	(287)	1155	(202)
	Speaker_O	980	(233)	1106	(181)

Table A3.4. Middle female speakers: Mean F1 and F2 values (Hz) for back mid-vowels.

Young speakers: mid-vowels

		/e/ μ	/e/ σ	/ɛ/ μ	/ɛ/ σ
F1	Speaker_Z	371	(54)	415	(75)
	Speaker_@	408	(56)	444	(55)
	Speaker_$	449	(68)	547	(95)
	Speaker_£	428	(92)	484	(92)
	Speaker_€	452	(40)	517	(71)
F2	Speaker_Z	1883	(171)	1778	(128)
	Speaker_@	1765	(100)	1729	(123)
	Speaker_$	2129	(140)	1908	(198)
	Speaker_£	1829	(127)	1805	(111)
	Speaker_€	1855	(140)	1764	(171)

Table A3.5. Young male speakers: Mean F1 and F2 values (Hz) for front mid-vowels.

		/e/ μ	/e/ σ	/ɛ/ μ	/ɛ/ σ
F1	Speaker_U	500	(42)	635	(107)
	Speaker_V	548	(73)	655	(113)
	Speaker_W	507	(73)	572	(99)
	Speaker_X	486	(71)	567	(79)
	Speaker_Y	424	(31)	536	(140)
F2	Speaker_U	2105	(288)	2024	(242)
	Speaker_V	2188	(230)	1965	(164)
	Speaker_W	2189	(188)	2022	(217)
	Speaker_X	2299	(236)	2166	(199)
	Speaker_Y	1825	(76)	1738	(122)

Table A3.6. Young female speakers: Mean F1 and F2 values (Hz) for front mid-vowels.

		/o/		/ɔ/	
		μ	σ	μ	σ
F1	Speaker_Z	376	(57)	413	(56)
	Speaker_@	408	(45)	450	(57)
	Speaker_$	443	(51)	498	(90)
	Speaker_£	380	(68)	478	(84)
	Speaker_€	444	(53)	489	(77)
F2	Speaker_Z	906	(222)	1071	(186)
	Speaker_@	991	(162)	1019	(94)
	Speaker_$	968	(209)	940	(142)
	Speaker_£	1021	(210)	1118	(149)
	Speaker_€	917	(202)	988	(124)

Table A3.7. Young male speakers: Mean F1 and F2 values (Hz) for back mid-vowels.

		/o/		/ɔ/	
		μ	σ	μ	σ
F1	Speaker_U	490	(56)	639	(127)
	Speaker_V	526	(87)	584	(121)
	Speaker_W	515	(78)	570	(102)
	Speaker_X	476	(74)	499	(81)
	Speaker_Y	475	(86)	525	(92)
F2	Speaker_U	1061	(172)	1322	(194)
	Speaker_V	1046	(268)	1087	(221)
	Speaker_W	1070	(239)	1144	(198)
	Speaker_X	1040	(275)	1196	(223)
	Speaker_Y	1056	(211)	1081	(201)

Table A3.8. Young female speakers: Mean F1 and F2 values (Hz) for back mid-vowels.

Middle speakers: nasal vowels

		[ɛ̃ N]	[œ̃ N]	[ɑ̃ N]	[ɔ̃ N]
		μ	μ	μ	μ
		σ	σ	σ	σ
F1	Speaker_P	374	369	551	388
		49	66	75	51
	Speaker_Q	486	471	566	426
		76	66	101	78
	Speaker_R	499	463	618	476
		66	18	51	52
	Speaker_S	502	455	559	410
		81	91	106	80
	Speaker_T	481	460	521	454
		63	69	74	85
F2	Speaker_P	1742	1288	1109	927
		177	133	94	120
	Speaker_Q	1574	1441	1096	898
		150	130	166	113
	Speaker_R	1769	1441	1137	921
		140	164	95	131
	Speaker_S	1726	1395	961	807
		279	251	151	106
	Speaker_T	1548	1254	1092	920
		220	134	99	138

Table A3.9. Middle male speakers: Mean F1 and F2 values and
standard deviations for nasal vowels in sequential [ṽN] nasal units.

		[ɛ̃]	[œ̃]	[ɑ̃]	[ɔ̃]
		μ	μ	μ	μ
		σ	σ	σ	σ
F1	Speaker_P	379	372	496	349
		62	59	74	40
	Speaker_Q	516	490	566	439
		65	44	122	78
	Speaker_R	454	482	617	461
		31	108	26	28
	Speaker_S	474	554	530	445
		107	—	107	121
	Speaker_T	507	483	482	465
		65	35	56	65
F2	Speaker_P	1782	1265	1106	1019
		231	85	138	165
	Speaker_Q	1487	1443	1116	911
		78	130	275	91
	Speaker_R	1619	1417	1055	986
		201	164	72	140
	Speaker_S	1684	1392	967	829
		169	—	109	159
	Speaker_T	1523	1387	1038	965
		135	298	56	97

Table A3.10. Middle male speakers: Mean F1 and F2 values and standard deviations for nasal vowels in non-sequential [ṽ] nasal units.

		[ɛ̃N]	[œ̃N]	[ɑ̃N]	[ɔ̃N]
		μ	μ	μ	μ
		σ	σ	σ	σ
F1	Speaker_K	588	531	721	574
		84	65	118	108
	Speaker_L	508	528	667	559
		62	53	50	61
	Speaker_M	682	589	785	608
		112	143	102	142
	Speaker_N	575	542	646	444
		84	105	106	98
	Speaker_O	570	512	706	546
		90	50	98	97
F2	Speaker_K	2085	1557	1282	1032
		254	187	210	150
	Speaker_L	1939	1653	1334	1034
		140	195	164	124
	Speaker_M	1891	1641	1269	1102
		282	262	136	167
	Speaker_N	1884	1670	1136	937
		140	235	304	127
	Speaker_O	1828	1549	1226	962
		193	221	150	108

Table A3.11. Middle female speakers: Mean F1 and F2 values and standard deviations for nasal vowels in sequential [ṽN] nasal units.

		[ɛ̃]	[œ̃]	[ɑ̃]	[ɔ̃]
		μ	μ	μ	μ
		σ	σ	σ	σ
F1	Speaker_K	695	577	591	533
		122	95	91	54
	Speaker_L	548	448	658	496
		84	96	135	69
	Speaker_M	758	656	771	598
		106	135	117	112
	Speaker_N	503	571	641	456
		92	86	132	127
	Speaker_O	581	570	637	546
		82	64	112	85
F2	Speaker_K	1800	1317	1147	1032
		192	96	156	147
	Speaker_L	1928	1635	1178	1043
		76	128	200	125
	Speaker_M	1672	1497	1230	1026
		133	156	132	165
	Speaker_N	1779	1664	1254	967
		343	223	359	151
	Speaker_O	1799	1439	1132	1014
		221	162	143	127

Table A3.12. Middle Female Speakers: Mean F1 and F2 values
and standard deviations for nasal vowels in non-sequential [ṽ] nasal units.

		[ɛ̃N]	[œ̃N]	[ɑ̃N]	[ɔ̃N]
		μ	μ	μ	μ
		σ	σ	σ	σ
F3	Speaker_P	2629	2512	2502	2599
		189	130	242	197
	Speaker_Q	2769	2787	2752	2667
		151	277	172	234
	Speaker_R	2524	2462	2578	2620
		135	96	229	277
	Speaker_S	2483	2342	2406	2318
		385	261	268	168
	Speaker_T	2564	2329	2432	2295
		238	280	341	213

Table A3.13. Middle male speakers: Mean F3 values
and standard deviations for nasal vowels in sequential nasal units.

		[ɛ̃]	[œ̃]	[ɑ̃]	[ɔ̃]
		μ	μ	μ	μ
		σ	σ	σ	σ
F3	Speaker_P	2586	2499	2618	2575
		214	205	224	115
	Speaker_Q	2899	2761	2749	2707
		64	310	160	272
	Speaker_R	2500	2545	2491	2607
		210	100	181	80
	Speaker_S	2405	2119	2264	2358
		388	—	298	259
	Speaker_T	2608	2804	2449	2462
		360	523	244	158

Table A3.14. Middle male speakers: Mean F3 values
and standard deviations for nasal vowels in non-sequential nasal units.

		[ɛ̃ N]	[œ̃ N]	[ɑ̃ N]	[ɔ̃ N]
		μ	μ	μ	μ
		σ	σ	σ	σ
F3	Speaker_K	3016	2897	2928	3061
		139	227	257	395
	Speaker_L	2654	2582	3187	2759
		206	152	215	210
	Speaker_M	3205	3094	3446	3136
		136	207	425	480
	Speaker_N	2769	2786	2853	2577
		302	227	551	581
	Speaker_O	2944	2952	3028	2948
		336	373	483	267

Table A3.15. Middle female speakers: Mean F3 values
and standard deviations for nasal vowels in sequential nasal units.

		[ɛ̃]	[œ̃]	[ɑ̃]	[ɔ̃]
		μ	μ	μ	μ
		σ	σ	σ	σ
F3	Speaker_K	3127	2928	3108	3072
		123	175	467	386
	Speaker_L	2736	2554	2813	2612
		222	193	206	173
	Speaker_M	3266	2990	3232	3318
		103	535	640	619
	Speaker_N	2446	2838	2853	2658
		701	344	541	376
	Speaker_O	2934	3020	2928	2945
		362	58	267	223

Table A3.16. Middle female speakers: Mean F3 values
and standard deviations for nasal vowels in non-sequential nasal units.

Young speakers: nasal vowels

		[ɛ̃ N]	[œ̃ N]	[ɑ̃ N]	[ɔ̃ N]
		μ	μ	μ	μ
		σ	σ	σ	σ
F1	Speaker_Z	460	445	522	460
		47	64	61	65
	Speaker_@	455	446	540	454
		38	84	47	40
	Speaker_$	564	563	649	533
		55	64	59	52
	Speaker_£	554	546	617	488
		43	35	29	61
	Speaker_€	580	534	594	530
		38	43	50	59
F2	Speaker_Z	1752	1695	1175	895
		156	241	252	153
	Speaker_@	1625	1387	1247	1080
		214	153	129	101
	Speaker_$	1876	1519	1179	1033
		230	169	154	118
	Speaker_£	1638	1467	1028	979
		176	126	56	103
	Speaker_€	1567	1539	1051	947
		208	133	222	195

Table A3.17. Young male speakers: Mean F1 and F2 values and standard deviations for nasal vowels in sequential [ṽN] nasal units.

		[ɛ̃]	[œ̃]	[ɑ̃]	[ɔ̃]
		μ	μ	μ	μ
		σ	σ	σ	σ
F1	Speaker_Z	431	461	557	433
		131	66	61	75
	Speaker_@	439	487	512	404
		19	62	39	52
	Speaker_$	564	527	636	507
		68	125	71	68
	Speaker_£	572	545	603	526
		61	93	40	84
	Speaker_€	554	567	625	544
		84	57	53	58
F2	Speaker_Z	1627	1485	1137	827
		292	142	394	133
	Speaker_@	1665	1385	1299	1142
		135	90	133	61
	Speaker_$	1771	1618	1163	1026
		177	250	108	178
	Speaker_£	1525	1484	1066	964
		160	148	207	152
	Speaker_€	1419	1471	1085	946
		96	146	256	186

Table A3.18. Young male speakers: Mean F1 and F2 values and standard deviations for nasal vowels in non-sequential [ṽ] nasal units.

		[ɛ̃ N]	[œ̃ N]	[ɑ̃ N]	[ɔ̃ N]
		μ	μ	μ	μ
		σ	σ	σ	σ
F1	Speaker_U	603	669	621	505
		89	77	58	51
	Speaker_V	686	626	829	660
		54	112	88	84
	Speaker_W	647	631	781	657
		68	122	52	126
	Speaker_X	637	631	707	558
		67	59	66	104
	Speaker_Y	598	510	709	562
		110	138	107	85
F2	Speaker_U	1867	1536	1268	1092
		280	161	141	131
	Speaker_V	1928	1615	1231	1032
		176	207	102	134
	Speaker_W	2047	1576	1244	1031
		104	175	111	167
	Speaker_X	1957	1879	1183	930
		234	290	231	143
	Speaker_Y	1747	1436	1105	1017
		186	171	96	186

Table A3.19. Young female speakers: Mean F1 and F2 values and standard deviations for nasal vowels in sequential [ṽN] nasal units.

		[ɛ̃]	[œ̃]	[ɑ̃]	[ɔ̃]
		μ	μ	μ	μ
		σ	σ	σ	σ
F1	Speaker_U	618	602	637	531
		103	163	68	88
	Speaker_V	769	618	805	654
		75	139	122	111
	Speaker_W	657	644	767	601
		85	123	59	102
	Speaker_X	699	651	736	623
		57	77	72	73
	Speaker_Y	613	570	705	611
		123	42	59	125
F2	Speaker_U	1699	1601	1195	1157
		226	188	115	177
	Speaker_V	1935	1590	1264	1013
		138	259	138	108
	Speaker_W	1886	1562	1234	1080
		213	168	130	120
	Speaker_X	1931	1779	1267	1145
		119	227	243	204
	Speaker_Y	1752	1481	1064	998
		128	55	65	69

Table A3.20. Young female speakers: Mean F1 and F2 values and standard deviations for nasal vowels in non-sequential [ṽ] nasal units.

		[ɛ̃ N]	[œ̃ N]	[ɑ̃ N]	[ɔ̃ N]
		μ	μ	μ	μ
		σ	σ	σ	σ
F3	Speaker_Z	2307	2143	2221	2287
		280	216	157	148
	Speaker_@	2287	2158	2274	2196
		319	124	131	121
	Speaker_$	2775	2680	2856	2577
		128	460	333	456
	Speaker_£	2312	1915	2108	2383
		160	153	118	131
	Speaker_€	2533	2418	2308	2459
		210	195	161	170

Table A3.21. Young male speakers: Mean F3 values and standard deviations for nasal vowels in sequential nasal units.

		[ɛ̃]	[œ̃]	[ɑ̃]	[ɔ̃]
		μ	μ	μ	μ
		σ	σ	σ	σ
F3	Speaker_Z	2325	1997	2275	2337
		597	161	170	242
	Speaker_@	2236	2184	2258	2196
		216	74	152	77
	Speaker_$	2733	2665	2859	2793
		105	27	229	166
	Speaker_£	2289	2130	2279	2389
		168	204	333	191
	Speaker_€	2455	2467	2332	2497
		214	241	171	161

Table A3.22. Young male speakers: Mean F3 values and standard deviations for nasal vowels in non-sequential nasal units.

		[ɛ̃ N]	[œ̃ N]	[ɑ̃ N]	[ɔ̃ N]
		μ	μ	μ	μ
		σ	σ	σ	σ
F3	Speaker_U	3139	2836	2832	2740
		294	285	323	188
	Speaker_V	3080	2852	2804	2865
		246	406	595	611
	Speaker_W	2818	2708	2670	2713
		325	178	150	112
	Speaker_X	3057	3043	2883	2660
		183	244	411	293
	Speaker_Y	2924	2701	3052	2869
		284	261	223	303

Table A3.23. Young female speakers: Mean F3 values and standard deviations for nasal vowels in sequential nasal units.

		[ɛ̃]	[œ̃]	[ɑ̃]	[ɔ̃]
		μ	μ	μ	μ
		σ	σ	σ	σ
F3	Speaker_U	2818	2866	2674	2852
		499	342	318	225
	Speaker_V	3156	2567	2747	3082
		96	812	580	569
	Speaker_W	2662	2473	2735	2813
		411	209	249	247
	Speaker_X	3123	3074	3066	3033
		71	81	407	310
	Speaker_Y	2994	2664	3018	2980
		302	196	220	123

Table A3.24. Young female speakers: Mean F3 values and standard deviations for nasal vowels in non-sequential nasal units.

INDEX

❖

www.ingramcontent.com/pod-product-compliance
Lightning Source LLC
LaVergne TN
LVHW061327060426
835511LV00012B/1896